Democratization and Development

PALGRAVE STUDIES IN GOVERNANCE, SECURITY, AND DEVELOPMENT

Series Editor: Dietrich Jung of the Danish Institute
for International Studies

This series contributes to the critical analysis of international affairs, linking the theoretical and the empirical, especially through comparative works. The focus is on three processes in international relations: *governance* involving both formal and informal institutions; *security*, meaning that of key actors in international society, with a focus on the distinctions and differences among security of and for individuals, groups, and states; and *development*, meaning the improvement of both political and economic conditions for individuals and groups. The links among the three will be a focus, pertinent given the interactions among them and among the levels of influence (from individual to global society).

Also in the series:

Aid Impact and Poverty Reduction
edited by Steen Folke and Henrik Nielson

Democratization and Development: New Political Strategies for the Middle East
edited by Dietrich Jung

Democratization and Development

New Political Strategies for the Middle East

Edited by

Dietrich Jung

Danish Institute for International Studies

DEMOCRATIZATION AND DEVELOPMENT
© Dietrich Jung, 2006.

First published in 2006 by
PALGRAVE MACMILLAN™
175 Fifth Avenue, New York, N.Y. 10010 and
Houndmills, Basingstoke, Hampshire, England RG21 6XS
Companies and representatives throughout the world.

PALGRAVE MACMILLAN is the global academic imprint of the Palgrave Macmillan division of St. Martin's Press, LLC and of Palgrave Macmillan Ltd. Macmillan® is a registered trademark in the United States, United Kingdom and other countries. Palgrave is a registered trademark in the European Union and other countries.

ISBN-13: 978–1–4039–7064–0
ISBN-10: 1–4039–7064–5

Library of Congress Cataloging-in-Publication Data

Democratization and development : new political strategies for the Middle East / edited by Dietrich Jung.
    p. cm.
Includes bibliographical references and index.
ISBN 1–4039–7064–5
    1. Middle East—Politics and government—1979–
2. Democratization—Middle East. 3. Democracy—Middle East.
4. Secularization—Middle East. I. Jung, Dietrich, 1959–

JQ1758.A58D46 2006
320.956—dc22   2006041589

A catalogue record for this book is available from the British Library.

Design by Newgen Imaging Systems (P) Ltd., Chennai, India.

First edition: August 2006

Printed in the United States of America.

Contents

Conclusions

Note on Contributors

Dietrich Jung is a senior research fellow at the Danish Institute for International Studies in Copenhagen where he is heading the research unit "Religion, Social Conflict, and the Middle East." He has been teaching at Aarhus University (Denmark), Bilkent University (Ankara), and the Universities of Copenhagen, Hamburg, and Southern Denmark. Dr. Jung has published on causes of war, theories of world society, and on conflicts in the Middle East. His most recent books are *Shadow Globalization, Ethnic Conflicts and New Wars. A Political Economy of Intra State Wars* (Routledge, 2003), *Contemporary Security Analysis and Copenhagen Peace Research* (Routledge, 2004; co-edited with Stefano Guzzini), and *The Middle East and Palestine. Global Politics and Regional Conflict* (Palgrave, 2004).

Maye Kassem holds a Ph.D. in Middle Eastern Comparative Politics from SOAS, University of London, and is currently an assistant professor at the Political Science Department of the American University in Cairo. She has published a number of articles on institutional reform and questions of governance in Egypt, Iran, and Turkey. Moreover, Dr. Kassem has published two books on Egypt: *In the Guise of Democracy: Governance in Contemporary Egypt*, London: Ithaca Press (1999) and *Politics in Egypt: The Dynamics of Authoritarian Rule*, Boulder, CO: Lynne Rienner Press (2004).

Ziya Öniş is professor of international political economy at Koç University in Istanbul. Previously he taught as professor of economics at Boğaziçi University, Istanbul. His recent research has focused on the interface between globalization and democracy, as well as patterns and paradoxes of democratization processes in developing societies. Previously Prof. Öniş was a Fulbright Fellow at Princeton University and a consultant to the World Bank and the OECD Development Centre. He has published numerous articles in international journals and his most recent book is *The Turkish Economy in Crisis*, London: Frank Cass (2003), edited together with Barry Rubin.

Jakob Skovgaard-Petersen is associate professor in middle eastern studies at the Carsten Niebuhr Institute of Copenhagen University and currently the director of the Danish-Egyptian Dialogue Institute in Cairo. His main fields of research are the modern history of the Middle East, mass media in the Arab world, sociology of religion, and modern developments in Islam. Dr. Skovgaard-Petersen wrote a series of articles on modern Islam and his Ph.D. thesis *Defining Islam for the Egyptian State. Muftis and Fatwas of the Dar al-Ifta* was published by Brill, Leiden in 1997. His last book was a text book on modern Islam in Danish (2003).

Thomas Scheffler is a visiting lecturer at the Carsten Niebuhr Section for Near Eastern Studies, Copenhagen University, currently working on religion, violence, and conflict management in Lebanon. He received his Ph.D. in Political Science at the Free University of Berlin and has been a senior researcher at the Center for Modern Oriental Studies, Berlin (1993–95), at the German Orient Institute in Beirut, Lebanon (1996–99), and at the Political Science Department of the Free University of Berlin (2000–01). In 2001–02 he was a Rockefeller Visiting Fellow at the Joan B. Kroc Institute for International Peace Studies at the University of Notre Dame, Indiana. He is the author of numerous studies on ethno-religious conflicts in the Middle East and on German Middle East politics. His books include *Religion between Violence and Reconciliation* (editor, 2002), *Baalbek: Image and Monument, 1898–1998* (co-editor, 1998), *German Social Democracy and the Algerian Liberation War* (1995, in German), *Ethnicity and Violence* (editor, 1991, in German).

Oliver Schlumberger is a senior research officer at the German Development Institute in Bonn. His research focuses on political change and authoritarianism in the Middle East and North Africa and he advises German development cooperation. Dr. Schlumberger received his Ph.D. from the University of Tübingen where he was an assistant professor at the Institute of Political Science. He is currently working on a collective volume on authoritarianism in the Middle East, and is finalizing a monograph on governance deficits in the region and their implications for development cooperation (in German). His scholarly articles comprise works on economic and institutional reform, on questions of political change/democratization in the Arab world, as well as on the Euro-Mediterranean partnership.

Søren Schmidt has been teaching history and politics of the Middle East at the Carsten Niebuhr Institute and the Institute for Political Science, Copenhagen University. He has recently finalized his Ph.D. from the Department of International Development Studies, Roskilde University. His fields of research are on state-building processes and the relationship between states and markets. Recently, Mr. Schmidt has written on democracy and state-building in Iraq and on the modern history of Syria. Prior to re-entering academia in 2000, Mr. Schmidt worked for several years as a senior officer with the European Commission in Jerusalem and Damascus.

Preface

> Bullied, nagged and cajoled by their superpower patron, the kings of
> Jordan and Morocco, the emirs of the Gulf, the Saudi crown prince and the
> ever-ruling presidents of Egypt and sundry North African states are forced
> in public to mouth the jargon of political reform and democracy while
> straining every muscle in private to ensure that their version of democracy
> denies the masses the one thing they most desire: a peaceful way to boot
> the said kings, emirs, crown princes and presidents out of office.

This assumption in a "leader" of *The Economist* is both right and wrong.[1]
Indeed, a large proportion of the people in the Middle East is sick and tired
of its incumbent political leadership and the hypocrisy regarding the
Western discourse on democracy and the Middle Eastern reality of political authoritarianism. In particular, the *Arab Human Development Report
2004* has emphasized the "longing for freedom and justice" in the region.[2]
Yet this leader of the Economist is utterly wrong in its simplistic approach
to democratization in the Middle East. Booting the current royal or republican patrons out of office does not necessarily mean voting a democratically minded and accountable leadership in.[3] The smooth and sudden shift
from deeply entrenched authoritarian rule to liberal democracy has no
historical precedence. Rather, this assumption is the result of a particular
kind of Western wishful thinking with respect to the political mess in
which postcolonial state building and international relations have led to in
the Middle East. In order to clean up this mess, however, wishful thinking
has to be substituted by informed analysis.

It is to this goal that this collection of essays aims to contribute. In shedding some light on the absence of democratization and development in the
Middle East, this volume rejects handy policy blueprints that are derived
from the post-1945 Marshall Plan, the Organization for Security and Cooperation in Europe (OSCE) process, or the transformation of Eastern
Europe. These completely disregard the radical differences of both the
socio-political and international contexts in which Middle Eastern states
have evolved. Contrary to the situation in post–Second World War Europe,
in many Middle Eastern countries the principle social order on which

successful policies of democratization rest—a consolidated modern state based on a minimum level of the rule of law—simply does not exist. Yet without a functioning state apparatus and a social order based on certain levels of economic and legal security, development remains absent and democracy tends to degenerate into an electoral smoke-screen, as previous liberalization policies have shown.

Therefore, this book investigates the economic, social, political, and cultural particularities that will essentially decide the prospects of demo-cratically inspired policies to support the ongoing state- and nation-building processes in the Middle East. The authors combine intensive and innova-tive research with practical and/or field experience in the implementation of public policies in their related fields. From different disciplinary angles, the chapters present new insights into the political economy of democrati-zation and development in the region. Applying a historical perspective, the authors shed new light on explanatory variables such as political institutions, economic structures, the media, civil society, and the interna-tional/transnational contexts in which the evolution of Middle Eastern statehood has emerged. The book is subdivided into two major parts, each comprising three important and interrelated aspects of current develop-ment processes.

After an introductory chapter on war-making and state-making in the Middle East, the first part of the book addresses the international and transnational contexts to which development strategies for the Middle East have to respond. In thematic terms, the three contributions will analyze external initiatives for the support of good governance in Arab states, the impact of transnational Islamist and Pan-Arab ideologies on democratiza-tion in the Middle East, and the role of new media, in particular satellite broadcasting, in the Arab world. The second part presents three case studies—Turkey, Egypt, and Syria—analyzing the specific political and economic environments in which liberalization processes in the Middle East have taken place. These three essays show that there is no linear trans-formation of so-called policies of liberalization into the democratization of societies. While in the case of Egypt liberalization became a means of stabilizing authoritarian rule, the Turkish reform process has not only decisively changed the institutions of the country but has also been accom-panied by the rise and fall of Islamic radicalism. The book concludes with some policy-relevant considerations regarding democracy promotion as a means of security politics and the choice of Middle Eastern actors to whom Western foreign policy initiatives should be directed.

The chapters of this volume were developed in a joint research process during the years 2004 and 2005. Being well aware of the time-absorbing nature of academic discussion and writing, I am deeply indebted to my colleagues who were willing to join this process and to bring it with their valuable contributions to a successful ending. My sincere thanks are yours for sharing with me both your knowledge and time. Moreover, I would like to thank the Danish Institute for International Studies (DIIS) and the Danish Social Science Council (SSF) for facilitating this research process. In particular I am grateful to SSF for funding a workshop and authors' symposium on the topic of Democratization and Development in the Middle East. Both took place at DIIS in March 2005 and gave the contributors of this book the opportunity to discuss their ideas intensively with a distinguished group of workshop participants from academia, politics, the bureaucracy, and various Nongovernmental Organization (NGOs). Thanks are also due to them for giving their valuable input to this book.

Last but not least, I am very grateful for the smooth and professional collaboration regarding the technical assistance for this book. As always, Catherine Schwerin was a reliable and quick language editor whose expertise was indispensable in putting the various manuscripts into a coherent English text. David Pervin and his Palgrave team were instrumental in turning the text into a book. Thank you very much for your professional support!

Preface

1. "Now please vacate your thrones," The Economist, May 28 to June 3, 2005, p. 16.
2. Arab Human Development Report 2004. Towards Freedom in the Arab World, New York: UNDP.
3. This longing for political change and "democracy" should not generally be equated with the desire to establish political systems that follow Western blueprints of liberal democracies (cf. Marc A. Tessler and Eleanor Gao (2005) "Gauging Arab Support for Democracy," Journal of Democracy, 16 (3): 83–97).

Introduction

I

War-Making and State-Making in the Middle East

Dietrich Jung

Introduction

The inherent relationship between war-making and state-making in European history was a core theme of historical sociology long before Charles Tilly put it in the rather ironic formula of "war making and state-making as organized crime" (Tilly, 1985; cf. Tilly, 1990). Tilly's insinuation that state-building processes are not only war-prone but also display patterns of organized crime, following in particular the logic of protection rackets, can be amply supported by historical evidence. Contrary to the national narratives of European state formation, the emergence of modern European nation-states was the construction of political territories and national identities by coercive means, rather than the political awakening of European peoples. Moreover, the democratic nation-state, based on a liberal market economy, representative political institutions, and the rule of law, was only a very late outcome of this violent historical process.[1]

In principle, contemporary state-building processes do not deviate from this conflict-prone and coercive European path. Looking at the wars that have accompanied the evolution of the postcolonial states of Asia, Africa, and the Middle East, it is not so much the patterns of violent conflict that differ. Rather, the cognitive and normative categories of our perception make the difference, as well as the rapidly changing international environment in which these state-building processes take place. Thereby both the perceptual categories and the legal, political, and economic constraints of the international system are closely related to the specific form of social order that European state formation brought about: the democratic nation-state. It is this changed context that largely prevents current state-makers from following the European path. In the present world, the determination of political territories and the shaping of national identities by coercive means have clear limits.

This new context for postcolonial state-building becomes apparent in current peace-making and peace-building operations in which a new alliance of states, as well as international and transnational organization, is engaged in fostering global peace through political and economic liberalization. From the perspective of the above-mentioned findings of historical sociology, these proponents of what Roland Paris once called the ideology of *Liberal Internationalism* have turned ends into means (Paris, 1997). This is the new *mission civilisatrice* of an admittedly heterogeneous global alliance which wants to use the normative legal framework and the institutional setting of consolidated democratic states as tools to support state- and nation-building processes in the former Third World (cf. Paris, 2002). The discursive dominance of this ideology of Liberal Internationalism is giving the answer to the question of why terms like "peace-building," "nation-building" or "state-building" have "today become so intimately intertwined with democracy-building." (Plattner, 2005: 7). And since September 11, 2001, it is in particular the Middle East that has become the center stage for this huge project of contemporary international social engineering.

To be sure, this critique of Liberal Internationalism is not directed against its vision. There is no doubt that a democratically ruled Middle East with a flourishing market economy is a desirable scenario. However, this author shares Roland Paris' reservations that at least some of these peace-building efforts are in danger of confusing means with ends. The prescription of competitive "market democracies as a remedy for conflict" is flawed because it disregards the "inherently destabilizing effects" that processes of political and economic liberalization have on conflict-ridden societies that are passing through the most critical phases of state- and nation-building processes (cf. Paris, 1997). The leading question of this anthology is therefore how can the "international community" support democratization and development in a region in which firmly consolidated modern state structures have not yet emerged.

In order to provide the reader with some critical insights into the current status of Middle Eastern state formation, this chapter will take up the central question of historical sociology with regard to the region. It investigates the relationship between war-making and state-making in the Middle East. This investigation will start with a brief presentation of some elementary conceptual tools necessary for the understanding of the crucial linkage between violent conflicts and state formation. Then a sketch of the historical origins of modern state-building in the region will follow. The major body of the chapter will present an analytically guided description of Middle Eastern warfare since the decolonization of the region after 1945. This description is subdivided according to five major spots of conflict in the Middle East: Palestine, Yemen, Kurdistan, the Gulf region, and the southern rim of the former Union of Soviet Socialist Republics (USSR). Furthermore, this section will discuss the periods of state decay in Afghanistan and Lebanon. In the light of the current international state-building operations in Afghanistan and Iraq, the chapter ends with some concluding remarks about the status of the state in the region.

War-Making, State-Building, and Democracy

It was Max Weber who defined the central feature of modern statehood— "the monopoly of the legitimate use of physical force within a given territory" (Weber, 1991: 78)—against the backdrop of the violent history of European state-building. In Weber's words, this war-prone formation of state monopolies of physical force was a long-lasting process of "political expropriation," gradually depriving all political communities other than the state of the means of coercion (Weber, 1991: 83). However, the establishment of state monopolies of physical force should not be conceptualized in mere power relations through which power holders carry out their will despite any resistance from the subordinated. In order to establish consolidated statehood, the factual monopoly of the use of physical force has to be considered legitimate by both rulers and the ruled. Stable systems of political authority do not only rest on a monopoly of coercion but this state monopoly also has to be anchored in a mutually accepted symbolic structure. A political order needs legitimacy.

Max Weber acknowledged the crucial role of this symbolic embeddedness of political authority in making legitimacy into a central category of his sociology of domination. Therefore, despite all difficulties in conceptualizing and measuring legitimacy, it would be a mistake to avoid the application of this concept at all (cf. Huntington, 1991: 46). Long-lasting political institutions require a stable set of rules that in normative and cognitive ways regulate the social conduct of rulers and the ruled. In referring to the inner justification of systems of domination, Weber precisely distinguishes political authority from mere power relations by the category of legitimacy. His concept of legitimacy is intended to give an answer to the question of when and why people obey (Weber, 1991: 78). In this sense, legitimacy is anchored in the normative and symbolic structures of society. To be sure, Weber does not deny the importance of material interests in the maintenance of authority structures. He actually distinguishes between two types of domination: domination by virtue of authority and domination by virtue of a constellation of interests. In empirical systems of domination, however, this analytical distinction between the two ideal types is blurred and the borderline between compliance owing to material benefits or to obeyed authority is fluid (Weber, 1968b: 943).

Focusing on the symbolic side of systems of domination, Weber distinguished three ideal types of legitimate political authority: first, legal or rational authority, which rests on the belief "in the legality of enacted rules and the right of those elevated to authority under such rules to issue commands;" second, traditional authority, which rests on the "established belief in the sanctity of immemorial traditions and the legitimacy of those exercising authority under them;" and finally, charismatic authority, which rests on the "devotion to the exceptional sanctity, heroism or exemplary character of an individual person" (Weber, 1968a: 215). In contrast to traditional and legal systems of domination, charismatic authority is not based on a shared set of rules and acts as a specifically revolutionary force in times of social crises. In the long run, however, charismatic authority has the tendency to become either traditionalized or rationalized in order to take on the character of a permanent political order (Weber, 1968a: 246). In the light of these concepts, we can conceptualize the processes of modern state formation as a gradual shift from forms of traditional authority to the rational/legal type—from absolutist states to constitutional monarchies, republican democracies, and welfare states (cf. Jung, 2001: 458–63)—whereas elements of the charismatic type are most likely to occur in the foundational phase of a newly emerging state.[2]

In the 1930s, Norbert Elias reformulated Weber's process of political expropriation as a "civilizing process." In doing so, he applied a double perspective. On the one hand, Elias examined in a Weberian way the macrosociological aspects of state formation and the emergence of the fundamental monopolies on physical force and taxation. On the other hand, Elias borrowed from Sigmund Freud and investigated the microsociological developments of this process, which he located in a peculiar molding of the human drive economy. In defining the immanent link between the macro- and microlevels as the conversion of outer constraints into self-restraints, Elias concluded that the formation of modern states has been reflected in increasingly differentiated patterns of self-control on the side of the individual (Elias, 1994: 443–56). The pacifying institutional setting of modern statehood was accomplished by a particular normative restriction of the public behavior of individuals. In this way, Elias perceived state formation as a process in which macro-and microsociological developments, as well as material and symbolic structures, penetrate each other.

Yet this gradual pacification of society and individuals has not been a peaceful process in itself. Elias traced the origin of both the modern state and the modern individual back to an unrestricted and violent elimination contest in which any individual or small group struggled among many others for resources not yet monopolized (Elias, 1994: 351). In abstracting from the European experience, in particular the history of France, Elias differentiated between two distinct phases in the emergence of the modern state monopoly of physical force. In the first phase, a factual monopoly of physical force is established. An increasing number of people lose direct access to the means of force, which progressively become centralized in the hands of a few and thus placed outside open competition. In the second phase, this relatively private control over the monopoly of physical force tends to become public, that is, it moves from the hands of state-makers into a political setting of legal institutions and appointed rulers under the control of the public. From this perspective, the monopoly of physical force becomes first "nationalized" and then, possibly, "democratized" (Elias, 1994: 345–55).

Given this focus on the relationship between war-making and state-making, it is surprising that the classical political sociologists paid so little attention to the role of the military in state-building processes. This dearth was partly filled by some studies carried out by military sociologists in the 1960s and 1970s. At that time, the concern of political scientists with the role of military institutions in postcolonial nation-building also led to a new interest in the military dimension of European state formation. Morris Janowitz, for example, argued that in spite of very different developmental paths, the "participation in armed conflict has been an integral aspect of the normative definition of citizenship" and emerged as a "hallmark of democracy" in Western states (Janowitz,1976: 190–1). This was partly due to the fact that the professionalization and technological advancement of the military in the nineteenth century was paralleled by the introduction of middle-class elements into the previously aristocratic armed forces.[3] In this sense, the monopoly of physical force and its instrument, the military, was gradually transferred to the whole of the "nation," "transforming the military from a distinct status group into more and more of a civil service organ of the state" (Janowitz, 1976: 200). Yet this nationalization and democratization of the state monopoly of physical force was externally accompanied by some of the most violent interstate wars of human history, which followed the pre- and post-Reformation periods of European "civil wars."

The European and American experiences show the relationship between the emergence of representative political institutions, democratically framed systems of rational authority, conscription, and the conduct of war. Moreover, European history demonstrates that there is no linear move from traditional authority to systems of legal authority exerted through the institutions of democratic politics. Modern states have appeared in both democratic and totalitarian garment and the liberal democratic consensus in Europe is a very recent phenomenon. Robert Dahl, the grand seigneur among scholars on democracy, pointed out that we have to understand democracy as a process, in particular as a process for making binding decisions (cf. Dahl, 1989). In a rather minimalist definition, the central procedure of democracy is therefore to select the decision makers "through competitive elections by the people they govern." These elections must be characterized by free contestation and participation, providing the opportunity for a change of government (Huntington, 1991: 6–7).[4] Yet the establishment of this kind of elective democracy rests in itself on historical conditions that are not the result of democratic decision-making. On the contrary, these conditions resulted from long and violent periods of social and political instability. It is crucial that we have these lessons of European state formation and their conceptual derivatives in mind while assessing both state-building processes in the Middle East and the prospects for democratic governance in the region.

History of Modernization in the Middle East

If it makes sense to periodize modernization at all, then the modernization of the Middle East took off in the course of the nineteenth century through both indigenous reforms and colonial interventions. In this context, the gradual demise of the Ottoman Empire provides us with the historical framework in which the modern state structure of the region evolved. The empire's involvement in the European power struggle, its unfavorable integration into a rising capitalist world market, as well as the dissemination of modern political ideologies and scientific thoughts, undermined the social foundations of traditional Ottoman rule. In order to counter the erosion of political authority, the Ottoman reforms attempted to monopolize the means of physical force and to reorganize the traditional political structure of the empire. Yet, the attempt to form modern state monopolies was counteracted by foreign interventions and the aspirations of regional actors who tried in turn to monopolize the resources of political and economic power. Contrary to Elias's ideal type of the first phase of monopoly formation, Middle Eastern state-building did not take place under the conditions of free competition. Rather, the Ottoman rulers and other regional state-makers were acting within a complex historical power structure, the so-called Eastern Question system, characterized by the interdependent actions of a multiplicity of players (cf. Brown, 1984). To a certain extent, the defensive modernization of the Ottoman rulers finally undermined its initial purpose to safeguard the traditional order through reforms from above.

From a state-building perspective, the nineteenth century modernization processes in Middle Eastern polities such as the Ottoman Empire, Egypt, Iran, or Tunisia can be summarized by seven fields of political reform:[5]

1. the creation of monetized and rationalized systems of taxation;
2. the secularization and formalization of both education and administration of justice;
3. the functional differentiation of branches of government;
4. the gradual establishment of a governmental division of power;
5. the introduction of constitutional rule;
6. the differentiation of the means of physical force according to separate realms of internal and external security;
7. the reform of provincial administrations.

These reforms introduced various elements of modern statehood to the region. However, these fragments of legal authority were often mere instruments for the stabilization of basically traditional, dynastic authority structures. In this way, the various reform processes created hybrid forms of political authority, confusing the only analytically distinguishable phases of Elias's monopoly mechanism. The decisive political division of the Middle East according to the model of the territorial state took place after World War I. It was in the period under British and French mandate that the principles of territorial domination, legal authority, and central administration were more firmly established. Between the two world wars, new patterns of regional conflicts also developed, patterns that have influenced Middle Eastern politics until today (cf. Podeh, 1998).

The eventual decolonization of the region after World War II affirmed the political landscape that had been shaped during the mandate period. From this time onward, the precepts of international law have guaranteed the external sovereignty of the newly established states. Internal sovereignty, that is, the construction of legitimate forms of legal authority, however, has been confined to the territorial limitations of these internationally granted state boundaries (cf. Jackson, 1990). This struggle for internal sovereignty is one aspect of the decolonization process that correlates with the shift from interstate wars to civil wars in international war development since 1945.[6] Moreover, the decolonization process was accompanied by the region's integration into the political coordinates of the Cold War. In this way, a regional system of great-power clientelism emerged in which Middle Eastern regimes operated as political rent-seekers on the international level while pursuing relatively independent interests in regional affairs. Domestically, some regimes were able to use these international resources for the consolidation of their rule, that is, to build up coercive forms of internal sovereignty, and to circumvent at the same time the second phase of Elias's monopoly mechanism. Against public pressure for the nationalization and democratization of state monopolies, Middle Eastern state-makers have frequently used the coercive means of their security apparatus and perpetuated a huge gap between state/regime and society.[7]

In applying the lenses of political sociology, we have to reject one of the most persistent myths associated with the political modernization of the region. It does not make much sense to blame the so-called "artificial state boundaries" for the violent political history of the region. First of all, this term is deceptive, as it implies something like the "natural" origin of state borders. These are, however, always the result of long and often violent historical processes. State borders are neither natural nor artificial, but historically and socially constructed. Second, it was the introduction of juridical and administrative elements of legal authority rather than the drawing of borders that already in the nineteenth century stirred upheaval among the region's ethnic, religious, and tribal communities. Both indigenous reforms and colonial interventions interfered in the traditional authority structures of the region. Finally, the artificial border argument relies heavily on the state-building experiences of the so-called Fertile Crescent—Iraq, Syria, Lebanon, Israel, and Jordan—whose modern political landscape does not show many historical or territorial references to precolonial times. Yet in Egypt, Afghanistan, Iran, Yemen, Saudi Arabia, and Turkey, we can easily detect continuities between the modern states and their premodern political predecessors (cf. Harik, 1990).

Taking the example of Afghanistan, the "fragmented unity" of the country is largely the consequence of outside challenges by Shiite Iran and the colonial ambitions of Great Britain and Russia. To a large extent, the lowest common denominator which the tribal confederation of Afghanistan has shared since the mid-eighteenth century is Sunni Islam. Against this religious backdrop, the Afghan mosaic of Pashtuns, Tajiks, Usbeks, Turcomans, and Belutshis has been able to perceive external aggressions as a common threat. Similar confederate mechanisms and the balancing of tribal assertions have characterized the state-building processes in the ethnically more homogeneous countries, Saudi Arabia and Yemen, whose political structures feature a peculiar blending of traditional and modern forms of authority. In the Fertile Crescent and the Caucasus, as well as in southeastern Europe, regional state formation was simultaneous to Ottoman state decay. By the end of the nineteenth century, most of the European provinces of the Ottoman Empire had already achieved independence. The separation of Albania, Macedonia, and Bulgaria preceded World War I. The previous Ottoman provinces in the Caucasus and Central Asia were under Russian domination and their contemporary territorial features resemble, in principle, the internal administrative divisions of the Soviet Union.

In contrast to the former Ottoman territories, Iran can look back on a centuries-long formation of its state and nation. The modern history of Iranian state-building commences with the patrimonial consolidation of Safavid rule in the early sixteenth century. Although still traditional in its authority structure, the Safavid state anticipated the territorial demarcation and the Shiite national identity of the modern Iranian polity. In the Qajar period (1796–1925) the nation-building process continued and was accentuated by the colonial confrontations with Russia and Great Britain. In the formation of the Iranian state, Shiite Islam became an integral element of national identity. Shiite clerics played leading roles in the country's modern national movement, and they were a mobilizing force, together with national Liberals and representatives of the Bazar milieu, in the political revolts of the late nineteenth and early twentieth centuries (Algar, 1969: 24). In the course of these rebellions, which opposed the despotic habits of Qajar rule and the growing influence of the great powers in Iran's political economy, a constitutional movement was formed. In 1906, this movement succeeded in proclaiming a first Iranian constitution that granted the function of a moral guardianship to the Shiite jurisprudents (Vakili-Zad, 1996).

In cultural terms, the modernization of the Middle East has been strongly conditioned by the import, dissemination, and reinterpretation of modern European discourses. Albert Hourani identified three subsequent phases in this process. In the first one (1830–79), largely congruent with the core period of Ottoman reforms—the Tanzimat, only the higher echelons of the Ottoman state bureaucracy and some intellectuals became aware of the fundamental societal developments in Europe. Then, in the second phase (1870–1900) Europe turned into both the imperialist enemy and the model for reform. This is documented by the constitutionalist and nationalist movements in their Ottoman, Egyptian, Iranian, or Pan-Arab versions, as well as by the emergence of "Islamic Modernism," an anticolonialist intellectual movement that is linked to names such as Jamal ad-Din al-Afghani and Muhammad Abduh. The subsequent division of Islamic Modernists into an Islamist and a secularist wing then marks the third phase of this appropriation, reinterpretation, and refutation of European ideas (Hourani, 1983), and in particular its Islamist successors have remained an important element in the political discourse of the region until today.

Similar to those involved in the intellectual debates of the nineteenth century, contemporary Islamists interpret Islamic history as a process of decline and alienation that led to colonial repression. Their search for an "authentic Islamic order" has to be understood within the context of Imperial domination. Yet Islamist ideologies are not only a reaction to the political, economic, and cultural dominance of the West. From the beginning, Islamist movements also turned against the religious establishment and the postcolonial elites of their own societies. In particular militant Islamist ideologies that are inspired by the writings of Abu al-Ala Mawdudi and Sayyid Qutb emphasize the struggle against the Westernized Muslim elites (Sivan, 1989: 2), and it is especially this struggle against indigenous elites that has been visible in a number of civil wars in the region.

In conclusion, the modernization of the Middle East displays an enormous unevenness regarding its political, economic, and cultural patterns. This is, for instance, apparent in comparing Egypt with the mountainous regions of Yemen. While Egypt experienced under Muhammad Ali (1804–48) a series of massive modernizing reforms, the traditional ways of life in Yemen remained in large parts of the country almost untouched until the second half of the twentieth century. From the 1930s onward, the export of crude oil has increasingly played a decisive role in shaping the region's asymmetric economic structures and its very particular integration into the world market. The territories previously under Soviet rule, finally, have been characterized by specific forms of communist top-down modernization that made them entirely dependent on the center in Moscow. It is this unevenness of the modernization process that has conditioned regional state formation and that is reflected in the conflictive political features of local, ethnic, and religious differences. The following survey on warfare in the Middle East will show how these features are visible in the various violent conflicts that have impacted strongly on our perception of Middle Eastern politics.

Wars and Conflicts in the Middle East

In geographical terms, this overview of wars and conflicts in the Middle East defines the region as follows. It comprises the Arab states of North Africa, the so-called Fertile Crescent, the Arab Peninsula, Iran and Afghanistan in the east, and Turkey in the north. Since the dissolution of the USSR, the Caucasian and Transcaucasian countries, as well as the states of Central Asia, can be added to a region that nowadays is called the "Greater" or "Broader" Middle East. Since the end of World War II the Working Group on Causes of War at Hamburg University (AKUF) has counted forty-eight wars in the Middle East; a number that corresponds to about 23 percent of the total number of wars that have taken place since 1945. Thus, the region is one of the most war-prone areas on the globe. Moreover, with a ratio of thirty-three civil wars and fifteen interstate wars, the violent conflicts in the Middle East reflect the general trend of global war development: a clear shift from the classical form of wars between states to different forms of intrastate war.[8]

Palestine[9]

The long and bloody history of the Palestine conflict has contributed considerably to corroborating the negative image of a region in which violence seems to be endemic. In terminating the Middle East Peace Process in September 2000, the "Al-Aqsa Intifada" marked another violent step in this conflict that has frequently escalated into warlike forms such as popular unrest, communal riots, anticolonial insurgencies, guerrilla and terror attacks, and civil and interstate wars. In Palestine, regional and international conflicts converge, and since the foundation of the Israeli state in 1948, the conflict between Israel, the Palestinians, and Arab states has led to seven wars: the first Arab-Israeli War (1948–49), the Suez War (1956), the Six-Days War (1967), the War of Attrition between Israel and Egypt (1969–70), the October War (1973), the Israeli-Palestinian War in Lebanon (1982–83) and the Al-Aqsa Intifada (since 2000). In addition, the Palestinian question has heavily impacted on the internal conflicts of the so-called confrontation states—Egypt, Lebanon, Jordan, and Syria—and it was inseparably linked to the war between the Jordanian regime and the Palestine Liberation Organization (PLO), the so-called Black September (1970–71), as well as the civil war in Lebanon (1975–90).

From an analytical point of view, the wars about Palestine show four interrelated dimensions of conflict:

1. The Israeli-Palestinian dimension, which comprises the relations between the Israeli state and the Palestinians who live either in Israel proper, in the occupied territories of the West Bank and Gaza, or as refugees and expatriates outside Palestine. This dimension of the conflict is of a territorial and political demographic nature, reflecting the mutually exclusive claims of the Jewish character of the

Israeli state and the rights of the Palestinians to their homeland, to political self-determination, and to the return of the exiled population.

2. The Israeli-Arab dimension, which represents the complicated relationship between Israel and the Arab states revolving around issues such as military security, border demarcation, water distribution, and territories under Israeli occupation. Moreover, this dimension has been relevant in an ideological respect. Based on pan-Arab claims to Palestine, the (at least rhetorical) support for the Palestinian case has been an important variable for both the domestic legitimacy of Arab regimes and the quest for leadership amongst them.

3. The Jewish-Islamic dimension of the conflict has left its traces on the relationship between Israel and the Muslim world. From an Islamic perspective, Palestine is an integral part of the *dar al-Islam*, the lands belonging to the Islamic community. In this sense, the existence of a specifically Jewish state on these territories poses a permanent challenge to the ideal of Islamic supremacy. Furthermore, ranking behind Mecca and Medina, Jerusalem represents the third most important place among the holy cities of Islam.

4. The colonial/Western dimension, which is a result of the historical trajectory that Israeli state formation has taken. Against the backdrop of colonial history, Arab nationalist and Islamist political narratives perceive Israel as an "outpost and symbol of Western imperialism." This perception has been further strengthened by the almost unconditional support that the United States have granted to Israel since the late 1960s.

In contrast to the Palestinian uprisings under British mandate, the Arab-Israeli wars after 1945 largely mirrored the second dimension of the conflict. Yet from the disastrous defeat of the Arab state in the Six-Days War (1967) onward, it is the PLO that has increasingly taken the political initiative and become the culmination point of a Palestinian national movement. The PLO has engaged in a form of state- and nation-building project without a real territorial base, ironically similar to the Zionist project seven decades earlier. In this context, the forms of conflict have also changed and the Israeli-Palestinian dimension has gradually superseded the Israeli-Arab dimension. In military terms, this was most visible in the fighting between the PLO and Israeli troops in Lebanon (1978 and 1982), as well as in the two Intifadas that began in December 1987 and September 2000.

The different dimensions of the Palestine conflict indicate that, in principle, the Palestinian question can only with difficulty be disentangled from other domestic and interstate conflicts in the region. Moreover, the

Palestine conflict is closely knitted into the power structures of the inter-national system and plays a key role in the rent-seeking strategies of regional states. The developments in Palestine, therefore, have been an important factor in Middle Eastern state-building. In this context, the impact of international politics on the region was twofold. On the one hand, the confusion of international and regional conflicts has contributed enormously to the militarization of Middle Eastern states, which have been able to use their political rents to build up huge security apparatuses. On the other hand, the international relevance of the confrontation between Israel and the Arab states has put major constraints on the military behavior of regional states, to a certain extent limiting the inter-state wars between Israel and Arab states in terms of duration and further escalation.

In addition, the critical status of regional state formation has been apparent in armed conflicts such as that between the Egyptian state and Islamist militants, the Syrian crack-down on the Muslim Brotherhood in Hama (1982), or the so-called bread riots in Jordan and terrorist incidents in Bahrain, Kuwait, and Saudi Arabia. In the complex setting of Middle Eastern politics, Israeli-Palestinian relations are a crucial factor that impacts on the region as a whole. However, these internal conflicts and, in particular, the developments on the Arab Peninsula also show that the rise of Islamist terrorism is not a result of the unsolved question of Palestine alone. Rather, it is proof of the limitations of the strategies of the rentier state under the conditions of accelerated social change (cf. Herb, 1999; Yamani, 2000).

The Gulf Region

The political history of the Gulf region is another genuine expression of the crossroads of internal and external conflicts in the Middle East. The changing coordinates of international politics are instrumental in under-standing why the Gulf area has developed into a major regional theater of war. The First Gulf War between the Islamic Republic of Iran and Saddam Hussein's Iraq (1980–88), the Iraqi occupation of Kuwait (1990), the Second Gulf War, in which an international alliance liberated the Emirate from Iraqi occupation (1991), the low-intensity warfare with which the US and Great Britain maintained the non-flight zones over Iraq, and, finally, the U.S.-led military intervention and occupation of Iraq (2003) are thereby inherently connected with each other.

In the First Gulf War, a territorial conflict found its military escalation, which to a certain extent had been looming since the Ottoman-Persian treaty of Zahab in 1639. In spite of a series of agreements between Iran, the Ottoman Empire, and later Iraq, the distribution of the lands around the Shatt al-Arab and the question of political hegemony over the Gulf has never lost its conflictive potential. However, the international power structures prevented large-scale interstate warfare in the region, as we know it from European state formation. Until the early 1970s, for more than 150 years it was Great Britain that exerted military control in the area. Since the end of World War II, the United States gradually took over the British role. Then, in the context of the Cold War, Gulf security was knitted into U.S. containment policies and Iran assumed the role of America's prime client in the region. Under this constellation, a military escalation of the traditional territorial conflict between Iran and Iraq was not possible. Yet this situation changed with the Islamic Revolution in Iran (1978).

Prior to the Islamic Revolution, the military battlefield between Iran and Iraq was in Kurdistan. In supporting the separatist aspirations of different Kurdish factions the two countries were engaged in a sort of war of proxies. This was the situation in which the then Iraqi Vice President, Saddam Hussein, signed the so-called treaty of Algiers (1975). In this treaty, which was signed at the Oil and Petroleum Exporting Countries (OPEC) summit in Algiers, the Shah of Iran basically got his way. Only six days before the start of the First Gulf War, in September 1980, Saddam Hussein, then President of Iraq, terminated this agreement. Against the revolutionary turmoil in Iran, the regime in Baghdad apparently sensed a chance to revise its previous foreign policy and to settle the conflict with Iran by military means.

The decision for war, however, is not explicable by the changing international environment and related geostrategic considerations alone. A central variable for the escalation of the conflict also lay in the particular rationality of action of Baghdad. Whether in domestic conflicts or in international competition about territories and resources, the Iraqi regime always followed a specific course of action. As long as the regime was in the weaker position, it conducted negotiations. Yet as soon as Baghdad subjectively perceived a chance of success, military means were applied (cf. Gause III, 2002). The rationality of the regime was based on the factual disposal and relentless application of the means of force and not according to the normative principle *pacta sunt servanda*. From a more scholarly perspective, the First and the Second Gulf Wars show the interlacement of micro- and macrosociological processes, which lead to war. In the context of international political change, it is, on the one hand, the specific perception of relevant actors that makes a difference. On the other hand, these strategies of action are only understandable against the background of the cognitive and normative social structures in which they are rooted. In this sense, the explanation of warfare must combine structural analysis with an adequate understanding of social action.

Kurdistan

In the course of regional state formation, the territories with predominantly Kurdish population were mainly distributed among three territorial states: Turkey, Iran, and Iraq. Since 1945, the conflict between these three states and Kurdish movements resulted in seven wars. Besides the wars in Turkey (1984–99) and Iran (1946–47 and 1979–88), the Kurdish conflict has been most belligerently fought out in Iraq, where four wars have taken place. The Kurdish conflict is essentially characterized by questions of territorial consolidation and political integration, in which the interest of the Turkish, Iranian, and Iraqi states clash with Kurdish aspirations for autonomy or independence. In all three cases, the national state-building process has been threatened by separatist tendencies among their Kurdish populations. With regard to interstate relations, the Kurdish issue has been instrumentalized in regional conflicts between Turkey, Iran, Iraq, and Syria, as the previous section on the Gulf has already shown. Supporting Kurdish movements in neighboring countries has been a frequently used tool in regional foreign politics.

The belligerency of the Kurdish conflict in Iraq reflects the relatively low level of political consolidation that has characterized the country since its independence.[10] In contrast to the situation of its neighbors Turkey and Iran, the Iraqi state-building process has never led to a significant degree of national integration. Generally speaking, the different regimes in Baghdad substituted legitimate political authority by a mixture of clientelistic networking and the application of brute force. In order to maintain this fragile system of power, it was crucial to exert complete regime control over the country's oil resources. Given the overlap of some of the Kurdish territories in northern Iraq with oil-rich areas, Kurdish autonomy aspirations threatened the regimes in Baghdad at the very foundation of their power. It is therefore not surprising that all Iraqi regimes—the monarchy before 1958, the al-Qasim regime, and the Baath dictatorship—were engaged in warfare with the Kurds. To this end, it was of utmost importance that Baghdad was able to utilize the deep-rooted factionalism among the Kurds.

Similar to the situation in the Kurdish revolts in the 1930s and 1940s, the political aspirations of the Kurds after 1945 were also essentially contradicted by their internal fragmentation.[11] Yet, while in the first half of the twentieth century the inner-Kurdish disputes mainly reflected traditional loyalties, differences between modern and traditional segments of the Kurdish population became more visible after World War II. In all three states, national education policies, the spread of state bureaucracies, and the region's integration into the world market have been accompanied by the emergence of modern middle-class actors amongst the Kurds who formed the social basis for a specific Kurdish national movement. In Iraq, these modern actors have been compelled to side with traditional Kurdish leaders such as the Barzani and Talabani families in order to withstand the permanent confrontation with Baghdad. Therefore, the frequent military escalations of the Kurdish conflict in Iraq on the one hand are a result of the massive repression by the Iraqi state elite, and on the other hand show that Baghdad has not been able to extend its factual monopoly of the means of force to the Kurdish areas. There, the expropriation of the means of force has never succeeded, and Kurdish militias applied military means not only, against Baghdad but also in their internal conflicts. The last internal Kurdish war that took place within the United Nations (UN) protection zone in northern Iraq (1996) is a particularly good example of this predicament (Gunter, 1996).

In contrast to the state elites in Iraq, those in Turkey and Iran have been able to at least partly integrate modern Kurdish segments into their state-building processes through economic and political participation, whereas radical groups have been contained by means of state repression. In the late 1970s, however, this relatively quiet phase came to an end. In both countries, the economic disparities between the Kurdish areas and other parts translated into ethnically perceived conflicts between winners and losers of the countries' modernization processes. In Iran, the Kurdish hope for more participation in economic and political power vanished after the revolution. While the Kurdish opposition participated in overthrowing the Shah, the new clerical state elite marginalized the Kurds in the consolidation phase of the revolution and, instead of granting limited autonomy, used the means of military suppression against the Kurds. In Turkey, the Kurdish nationalist movement developed and radicalized under the political turmoil of the 1970s. After the military coup of 1980, only the radical Kurdish Workers Party (PKK) was able to reorganize and started a guerrilla war against the Turkish state in 1984. This war lasted until the capture of its leader, Abdullah Öcalan, in 1999. In the context of Turkey's candidacy for European Union (EU) membership, a large part of the Kurdish movement has abandoned previously held separatist aspirations, now claiming cultural autonomy for the Kurds within a democratic and pluralistic Turkey. Apparently, the prospect of future EU membership is a conducive context in which the second phase of Turkish state formation can take place. In this way, the Turkish example could prove that Kurdish separatism was not so much the result of insurmountable ethnic differences but rather the effect of state-building processes that generated modernized Kurdish constituencies without integrating them into the political and economic structures of the modern state.

Yemen

Until the suicide attack against the destroyer USS Cole in the port of Aden, on October 12, 2000, the Arab Republic of Yemen tended to be at the margin of international attention. This applies specifically to the series of ten wars that have taken place in this south-western corner of the Arab Peninsula since 1945. The general core of conflict in Yemen has been related to the fragmented tribal nature of its society and the attempt of the state authorities to establish a factual monopoly of physical force. However, these internal conflicts of Yemeni state formation have frequently been aggravated by foreign intervention. During the civil war between 1962 and 1967, the republican government in Sanaa was directly supported by Egyptian troops, while Saudi Arabia backed Yemen's traditional political forces. In the previously independent state of South Yemen, the decolonization process was accompanied by two wars between indigenous militias and British troops (1956–58 and 1965–67). In 1994, the conflicts about the distribution of power after the unification of Northern and Southern Yemen (1990) escalated into a civil war in which the insurgent forces again found the support of Saudi Arabia.

In precolonial times, Yemen was formally a part of the Ottoman Empire. However, the Ottoman administration was never able to put the country under its direct control, but ruled indirectly through local leaders. In the northern parts of Yemen, the tribal units formed an alliance under a Zayidi Imam who was chosen by religious dignitaries and tribal leaders, whereas the southern parts were ruled by a number of autonomous tribes. In 1839, Great Britain occupied the coastal town of Aden and declared the protectorate a British colony in 1935. The Imamate in the north became independent in 1911 after driving the Ottoman troops out. The southern parts reached independence after protracted anticolonial warfare (1963–69) under a joint liberation front of trade unionists and Nasserist Arab nationalists.[12]

The central line of conflict in Yemen's internal wars runs between traditional tribal and religious authorities and the emerging modern stratum of society. In the second half of the twentieth century, this new middle class of military officers, bureaucrats, intellectuals and trade unionists demanded political power in the name of republican ideas. While the Imamate was restored in North Yemen after the civil war in 1948, in the second civil war (1962–67) the republican forces gained the upper hand, and the abolishment of the Imamate was eventually agreed on at a reconciliation conference in 1969. Yet in stabilizing state power, the republican wing had to make compromises with traditional forces, and until now the political authority of the state has rested on a precarious compromise between the modern state elites and traditional tribal chiefs. This precarious relationship has also been a recurrent feature in the political developments in South Yemen, where the National Liberation Front and later the Socialist Party took over the British colonial state.

In Yemen, modern statehood is still in an early process of consolidation. As such, not even the first stage of Elias's monopoly process has successfully ended. In some parts of the country, the means of physical force have remained in tribal hands and local customary law rivals with state jurisdiction. The majority of the population lives in the countryside and largely follows the rules of long-established traditions. Ironically, the monetization of trade and economic exchange has strengthened traditional social ties rather than fostering the modernization of the country. This is due to the fact that a large proportion of financial means flows as remittances from expatriates into the country. This financial influx has so far bypassed state administration and provided traditional authorities in the countryside with modern economic means. In this way, the swift support for the U.S.-led war against terror by the ruling elite in Sanaa might indicate a very new context for Yemeni state formation in which the state elite can capitalize on military and economic means offered by international politics.

(Trans)Caucasus and Central Asia

The end of the Cold War did not open a chapter of peaceful international relations as the developments in the former Soviet territories of the (Trans)Caucasus and Central Asia aptly show. The dissolution of the Soviet Union and the formation of independent states in this area resulted in nine wars related to the redistribution of territories and the establishment of new forms of political authority. In general, the core conflicts revolved around the legitimacy of the post-Soviet regimes, the territorial integrity of the former Soviet republics versus territorial claims of neighboring states, or the separatist assertions of some subordinated provinces. These issues of conflict did not only affect the newly independent republics, namely Armenia/Azerbaijan (1990–94), Georgia/South Ossetia (1990–92), Georgia (1991–93), Georgia/Abchasia (1992–94), Tajikistan (1992–98), and Uzbekistan (1999–2000), but also the Caucasian rim of the

Russian Federation (North Ossetia 1992–94 and Chechnya 1994–96 and since 1999).

While the interest of Russia shapes the particular context in this region, struggles for territories and scarce resources were at the heart of these wars. Moreover, the demise of the USSR led to a diffusion and privatization of physical force that also left its mark on the Russian Federation. In particular, the war in Chechnya shows signs of the (at least temporary) erosion of Russia's monopoly of physical force and its control by the center in Moscow. Since Russian troops reoccupied Chechnya in October 1999, they have been drawn into a war of attrition that shows criminal features of extortion, random assassinations, kidnappings, and terror against civilians on both sides. Apparently, in the course of the "war against terror" the Russian government has assumed a free hand in the dirty war in Chechnya. Yet a military success against the mobile insurgent troops still seems far away. Rather it will be the civilian population that continues to pay a heavy price for the "military solution" in Chechnya (cf. Dunlop, 1998; Sapir, 1996; Smith, 2001).

From an analytical point of view, these wars on the territories of the former USSR also display rather typical patterns of conflict for postcolonial state-building processes. First, we observe the struggle for territorial consolidation and the establishment of a factual monopoly of physical force. After the newly established state apparatus has received international recognition, it is the form of government and control over state institutions that is contested by various domestic forces. In this way, the consolidation of modern statehood and the associated violent conflicts move inside internationally guaranteed borders. While external sovereignty was granted from outside, internal sovereignty, the establishment of legitimate authority, has yet to be achieved. However, the cases of Lebanon and Afghanistan show that the internal consolidation of statehood can also lead to fragmentation and state decay.

State Decay in Lebanon and Afghanistan

The wars in Lebanon (1975–90) and Afghanistan (since 1978) are paradigmatic for processes of state decay. Yet in both cases it is rather questionable whether a consolidated state really existed in pre-war times. Despite its formal democratic institutions, the political system in Lebanon was based on a network of patron-client relationships that distributed resources in exchange for political loyalty. These networks were stabilized by Lebanon's system of proportional representation, which placed conflicts about public resources within religious communities whose internal structure was characterized by competing family networks. Given the fact that most of these families also had means of physical force at their disposal, a legitimate state monopoly of violence never existed. Rather, Lebanon was characterized by a precarious balance of power between traditional families and sectarian leaders.

Against this background, Michael Hudson compared Lebanese politics with the anarchical power structure of the international system. According to him, the Lebanese system was not based on a democratic balance of power, but on a balance of threats (Hudson, 1985: 6). The gradual erosion of this political structure in the early 1970s led to its break-down in 1975 and to a civil war with shifting alliances and foreign interventions by Israel, Arab states, and multinational troops.

In Afghanistan, formal democratic institutions such as in Lebanon can arguably be said to have barely ever existed. Neither the monarchy nor the Afghan republic that was established in a military coup in 1973 had developed the consolidated features of a modern state. The decisive forms of social and political integration were based on personalistic relationships that formed regionally based units of traditional authority. The republican circles only represented a tiny minority of the population, a thin stratum of an urban middle class of officers, bureaucrats, and intellectuals. It was their attempt to centralize state power and to assume control over public resources that raised the resistance of Afghanistan's traditional provinces.

The clash of these modern and traditional forces led to open warfare in the course of the Soviet intervention. From this point onward, the domestic conflict was fought out within the coordinates of the East-West conflict, leading to a total fragmentation of the country in protracted warfare. After the Taliban militias, trained and ideologically schooled in Afghan refugee camps in Pakistan, were able to conquer Kabul in 1996, they gradually established military control over 90 percent of the country (Allix, 1997). Yet this control almost entirely lacked patterns of legal authority and became increasingly entangled in the structures of transnational Islamist terror groups, epitomized in the person of Osama bin-Laden. The archaic Islamist rule of the Taliban ended with the U.S. intervention after the terror attacks against New York and Washington on September 11, 2001. It remains to be seen whether the international community that took on the responsibility of rebuilding Afghanistan has the persistence and will necessary to establish state-like institutions in the country. Either a gradual consolidation of state institutions or a collapse and a return to regional and ethnic fragmentation are likely scenarios for Afghanistan's future (cf. Dorronsoro, 1996 and 2005; Roy, 1991; Rubin, 1995).

Conclusions: State-making and the Prospects for Democracy in the Middle East

The modern, liberal, democratic nation-state serves as a kind of institutional blueprint for the proponents of Liberal Internationalism. This model-state brings together the idea of the "rule by the people" with the institutions of modern statehood, based on the legitimate monopoly of physical force that the state administration exerts over its people and its territory. In comparison to this ideal type, this overview of the relationship between war-making and state-making in the Middle East shows that most of the regional states lack essential preconditions for a democratic polity and that some of these states exist only as internationally accepted territories. In Yemen, for example, the state has not yet been able to effectively control the means of physical force and to administer its territory and people. In the peace-building operations in Iraq and Afghanistan it is indeed difficult to define a people who should eventually rule themselves. Moreover, the international military interventions destroyed existing state structures and the current attempts to establish monopolies of physical force by international forces have not yet succeeded. After the Lebanese state decayed in fifteen years of civil war, its state monopoly of physical force was established from outside. Yet this domination of the Lebanese state by Syria was not able to gain permanent legitimacy. It remains to be seen whether the withdrawal of the Syrian troops in spring 2005 will lead to more democracy or to the gradual erosion of the state monopoly and the resurgence of violent sectarian and political conflicts. Finally, in Palestine the Al-Aqsa Intifada has partly destroyed the state-like institutions that the PLO built up in exile and transferred to the occupied territories under the Oslo process.

In states with a higher level of political integration such as Egypt, Iran, Jordan, or Syria, where the first phase of the formation of state monopolies has taken place, state-society relations are still characterized by the detachment of the state authorities from their people. Norbert Elias's second phase of the monopoly process, the nationalization and democratization of modern state monopolies, has not yet started or has been put on hold. In contrast to their European predecessors, these Middle-Eastern state-makers were not allowed to fight the same large-scale state-building wars.[13] Under the impact of international norms and great power policies, Middle Eastern state formation was not able to operate by the same rules (Lustick, 1997). Thus, Tilly's mechanism according to which protection rackets turn into state-like organizations does not apply to Middle Eastern state-building, one factor that explains the legitimacy deficit of many regional states. Moreover, the armed forces of these states have not lost their praetorian character. In the Middle East, a comparable relationship between participation in armed conflict and the normative definition of citizenship, as Janowitz described for Europe, has therefore not developed. Or in Raymond Hinnebusch's words, "the relative incongruity of state and identity is perhaps the most distinctive feature of the Middle East states system" (Hinnebusch, 2005: 153).[14] In regional states which were able to establish monopolies of physical force, the crucial question will therefore be whether the second phase of state formation will bring about the transformation from authoritarian to democratic rule or whether this process will turn into the violent destruction of established state structures.[15]

This question is paradigmatic for the situation in Iran, one of the region's most integrated states in national terms, where the experiment of an Islamic democracy has reached an impasse. In recent years, the political constraints put on the reform movement have steadily increased. Apparently, the Islamist state apparatus, represented by institutions such as the Supreme Leader, Ayatollah Khamenei, the judiciary, the Guardian Council or the Pashdaran, has not been willing to relinquish its almost absolute power and its economic privileges. Although article 113 of the Iranian constitution declares the President to be second in the state hierarchy, the political power of the President, his government, and the parliament is heavily curtailed. The formal existence of an institutionalized system of balance of power is actually superseded by the absolutist powers of the Supreme Leader (Mehpour, 1999–2000: 553). President Khatami's two periods in office showed that the Iranian executive is not able to implement policies without the consent of the Supreme Leader, who also limits the legislative power of the parliament through the Council of Guardians.

Despite the encouraging, lively political discussion in the country, the democratization of state monopolies in Iran has so far been limited to electoral processes of political bodies which are rather marginal within the overall power structure of the country. Thus the influence of the people on actual political decision-making has remained weak. However, given the enthusiastic involvement of the public in the electoral campaigns of the late 1990s, it would be a grave error of the conservative wing to continue to perceive electoral processes only as handy tools to channel popular dissatisfaction. In fact, since the first election of the former President Khatami, the politicization of the public has raised expectations in the political and economic fields which are difficult to contain. Apparently this was also the case in the presidential election of June 2005, in which the ultra-conservative candidate Mahmud Ahmadinejad was able to mobilize the poor and to win the second round of the polls against the former president and chairman of the Expediency Council, Akbar Hashemi Rafsanjani. So far, political competition has largely been articulated within the confines of the

Islamic system. Yet should the experiment of gradually transforming the *vilayet i-faqih* into an Islamic democracy fail, it could soon be the Islamic system as a whole that is put at stake. In the light of continuing violent state repression and an increasing disappointment of the public in fake democratic procedures, it is not unlikely that violent unrest will take the place of electoral democratic procedures.

The general dilemma that the proponents of Liberal Internationalism are facing is apparent in the "new protectorates" in Afghanistan and Iraq. In providing military security, state administration, economic prosperity, individual freedoms, and the rule of law at the same time, these current peace-building efforts resemble attempts to square the circle. Far from being state-like forms of political authority, the situation in Afghanistan and Iraq appears to be more a kind of "controlled anarchy" in which the interests and competencies of international, transnational, regional, national, and local actors compete with each other (Schlichte, 2003: 40). From the theoretical perspective applied here, the two phases of the monopoly mechanism have been fundamentally confused. The political expropriation of physical force has been taking place parallel to the introduction of democratic institutions that theoretically should be the outcome of the nationalization of a state monopoly, a state monopoly that does not yet exist in either state. Patterns of traditional and legal authority overlap and the normative attitudes of international actors clash with the social logics of local communities (cf. Dodge, 2005). In order to make democracy-building work, international policies have to follow specifically designed strategies that take the different social and international environments into account under which individual Middle Eastern polities function.

Regarding the state- and nation-building efforts in Iraq, this insight has been reflected in recent analyses made by both practitioners and academics. Hilary Synnott, for example, served for six months as the Coalition Provisional Authority's Regional Coordinator for four provinces in southern Iraq (Synott, 2005: 35). In his assessment of the coalition's state-building efforts, Synnott concludes that their fundamental shortcomings were due to the lack of "an accurate view of the political and socio-economic situation in Iraq." He continues that "facile comparisons with the reconstruction challenges in post–World War II Germany and Japan showed insufficient awareness of the profound differences of culture and heritage, and the fact that the Iraqis were not a defeated people" (Synott, 2005: 54). According to Eva Bellin's historical analysis, this comparison with democratization in the post–World War II period is clearly ill-conceived. Iraq had never achieved the level of economic development, the degree of ethno-national homogeneity, or the advanced standard of bureaucratic state-institutions that Germany and Japan had. In addition, Iraqi society was lacking adequate political leadership and previous democratic experience (Bellin, 2004–05: 596–601).

It is the common denominator for the authors of this book that we see the inadequacy of deriving a blue-print for democratization from the historical experience of Europe. Rather, state-building and democratization processes in Europe provide us with theoretical concepts and empirical evidence for the understanding of the different conditions under which current state- and nation-building processes are taking place in the Middle East. The following chapters will shed some light on the differences between the European and the Middle Eastern contexts. However, in the same manner as the present overview on war-making and state-making in the Middle East, the contributions of this book will draw attention to the different trajectories of state formation in Middle Eastern states. Unfortunately, the relevance of the particularities that distinguish individual Middle Eastern states from each other has been clouded by debates about Arab and/ or Muslim exceptionalism as a cause for the resilience of authoritarian rule (Stepan and Robertson, 2004). In particular the case studies in the second part of the book will indicate that this homogenizing view of Middle Eastern politics is wrong. In this way, the following studies also attempt to raise our awareness for the fact that the democratization of the region tends to follow the same unevenness and selectivity that has characterized modernization in the Middle East so far. It is this heritage of the modern Middle East that successful policy strategies for democracy and development have to take into account.

Notes

1. It makes sense to see this rise of a liberal and democratic Europe as a basically post-World War Two development, in which the formation of the European Union and its gradual enlargement has played a key role.

2. The basic sociological concepts of Max Weber are in principle all ideal types. They are not descriptions of reality, but one-sided logical accentuations of significant historically individual phenomena. Ideal types are "mental constructs" that serve us as heuristic instruments for the development of relevant hypotheses (cf. Weber, 1949: 89–94). In this respect, historically real forms of authority, for example, do not fully correspond with the exactly defined types of traditional, legal and charismatic authority. They may tend to combine aspects of all of them, and the ideal types serve as a means of measurement and comparison. Unfortunately, the application of ideal types is very often confused by the "naturalistic predisposition" to portray them as historical reality or as the "real forces" that operate behind the historical passage of events (Weber, 1949: 94).

3. For an account of this relationship between the professionalization of military institutions and the increasing differentiation of modern society, see van Doorn (1975).

4. Huntington distinguishes this procedural definition of democracy from definitions by source or by purpose that in his eyes lack analytical precision. Yet he also admits that democratic systems imply other societal power holders that balance the power of elected decision makers (Huntington, 1991: 10).

5. For a more detailed, sociologically guided analysis of the Ottoman reforms, see: Jung with Piccoli (2001: 28–58).

6 For some statistical surveys of major trends in global war development, see the data sets produced by the respective research units at the universities of Uppsala (Eriksson *et al.*, 2003, Gleditsch *et al.*, 2002), and Hamburg (Gantzel and Schwinghammer, 2000).

7. For an excellent compilation of case studies on the foreign policies of individual Middle Eastern states, see: Hinnebusch and Ehteshami (2002).

8. The war statistics of the AKUF are accessible via the AKUF website: www.akuf.de. The following survey on wars and conflicts in the Middle East is based on my chapter in Jung, Schlichte and Siegelberg (2003: 251–300)

9. This chapter builds on Jung (2004).

10. Toby Dodge's study gives a detailed account of state-building efforts in Iraq under the British mandate and the way in which these contributed to the failure of Iraqi state- and nation-building (Dodge, 2003). For politics in independent Iraq, see Tripp (2000).

11. For more detailed analyses of Kurdish history and society, see McDowall (1996).

12. For the modern history of Yemen, see the standard textbook by Dresch (2000), for the civil wars and the phase of decolonization, see Halliday (1974).

13. The only exception is the first Gulf War, in which, due to the specific international context, Iran and Iraq were engaged in a kind of warfare that resembled the European experience. However, this war was also contained by international forces in the sense that it could not spread in the region.

14. For a discussion of the political economy of Arab states and the way in which they are ill-prepared to face the challenges of economic globalization, see Henry and Springborg (2001).

15. In this process, Elias' micro-sociological aspects of state formation also are a crucial factor. The peaceful nationalization of state monopolies depends to a certain extent on the level of self-control previously established among the people.

References

Algar, Hamid (1969) *Religion and State in Iran* (1785–1906). *The Role of the Ulama in the Qajar Period*, Berkeley and Los Angeles: University of California Press.

Allix, Stephane (1997) "De la resistance à la prise de Kaboul, l'histoire secrete des talibans," *Le Monde Diplomatique*," January 1997.

Bellin, Eva (2004–05) "The Iraqi Intervention and Democracy in Comparative Historical Perspective," *Political Science Quarterly* 119 (4): 595–608.

Brown, Carl L. (1984) *International Politics and the Middle East. Old Rules, Dangerous Game*, Princeton: Princeton University Press.

Dahl, Robert A. (1989) *Democracy and Its Critics*, New Haven and London: Yale University Press

Dodge, Toby (2003) *Inventing Iraq: The Failure of Nation Building and a History Denied*, New York: Columbia University Press.

—— (2005) *Iraq's Future: The Aftermath of Regime-Change*, Adelphi Paper 372, London: The International Institute for Strategic Studies.

Doorn, Jacques van (1975) *The Soldier and the Social Change*, Beverly Hills and London: Sage.

Doronsoro, Gilles (1996) "Afghanistan: des résaux des solidarité aux espaces régionaux," in: Jean, F. & J-C. Rufin, ed. 1996. *Économie des guerres civiles*, Paris: Pluriel.

—— (2005) *Revolution Unending. Afghanistan: 1979 to the Present*, translated from the French by John King, London: Hurst & Company.

Dresch, Paul (2000) *A History of Modern Yemen*, Cambridge: Cambridge University Press.

Dunlop, John B. (1990) *Russia Confronts Chechnya. Roots of a Separatist Conflict*, Cambridge: Cambridge University Press.

Elias Norbert (1994) *The Civilizing Process. The History of Manners and State Formation and Civilization*, Oxford: Blackwell.

Eriksson, Mikael, Peter Wallensteen and Margareta Sollenberg (2003) "Armed Conflict, 1989–2002," *Journal of Peace Research* 40 (5): 593–607.

Gantzel, Klaus Jürgen and Schwinghammer, Torsten (2000) *Warfare since the Second World War*, New Brunswick and London: Transaction Publishers.

Gause III, Gregory F. (2002) "Iraq's Decision to Go to War, 1980 and 1990," *Middle East Journal*, 56 (1): 47–70.

Gleditsch, Nils Petter, Peter Wallensteen, Mikael Eriksson, Margareta Sollenberg and Håvard Strånd (2002) "Armed conflict 1946–2001. A New Dataset," *Journal of Peace Research* 39 (5): 615–637.

Gunter, Michael M. (1996) "Civil War in Iraqi Kurdistan: The KDP-PUK Conflict," *Middle Eastern Journal*, 50 (2): 225–42.

Halliday, Fred (1974) *Arabia without Sultans*, Harmondsworth: Penguin Books.

Harik, Iliya (1990) "The Origins of the Arab State System," in Giacomo Luciani (ed.): *The Arab State*, Berkeley: University of California Press: 1–28.

Henry, Clement M. and Robert Springborg (2001) *Globalization and the Politics of Development in the Middle East*, Cambridge: Cambridge University Press.

Herb, Michael (1999) *All in the Family. Absolutism, Revolution, and Democracy in the Middle Eastern Monarchies*, New York: State University of New York Press.

Hinnebusch, Raymond and Anoushiravan Ehteshami (eds.) (2002) *The Foreign Policies of Middle East States*, Boulder: Lynne Rienner.

—— (2005) "The Politics of Identity in Middle East International Relations," in Louise Fawcett (ed.), *International Relations of the Middle East*, Oxford: Oxford University Press.

Hourani, Albert (1983) *Arabic Thought in the Liberal Age*, 1798–1939, Cambridge: Cambridge University Press.

Hudson, Michael (1985) *The Precarious Republic. Political Modernization in Lebanon*, Boulder: West View.

Huntington, Samuel P. (1991) *The Third Wave. Democratization in the Late Twentieth Century*, Norman and London: University of Oklahoma Press.

Jackson, Robert H. (1990) *Quasi-States: Sovereignty, International Relations, and the Third World*, Cambridge: Cambridge University Press.

Janowitz, Morris (1976) "Military Institutions and Citizenship in Western Societies," *Armed Forces and Society*, 2 (2): 185–204.

Jung, Dietrich (2001) "The Political Sociology of World Society," *European Journal of International Relations*, 7 (4): 443–474.

—— (2004): "Global Conditions and Global Constraints: The International Paternity of the Palestine Conflict," in Dietrich Jung (ed.): *The Middle East and Palestine: Global Politics and Regional Conflict*, New York: Palgrave.

Jung, Dietrich, Klaus Schlichte and Jens Siegelberg (2003) *Kriege in der Weltgesellschaft. Strukturgeschichtliche Erklärung Kriegerischer Gewalt (1945–2002)*, Wiesbaden: Westdeutscher Verlag.

Jung Dietrich, with Wolfango Piccoli (2001) *Turkey at the Crossroads. Ottoman Legacies and a Greater Middle East*, London: ZED books.

Lustick, Ian S. (1997) "The Absence of Middle Eastern Great Powers: Political 'Backwardness' in Historical Perspective," *International Organization*, 51 (4): 653–83.

MacDowell, David (1996) *A Modern History of the Kurds*, London: I.B. Tauris.

Mehpour, Hossein (1999–2000): "Responsibilities of Iran's President for the Implementation of the Constitution," *Iranian Journal of International Affairs*, 11 (4): 541–582.

Paris, Roland (1997) "Peacebuilding and the Limits of Liberal Internationalism," *International Security*, 22 (2): 54–89.

—— (2002) "International Peacebuilding and the 'Mission Civilisatrice'," *Review of International Studies*, 28 (2002): 637–56.

Plattner, Marc F. (2005): "Introduction," *Journal of Democracy*, 16 (1): 5–8.

Podeh, Elie (1998) "The Emergence of the Arab State System Reconsidered," *Diplomacy & Statecraft*, 9 (3): 50–82.

Roy, Olivier (1991) *The Lessons of the Soviet/Afghan War*, London: Elsevier.

Rubin, Barnett R. (1995) *The Fragmentation of Afghanistan: State Formation and Collapse in the International System*, New Haven: Yale University Press.

Sapir, Jacques (1996) "La prise de décision en matières de sécurité en Russie: enseignements de la guerre en Tchétchénie," *Memento GRIP 1995–96: L'Europe et la sécurité internationale*, Brussels.

Schlichte, Klaus (2003) "State Formation and the Economy of Intra-State Wars," in Dietrich Jung (ed.): *Shadow Globalization, Ethnic Conflicts and New Wars: A Political Economy of Intra-State War*, London and New York: Routledge.

Sivan, Emmanuel (1989) "Sunni Radicalism in the Middle East and the Iranian Revolution," *International Journal of Middle East Studies*, 21 (1989): 1–30.

Smith, Sebastian (2001) *Allah's Mountains. Politics and War in the Russian Caucasus*, London: I.B. Tauris.

Stepan, Alfred and Graeme B. Robertson (2004) "Arab, Not Muslim, Exceptionalism," *Journal of Democracy* 15 (4): 140–46.

Synnott, Hilary (2005) "State-building in Southern Iraq," *Survival* 47 (2): 33–56.

Tilly, Charles (1985) "War Making and State Making as Organized Crime," in Peter B. Evans, Dietrich Rueschemeyer, and Theda Skocpol (eds.): *Bringing the State Back In*, Cambridge: Cambridge University Press.

——(1990) *Coercion, Capital and European States, AD 990–1990*, Cambridge: Basil Blackwell.

Tripp, Charles (2000) *A History of Iraq*, Cambridge: Cambridge University Press.

Vakili-Zad Cyrus (1996) "Collision of Consciousness: Modernization and Development in Iran," *Middle Eastern Studies*, 32 (3): 139–160.

Weber, M. (1949) *The Methodology of the Social Sciences*, New York: The Free Press.

—— (1968a) *Economy and Society. An Outline of Interpretive Sociology*, ed. Guenther Roth and Claus Wittich, Volume I, New York: Bedminister Press

—— (1968b) *Economy and Society. An Outline of Interpretive Sociology*, edited by Guenther Roth and Claus Wittich, Volume III, New York: Bedminister Press

—— (1991) *From Max Weber: Essays in Sociology*, edited, with an introduction by H.H. Gerth and C.Wright Mills, with a new preface by Bryan S. Turner, London: Routledge.

Yamani, Mai (2000) *Changed Identities. The Challenge of the New Generation in Saudi Arabia*, London: The Royal Institute of International Affairs.

Part I

Transnational and International Contexts

2

Dancing with Wolves: Dilemmas of Democracy Promotion in Authoritarian Contexts

Oliver Schlumberger

Introduction: Arab Political Change and External Efforts at Promoting Democracy[*]

This contribution deals with the international dimension of political change in the Middle East, and more specifically with external efforts to promote democracy. While democracy promotion (DP) in this region is not new, the recent international discourse (cf. UNDP, 2002a, 2002b and 2005; World Bank, 2003), as well as Arab and Western initiatives on Arab political reform, underlines the importance of this topic. Western and Arab programs, initiatives, and declarations referring to the need for political reform have emanated in hitherto unknown numbers over the past few years from Paris, Washington, Cairo, Sanaa, Alexandria, Beirut, Tunis, and elsewhere; they were voiced by national, international, and nongovernmental political actors such as the UN, the OECD, the Arab League, NGO networks, and individual governments. For the first time in decades, social unrest in countries such as Lebanon, Egypt, or Bahrain has shifted to decidedly anti-regime political protest (as opposed to bread riots, for instance), while changes engineered by incumbent autocrats continue to be in the direction of adapting formally democratic institutions without according them any content that would redistribute power, install guaranteed rights, or enhance participation.

Two things are far from clear: first, it is not certain whether such changes have anything to do with democratization—which most scholars today agree is not the case[1]—and second, the more complex question of whether these changes can be geared toward democratization by external actors remains unanswered. With the renewed international focus on Arab political change, this second question has gained dramatically in importance for both the academic and the policy-making communities (see, e.g., Carapico, 2005) and will be focused on here.

Taking up the assumption that political liberalization as initiated by incumbent regimes is a survival strategy to maintain power,[2] it seems necessary to know more about how external DP works and, more importantly yet, when and why it does not trigger the expected results. All Arab regimes are nondemocratic; no peaceful transfer of power has taken place in any Arab country for decades (except intergenerational such as in Jordan, Syria, Morocco, or Bahrain). Therefore, political cooperation with precisely these regimes and their incumbents evokes the image of donors "dancing with wolves," wishing them to transform into sheep. With this in mind, a brief review of the state of illiberalism in the Arab world in comparative perspective is followed by a discussion of three crucial dimensions of currently pursued strategies of DP.

First, the criticism that has been brought forth against democracy promotion as a secondary goal for donors when compared to short-term stability considerations.[3] This includes uneasy but inevitable questions which Western policy makers usually avoid. Second, a look inside the donors' perspective reveals conceptual challenges and shortcomings in the design and formulation of DP strategies, two of which are discussed in detail. The first is related to structural factors, namely to the fact that the causes of Arab authoritarian durability are mostly ignored in current DP strategies, which raises concerns about democracy promoters' awareness of the political environment in which they intervene. The second is related to the constellation of political actors, and more specifically to the fact that incumbent regimes act as veto-players able to render external efforts at more transparent and accountable governance ineffective, which is too little reflected in donor policies.

The chapter concludes that DP as practiced today is unlikely to contribute to democratization on a macrolevel. For more coherent Western policies, both foreign-policy priorities and DP concepts would have to be thoroughly revisited. None of this is easy, but revisiting DP concepts is less difficult than changing established policy priorities. However, there is no doubt that such improvements in donor strategies will be futile unless donors are ready to prioritize good governance over short-term stability considerations in a manner in which actual political positions and actions are more consistent with political rhetoric.

The State of Illiberalism in the Arab World

Looking at the Arab world and comparing political developments in the direction of democracy, available indicators of political and civil rights speak a clear language: the Arab countries, as a whole, not only make up the world's most unfree region, but also have not liberalized politically over the past one and a half decades—in contrast to all other developing regions. Of course, nothing is black and white, but to gain a rough idea of where the Arab world stands, a look at some of the most widely used indicators may be helpful.

Figure 2.1 uses aggregate data provided by Freedomhouse in a cross-time comparison of Arab countries with other world regions. It clearly demonstrates that all developing regions experienced significant political liberalization between the late 1980s and the early 2000s, that is, a greater degree of civic rights and political liberties. The only exception is the Arab world, where, according to Freedomhouse, the degree of rights and liberties did not augment, but in fact decreased, albeit slightly.

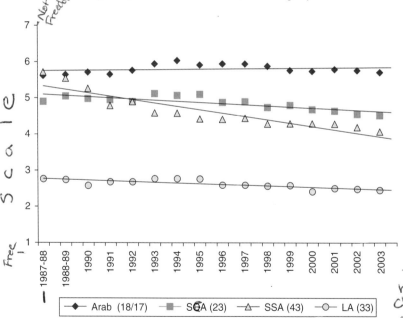

Figure 2.1 Political rights, civil liberties in inter-regional comparison, 1988–2003.

Note: In black: linear trend lines for individual regions. Values represent the regional averages for Arab countries, South-East Asia (SEA), Sub-Saharan Africa (SSA) and Latin America and the Caribbean (LA). The numbers in brackets are the number of countries on which the regional average is based, as calculated by the author.

Source: Freedom House (2004).

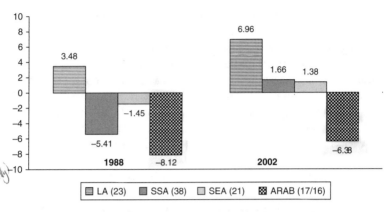

look of DP (however...)

looking

for Stability!

Figure 2.2   *Polity* values in inter-regional comparison (1988/2002).

Note: Regional averages: Author's calculation from *Polity* Database.

Source: *Polity IVd* (2003).

Even when these figures are compared to other indices, the broad picture remains the same. Taking the *Polity IVd* dataset, the impression diverges from the one Freedomhouse gives insofar as all regions seem to have become more liberal.[4] However, the positions of the world regions as indicated in figure 2.2 reveal that, while in the late 1980s three out of four developing regions had negative (i.e. less liberal) *Polity* values, in 2002 the Arab world was the only region that remained firmly rooted in the negative range. What is more, in terms of the positions of developing regions *relative* to one another, figure 2.2 shows that the "governance gap" between the Arab world and all other developing regions had widened instead of narrowed. This means that while *Polity* saw all developing regions more liberally in 2002 than in 1988, the Arab world had liberalized less than all other world regions.

This stands in slight contrast to the observations made on the Arab world in political science literature, which concentrated on tracking the processes of political liberalization, at least from the late 1980s and into the first half of the 1990s, before scholars started to realize that there was also an opposite trend, starting with Eberhard Kienle's (1998) essay on the political de-liberalization of Egypt in the 1990s. Freedomhouse (2004) gives individual figures for all Arab countries that have been considered for figures 2.1 and 2.2 in this chapter and demonstrates, too, that there are no easily discernible patterns of liberalization or de-liberalization in the Arab world as a whole. Furthermore, it undeniably demonstrates that no single Arab country has ever reached a state in which its polity could reasonably be considered "democratic."[5] Even the most liberal ones such as Bahrain, Jordan,

Morocco, or Lebanon clearly fall within the range of authoritarian regimes according to Linz's classical definition (1964 and 1975: 264ff.). More detailed empirical case studies on individual countries confirm the picture emerging from the most commonly used indicators (El-Khazen, 2003 on Lebanon; cf. Lawson, 2003 on Bahrain; Hammoudi, 1997 and Maghraoui, 2001 on Morocco; Schlumberger and Bank, 2002 on Jordan).[6] Analysts of Arab politics are therefore well advised not to look at Arab politics from the narrow perspective of democracy and democratization only, but rather inquire into the kinds of changes that are actually taking place (Schlumberger, 2000a; Heydemann, 2002; Schlumberger and El-Khazen, 2004; Albrecht and Schlumberger, 2004; Guazzone and Pioppi, 2004; Hinnebusch, 2004; Lust-Okar, 2004; Pioppi, 2004).

The astonishing fact about illiberalism in Arab countries is that this picture was not taken before democracy promotion in Arab countries set in, but more than a decade later, after hundreds of DP projects had been conducted, and after hundreds of millions of dollars had been spent on supporting and promoting democratic governance in that region. Apart from a forceful testimony to the resilience of authoritarianism in this part of the world, this raises serious concerns about the effectiveness of DP. Independently of the success or failure of individual projects (which often tend to be evaluated as "success" by precisely those donor institutions that designed, financed and implemented them), on a macrolevel of analysis, DP has clearly not been successful in achieving more liberal governance in Arab countries. Brouwer's statement that "civil society assistance and other forms of democracy promotion have not been able to bring about political liberalization and democratization in . . . any Arab country" remains true (2000: 33). The question is: Why?

Fundamental Questions on Democracy Promotion

First and foremost, there is the question of whether the goal of promoting democratic governance actually receives priority within the broad range of foreign policy goals of donors' external policies. While some 250 million USD that USAID alone spent in the Arab world on projects and programs related to DP certainly seems more than a negligible amount of money, this must be contrasted with the roughly one billion USD the United States spends each year in Egypt alone—on military aid for the Mubarak regime. Some observers have recently depicted the "forward strategy for freedom" in the Middle East announced by the Bush administration as a major shift from former U.S. policies toward the region, emphasizing today the importance of democratic rule as opposed to former strategies based on the primacy of stability over democracy. The administration itself has lent credibility to this argument, stating its desire to "use this moment of opportunity to extend the benefits of freedom across the globe" (USA, 2002: 4).

However, current practices have not yet proven that U.S. domestic political rhetoric results in significant changes to past external policies, which then as today relied on the exercise of influence in the "national interest," including military intervention, and were based on the support of regimes that would, in their turn, secure the stable influx of mineral resources on which the industrialized world continues to depend. The nondemocratic nature of such regimes, by contrast, was no impediment to these policies. Successive U.S. administrations have supported "friendly tyrants" as long as they were perceived as guarantors of stability. The current administration continues these policies by supporting Mubarak's authoritarian regime in Egypt, or by recently agreeing to military cooperation with Algeria's autocratic ruling clique made up of a military-entrepreneurial alliance, to name but two examples. Amidst "all the talk about Washington's newfound desire to foster democracy" (Carothers, 2002: 7), and some interventions by the president on behalf of jailed individuals notwithstanding, there is thus also a degree of continuity in U.S. Middle East policy, in which support for autocratic regimes still overrides the desire for democratic partners. The perceived shift may in fact not be as large as some scholars have recently tended to assume. Therefore, it cannot be dismissed as merely an ideologically biased view when countless scholars unremittingly point to the fact that "a revision of the overall foreign-policy objectives would have the most significant impact on democratization" (Brouwer, 2000: 36).

The EU, another major player in the region, is keen on demonstrating that its approach to political change in the region differs from the American strategy: it places dialogue, cooperation, and mutual understanding higher than intervention by force. However, there is hardly any doubt that the EU's own economic interests of opening up export markets range higher on the list of priorities than the promotion of good governance, as a glance at the distribution of aid spent on economic restructuring versus aid for political change easily demonstrates (cf., e.g., Schlumberger, 2000b). This is also illustrated by looking at the content of the three baskets the Barcelona Process has been built on, where the political/security and social/cultural baskets, ten years after their initiation, still have gained only negligible weight when compared with the economic one. To be sure, money is not everything and a word might be worth many dollars, but strikingly, the EU's association agreements with Arab partners provide the

European side with a strong instrument for conditionality that has never been used. Article 2 of these agreements stresses the importance of respect for human rights and good governance; it opens the way for sanctions against noncompliant regimes. But while no Arab signatory has ever lived up to its obligations, there is not a single instance of EU intervention against the clear and persistent violations of this article by all Arab regimes. The EU's willingness to prioritize good governance in partner countries over its own economic interests is thus doubtful, to say the least.

While all Western donors say that they would wish to see their partner countries become democratic, none of them seems to take into account that transitions to democracy by definition include the demise of a prior regime and, therefore, a period of uncertainty that collides with the desire for political and economic stability (cf. Przeworski, 1991: ch. 2).[7] In fact, short- to medium-term political stability and democratic transition are mutually exclusive policy goals; only a choice between the two will determine which goal donor governments wish to achieve (cf. also Carothers, 2002). Both are uncertain, but clearly "political reform and democratization were sacrificed to regional stability" (Norton and Kazemi, 2004: 87). If the current (rhetorical) emphasis on political reform continues to avoid the key question of the distribution of power (political, as well as economic), this will certainly not help Arab democratizers.[8] By contrast, policies that avoid this question of power are most likely to stabilize authoritarian rule and thus continue to erode the credibility of the commitment to political reform that donors reiterate. In none of the Arab countries has there been a peaceful redistribution of core decision-making power over recent decades. Today, "most analysts feel that the reforms carried out or underway neither represent a real process of democratization nor are preliminary to it, and that they configure and legitimize a restructuring of the power system that does not change the authoritarian and neo-patrimonial nature of the regime[s] but, on the contrary, contribute to [their] permanence" (Guazzone and Pioppi, 2004: 94). Unless they explicitly and directly tackle this core issue of the concentration of economic and political power in the hands of Arab elites, donors risk their DP programs and projects being perceived as a mere cover-up for other, far less altruistic objectives in both Arab and Western societies.

It is thus fairly safe to conclude that overall Western policies toward the region have contributed to the persistence of authoritarian rule rather than working in favor of democratization, and that, despite political rhetoric, they might trigger change, but this will not necessarily lead to the emergence of democracies. However, these problems are only one out of three foci of the present contribution.

Problems within the Logic of Democracy Promotion

Even if DP were the only objective external powers pursued in the Arab world, and if they did so wholeheartedly, major conceptual challenges remain for democracy promoters to which answers have yet to be formulated in a way that they could trickle into the design and implementation of donor policies. More specifically, there are at least two key aspects that have hitherto received too little attention from policy makers and policy researchers. One of them is rather a structural factor, related to the intellectual bases of democracy promotion as it is currently practiced. The second focuses on agency and asks about preferences of actors involved in the game of international DP.

Donor Policies between Political Theory and Empirical Reality: A Troublesome Inter-Relation

One may question the general framework of democracy promotion and whether the major donors to Arab countries really wish to see processes of democratization with uncertain outcomes. One can also ask whether it is reasonable to regard the current levels of financial resources that donors commit to such a complex task as conducive to triggering the expected processes, or whether these amounts are more likely to result in cosmetic changes at best. Yet, the fact that DP has become a sizable industry of its own over the past decade or so is hardly debatable. Some authors even speak of an "international democracy promotion regime" that has emerged, which has its own agenda, preferences, and strategies (Carapico and Amawi, 2005). But what do donors actually *do* when they promote democracy? The consensus about good governance being vital for socioeconomic and human development is more far-reaching than just stating it. When looking at the issue areas that are in focus within the frame of DP, there is a broad consensus at least between the major bi- and multilateral donor organizations that comprises (at least) the following issues:

- strengthening respect for human rights, including women's rights and the rights of the child (support for compliance with human rights norms and conventions);
- civil and political rights such as freedom of the media, the right to participate actively in public and political life, mainly through competitive elections, eligibility for public office, and the like (support for democratic elections and the preconditions of their being meaningful, i.e., enhancing participation);

[handwritten marginalia: "Donors aren't asking these questions..."; "if McD's were on every corner, belief that ppl's diets will change"; "establishment → practice/change in act."; "? interrelationship - how produced - how connected - order?"]

- strengthening opportunities for the voluntary association of citizens for purposes of public interest, and facilitating their inclusion in decision-making processes in public affairs (support for civil society);
- support for an independent judiciary, for the equitable application of laws, and citizens' access to the judicial system (support for judicial independence and the rule of law);
- avoiding the concentration of power in the hands of a few and bringing "the state" closer to its citizens not in the sense of being a controller, but as being a service provider, especially to the poor and those remote from the central decision-making circles (support for political, administrative and fiscal decentralization).

In a more general sense, some would add to this list two further points, namely

- the ability of the ruled to hold accountable the rulers for the authoritative decisions (strengthening accountability);
- access to all relevant information which helps identify those who are responsible for decisions taken in public office, which is a necessary pre-condition to holding the rulers accountable (strengthening transparency and combating corruption).

Even though this list may not be exhaustive, little surprisingly, it appears to be a list of democracy's key dimensions. In fact, when comparing it with typical definitions of democracy, such as Dahl's (1971: ch.1) or the one used by Diamond, Linz, and Lipset (1988: xvi), it soon shows that what donors try to promote is a neat collection of individual elements that are thought to make up, in their sum, a functioning and liberal democracy like those known from Europe and North America.

One might thus argue that at the beginning of any design of strategies for the promotion of good or democratic governance stands a process of "self-awareness raising" by the donor community itself about what makes a "good" democracy. The suspicion arises that what donors have in mind when they try to assess what makes democracies work are, in fact, their own Western home countries. The elements of this type of political regime are then identified as the ones to be supported (or even exported), and are added to one another, much as in the list given above. Arguably, thus, the themes of DP strategies are essentially derived from democratic theory— or at least from some popular notion of democratic regimes and the mechanisms according to which they work.

Unfortunately, many, if not most, countries display only some or even none of the democratic attributes the donor community has come to regard as essential requisites for development. While this observation is banal, the ensuing question of how to get these elements to take hold where they are absent is extremely difficult to answer. Democratic theory may tell us about individual elements of democratic regimes and in how far they are defining or non-defining characteristics of democracies, but theories of democracy do not tell us anything about how these elements evolve in a given social, economic, political, or historical context. This leaves democracy promoters with a number of serious problems. First, little is known about the relative importance of individual elements of democracy for the process of democratic transition. Carothers (2002), for instance, vehemently complains about donors notoriously overestimating the role of competitive elections, to give but one example. Second, there is no certainty whether or not all elements that play together in the making of democracies are really on the agenda of democracy promoters. Third, we do not know much about the ways in which these elements are interrelated—something that would necessarily have to be known if the task was "to craft democracies," as Di Palma (1990) put it.

In sum, while donor agendas are filled with singled-out ingredients of democracy, there is no general recipe that would tell us, figuratively speaking, at what time to cut the onions (or whether one could maybe do without and use garlic instead), when to boil the water, what to fry in the pan, how much salt and spices to add, plus, maybe most importantly, in which ways all the ingredients should be mixed at what point in time in order for a digestible meal to result from the exercise.

Such a recipe could only then be convincingly provided if there were a clear and consensual understanding of how, when, and under what circumstances and conditions a systemic transition to democracy is certain or even likely to take place, what factors bring about the downfall of a given regime, and which actors, constellations, and structural conditions were needed, independently of time or space, in order to spur democratic transitions. In brief: What would be needed are the universal laws of democratic transitions. The strand of research committed to the search for such laws has often been called "transitology." Yet, not only is this research relatively new (it began only in the late 1950s), but also there is a broad range of competing theoretical approaches that differ in their underlying assumptions about the relative importance of the many possible variables that might play a role in explaining democratic transition, and, in fact, different premises about human behavior as such. Each of them either explicitly or implicitly draws on different theoretical models of the emergence of democratic regimes. However, this is precisely where the problem lies: there are competing explanations for the emergence of democracy, and none of them can claim to satisfactorily explain systemic political transitions in a general manner that would allow us to formulate "laws of transition."[9]

Contrary to Carother's (2002) claim, transitology has not entirely failed and we are not facing "the end of the transition paradigm."[10] We know that under certain conditions, democratic outcomes are more likely to occur than under others (for instance when old dictatorial elites are negotiated out of office rather than washed away through revolution), and that democratic consolidation is more likely to be achieved in certain circumstances than in others (e.g., if external material incentives for democracy are large, such as in the case of the Spanish democratization). However, these are but pieces of knowledge. Without going into a sophisticated theoretical elaboration on each of the strands of transitology, it can safely be said that research has not found the "laws of transition"—let alone laws about how to steer such processes from the outside.

Figure 2.3 depicts this dilemma visually. As can easily be seen, there is a "gap" between what we know about the ingredients of democracy on the one hand (upper line), and the empirical reality of durably authoritarian regimes in the Arab world on the other (lower line). The initial puzzle is at question mark?1 in the middle of the table. The subdiscipline of transitology is located in between democratic theory (upper line), on which democracy promoters draw in selecting the issue areas they intervene in, and the empirical reality of persistent authoritarian rule in the Arab world.[11] Transitology can therefore be regarded as the subdiscipline that sets out to bridge the gap between the two, to become a theory not of democracy but of the process of democratization and thereby to solve the first puzzle.[12] However, since transitology has not, as of yet, found the type of laws that would be needed to provide policy makers with the knowledge of when, how, and why transitions take place, there is today no reasonable way of deriving an overall strategy of democracy promotion from the insights of transitology (question mark ?2 in the table). And while transitology does help in formulating policies which can at least be hoped to address issues relevant for the emergence of democracy, we do not know whether these issues are those that can be supported externally at all, nor under which circumstances they might be amenable to such support.

As with other highly complex processes, the problem is that political transitions are characterized by the interplay of a multitude of variables (we do not know how many) of different relative weight (we do not know how to assess that relative weight) under different conditions (we do not know which conditions are relevant in which contexts). Thus, there is a problem inherent in the very logic according to which DP today is implemented. But one thing can be said: While current strategies of DP are built on democratic theory, obviously this is not the theoretical frame that could

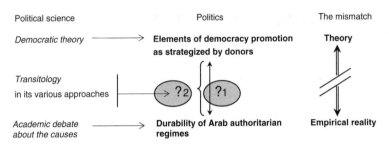

Figure 2.3   The dilemma of the intellectual bases of democracy promotion.
Source: Author.

be expected to help establish sound policies to support or catalyze transition *processes* away from authoritarian rule where the latter is firmly established. Nor does transitology provide donors with answers on how to engineer political transitions.

Which Partners? The Dilemma of Actor Constellations in Democracy Promotion

Civil society in the Arab world: A viable partner for democracy promoters?

The problem addressed here is related to the constellation of actors typical of development cooperation: Most of the projects and programs that are run under the header of DP are agreed upon through international contracts between the governments of donors and recipients. By contrast, democracy promoters are keen on supporting and cooperating with "civil society." Civil society, in turn, is a problematic concept which has no consensually agreed upon definition.[13] In development practice, its notion has often been restricted to nongovernmental organizations (NGOs) as potential partners eligible for foreign funding. Thus, the broader meaning of civil society is often reduced to advocacy groups which are formally institutionalized, enjoy the support or at least complacency of the regimes who rule their countries, and have personnel with the formal education to write proposals, master the jungle of, say, EU online application forms, know donors' management style, and therefore are able to apply for foreign funding. Such organizations tend to be elitist in nature; they often function precisely the opposite way Western donor organizations presume civil society to work: Rather than functioning as the kind of voluntary associations of free citizens which unite at the grassroots level in order to articulate aggregate societal interests (and which donors know from authors who wrote on Western societies, e.g., Tocqueville [1835] or Putnam [1993]), NGOs in predominantly informally organized societies often serve as vehicles for the promotion of particularistic or even individualistic interests of educated individuals or elitist groups. Through their NGO activities, they can not only earn themselves a good living with the possibility of frequent traveling, but come to enjoy privileges that have nothing to do with the cause they are formally advocating. The dilemma is that, leaving aside the question of whether there is any civil society at all in the Arab world (Albrecht 2005), the structure of Arab civil society often does not match with donor expectations. In short: "The civil society donors want does not exist, and the civil society that does exist is not wanted by donors," as Lingnau (2003: 234) writes.

By contrast, social movements that are rooted in society are often informally organized, thus hard to recognize for donors, and yet more difficult to fund or support. If rooted in society, pamphlets and documents are likely to be written and published in Arabic, which, in turn, makes it difficult for donors to correctly assess their content and impact. Their personnel's English language skills are often insufficient to live up to the requirements of governmental donors. Second, such organizations, should they really be independent from the regime, frequently declare the illegitimacy of incumbent rulers and are therefore outlawed by the latter—which in turn renders them ineligible for foreign funding. To be fair, there are significant differences between individual donors as regards their understanding of the complexity of the social fabrics they intervene in (cf. e.g., Challand, 2005). Yet, what remains problematic in all cases where some vague notion of "civil society" is funded in non-democracies is that those "non-governmental" bodies funded often turn out to be, upon closer inspection, really government-owned, controlled, or even -run organizations (Carapico, 2002; Schlumberger, 2000b). Third, donor assistance in many cases (and this holds not only for Islamist groups) is not even sought or desired by the few autonomous groups that exist in Arab countries as a counterweight to incumbent regimes. Foreign funding bears the danger of delegitimizing groups that were originally rooted within local society precisely because Western aid has come to be seen, among large parts of the population, as a mere instrument for the exercise of foreign influence and for the promotion of neo-imperial Western interests such as geostrategic aims, creating and securing export markets, and securing constant resource flows to the industrialized world (oil and gas).

However, the point to be made here is not that there are deficiencies in the donors' actual implementation of their strategies and programs, but that their strategies are deficient from a conceptual viewpoint. When donors support civil society organizations in Latin America's young democracies, they do something structurally different from when they support civil society organizations in, say, Egypt, Tunisia, or Jordan. In the former case, they support social groups that operate within a not only formally democratic but also competitive setting that does not allow the regimes to suppress societal interest articulation and organization at any minute just because incumbents might dislike such organizations' autonomy. In Latin America and other democratic contexts, supporting civil society organizations may arguably contribute to the building of a civic culture which in turn may enhance possibilities of holding governments accountable to their citizens. When donors fund NGOs in authoritarian settings, they support social groups that necessarily have the approval of autocrats. This fact in itself casts grave doubts on the donors' perception of civil society organizations in the Arab world (and in other authoritarian settings) as "spearheads" of democratization. There is, thus, a categorical difference between things that are called by the same name ("strengthening civil society"). However, this is just one instance of a much deeper problem donors face when they try to promote democracy in nondemocratic contexts: Their core partners are not NGOs, but states and governments.

Problems of government-to-government cooperation in
promoting democracy
In authoritarian and democratic polities alike, governments are the first and major partners for Western donors. But what are the consequences when recipient countries are ruled by strong, stable, and fully effective autocrats?

Despite the fragility of the demographic, social, political, and economic equilibria in the Middle East, despite the numerous internal and international conflicts in this region, there is no denying the fact that the Arab countries are ruled by the world's most durable political regimes where incumbents, all autocrats, have the highest YIPPI-scores ("years in power per incumbent"), as Volker Perthes once put it ironically. But even beyond the Arab world, this general question is highly relevant.[14]

Rational choice theory tells us that humans choose, from among perceived alternatives, the one that best serves their own interests. The ruling positions of Arab autocrats and their respective elites not only guarantee them power, control, and prestige, but also tremendous opportunities for self-enrichment and a life in luxury. Elsenhans (1991) points to the fact that often it is wealth gained not through entrepreneurial activity, but through the position in the state that allows what he calls the "state class" (the state bourgeoisie) to prosper. Today, not only is the top political elite able to acquire material wealth through state positions, but also, not least due to economic structural adjustment policies, the top segment of a largely politically dependent bourgeoisie benefits from the authoritarian status-quo.[15] For regime members and their clients, it is usually the politically ensured absence of competition that makes autocrats' and their clients' or family members' private businesses profitable. The Arab world has thus witnessed an amalgamation of economic and political power in the hands of incumbent elites (cf. also Perthes, 2004). This core politico-economic elite, that is, the partners of Western donors, tend to see political control as a zero-sum game in which they could only lose once they accept playing it. Assuming autocrats and their clients would cooperate in DP therefore is expecting them to undermine their own existence.

By contrast, the scenario of democratization by definition requires the demise of the previous authoritarian regime (Przeworski, 1991: ch. 2). This essential fact is often overlooked by advocates of a gradualist approach to democratization who prefer to refer to the "progress" or "setbacks" of individual countries on numerical indices such as the ones provided by Freedomhouse, by the World Bank, or the newly established but highly problematic Bertelsmann Transition Index (BTI). As Pioppi and Guazzone point out correctly: "the transition will necessarily damage the interests . . . of the governing elite" and therefore, "democratization . . . must be considered the outcome of a systemic change in the country's structure of political and economic power" (Guazzone and Pioppi, 2004: 93).

If there is any point to the assumption of rational actors, on what assumption do democracy promoters build their idea that partner governments would act in favor of their own demise? What incentives do we assume Arab rulers to have that we would assume them to be willing to commit the political and economic suicide that a democratic transition may bring for them? I have not yet met anybody who could provide a convincing answer to that simple question. Hence, in dictatorial regimes with functioning statehood, it is against all odds to assume that autocrats would somehow magically turn into democratizers. Anybody who claims that democracy is a matter of informing, building capacity, training the trainers, and the like, would at the very least have to provide a convincing answer to the question of what the incentives for rational autocrats and their co-opted elites are to engage in such a potentially dangerous endeavor. As long as the authoritarian state is effective, it is also (by definition) characterized by a concentration of power, information, and repressive capacities which allow it to maintain the privileges associated with the exclusive control of power, the political and economic dimensions of which are closely intermarried in all Arab countries.

The effective authoritarian regime is the strongest actor in its country by far, and therefore not only the most powerful player, but a powerful veto-player.[16] Without its consent, donors are utterly unable to engage into cooperation with civil society organizations. The regime decides on the legal status of such organizations and can easily outlaw them should it not want donors to support them. Donors can hardly support legislative development or judicial reform when judges know they risk their positions or more if they judge independently; they cannot effectively undertake measures to combat corruption, and cannot work against human rights abuses, for these are crucial elements in neopatrimonial regimes' survival strategies (cf. Bratton and Van de Walle, 1997 and 1994; Brownlee, 2001). Without the authoritarian veto-players' consent, there will be no transparency or accountability, no meaningful elections or their monitoring, no truly independent media, and, in short: no effective democracy promotion. What is more, even if a nondemocratic regime does accept DP measures on paper, there are dozens if not hundreds of instances where in reality the regime has done everything to avoid the undesired outcomes of such measures.[17]

In sum, these and a large number of similar observations (which are well recorded and documented in the relevant literature on civil society, governance, and the question of democratization in authoritarian settings) demonstrate one thing that, as trivial as it sounds, has yet to trigger its consequences in strategies of democracy promotion: A strategy that works in one setting under specific circumstances and conditions may not produce similar outcomes in a qualitatively different regime context. Arguably, development cooperation needs partners and local stakeholders. Democracy promotion, then, needs local actors who are supportive of democracy and good governance as an outcome. Put more generally: Local actors, their organizational capacities, interests, and preferences matter for the outcome of DP policies. In a very preliminary and general first step, one might conceive of six different patterns of constellations in which collective actors can be grouped.[18] Depending on these constellations, possible chances of success of DP strategies as hitherto prescribed can roughly be assessed.

Figure 2.4 visualizes this point in an easy-to-grasp fourfold matrix. The boxes shaded in gray are those for which current strategies of DP have little prospect of success. While there is no room to discuss the first column (DP in already democratized regimes) the other two deserve some attention: In the authoritarian setting, "the state," that is, the government, top elite, or ruler alone, has the power to accept or refuse resources aimed at aiding democracy, and, as a consequence, to determine the channels and directions democracy funds may take into the country. As outlined earlier, effective cooperation with nongovernmental actors requires a political regime that tolerates and accepts the legitimacy of autonomous political

		Political Regime		
		Democratic	Authoritarian	in Transition
Civil Society/ Political Opposition	Pro-active in advocating democracy	✓	(✓/✗)	✓
	Dormant/ Not tolerated/ Neutralized by regime	✓	✗	✓

[handwritten annotations: "can be trusted"; "Islamist Organizations"; "they have space to form"; "have a relationship ... closely related to state"]

Figure 2.4   Democracy promotion and the problem of authoritarian settings.
Source: Author

actors beyond its own boundaries. Typically, regimes that display that trait are democracies. But many regimes in which donors wish to intervene to support democracy, and certainly the Arab regimes, are not. Put somewhat provocatively, donors have good reason to question their own projects for DP should their authoritarian partners lend their support: This is often a signal of the fact that the recipient regime sees no threat to authoritarian rule arising from the respective measure. But of what use is DP if it does not challenge authoritarianism? Thus, DP strategies as currently implemented are not designed to work in authoritarian regimes.

In cases where a *political transition* is ongoing, the rules of the political game are uncertain. The number of options for foreign intervention is usually higher since capacities for control and repression by an either weakened or already overthrown nondemocratic regime are low. The words of former East Germany's chief of intelligence, Mielke, to former head of state Erich Honnecker in the night when the Berlin wall fell in 1989 ("Erich, we cannot shoot a hundred thousand people!" as quoted in Przeworski, 1991), have become famous testimony to this type of situation. Manifest opposition had already become too big in size, and the costs of repression had mounted too high for the regime to consider it a realistic choice.

Second, the range of active political actors tends to be larger during phases of political transition than in established systems. There is no single case worldwide where citizens did not make use of such spaces and organized themselves autonomously once the sphere for political organization outside the regime widened. As the space for oppositional actors widens, citizens' costs to engage politically decrease because the perceived risk of repression for the individual is reduced. This results in more and more citizens joining the opposition, which further augments the costs of repression for the regime (cf. Przeworski, 1986). Popular committees, associations, political parties, and the like mushroom in such situations. While only some of them will succeed in playing a significant role in the new regime, this is the necessary process of differentiation of political forces that takes place once the authoritarian regime's monopoly on the political organization of interests ends. In such contexts, therefore, democracy promoters still have a relatively "easy" game since they can wait until such endogenous political organization occurs and then support those forces whose programs are compatible with democratic governance; they can also act as "honest brokers" between competing social forces in order to help them arrive at a new democratic consensus so that more technical questions such as constitutional design can be tackled.

Yet, the transition scenario has become less frequent since the former Soviet bloc re-consolidated, either democratically (Poland, Hungary, the Baltic states), or autocratically (Belarus and others). Much more often, DP today faces authoritarian contexts. Nobody has captured the dilemma that exists here more precisely than Carothers (2000: 224f.):[19]

> The core issue in trying to promote democracy in semi-authoritarian contexts is power, or more particularly, the strong concentration and entrenchment of power characteristic of semi-authoritarian regimes. The basic democracy transition model on which conventional democracy aid programmes have been built over the past ten years assumes that authoritarian power structures have already been broken up.... The transition process, which the democracy aid programmes attempt to advance, is then supposed to be about distributing and channelling power.... But in semi-authoritarian countries power remains highly concentrated.... Conventional forms of democracy aid are therefore problematic in semi-authoritarian contexts. Their basic purpose of helping redistribute power is thwarted by the fact that power is still locked in place.

Again, we are referred to the essential question of the distribution of power, which has already been discussed above (section 3). The key question then is: What strategy should donors pursue when dealing with non-democratic partner governments? This question has hardly ever been posed explicitly, nor has any conceptually sound answer been suggested.

Reflecting on Challenges for Donors and Researchers

"As the lessons from the last decade or so become clearer, it is ... probably fair to say that we now think we understand more about how *not* to go about that challenge than we confidently know how to do it," says Peter

Burnell on the challenge of democratizing authoritarian regimes (2004: 100). This contribution, while having made a few points that underpin such a pessimistic opinion, should enable us to draw some conclusions on what should be done in terms of revisiting the political and conceptual bases on which DP has been built for the past decade.

First, it is a precondition for the success of DP in the Middle East that Western donor governments answer questions concerning their policy priorities unambiguously. Only if they prioritize democratic change in the Middle East (even though outcomes are uncertain) and simultaneously downsize support which benefits primarily incumbent elites will DP stand a chance of contributing to long-term stability based on different Arab regimes than the ones in power today. This would require coherent political positions, a fundamental change in foreign-policy priorities, and certainly also a multiplication of the resources hitherto devoted to the support of democratic governance. Should Western governments conclude that this is too high a risk (and there may be good reasons for such a conclusion), then the question is whether democracy should be promoted at all. As several studies cited here have shown, strategies to date, after roughly one and a half decades, have not resulted in structurally enhanced liberties in any Arab country, let alone in anything close to democratization on a macrolevel. If short-term stability is the overriding objective, it might be wise to disengage from DP (which, of course, would hardly be acceptable in Western public opinion).

Second, one level below (inside the logic of DP), there is a need to distinguish between systemically different contexts of intervention. Intervening in a new democracy is totally different from trying to promote democracy in durably authoritarian contexts. Up to now, no coherent strategies have been formulated that would allow donors to follow a clear path in their engagement with nondemocratic partner regimes in the field of democracy promotion. And while it is beyond the scope of this chapter to suggest any overall strategy, several issues have been discussed which suggest at least a broad focus and some directions which such a strategy might take.

Third, cooperation with nongovernmental actors can only take place to the extent that the regimes grant a wide-enough space for the organizations of societal interests autonomous of the regime. The Western dichotomy of a "bad" state versus a "good" civil society is not helpful in a setting where society is organized in a predominantly informal fashion and where social groups are routinely co-opted by incumbent nondemocratic regimes. Therefore, civil society assistance should be much more carefully and cautiously distributed than before. In fact, support for nongovernmental actors requires an intimate knowledge of the recipient country's society and its organizations—a knowledge the personnel of implementing agencies possess only in very rare exceptions.

On the other hand, a crucial and maybe the largest part of the story of DP in Middle Eastern countries is not about technical advice such as delivering election equipment or building capacity in state administrations. Many actors involved, including nongovernmental ones, belong to their home countries' elites and have a very clear understanding of how their own social and political systems work as well as how, theoretically, democracies work. There is hardly much use in training state bureaucrats in the methods of central auditing as long as parliaments are not allowed to approve the budget, or in "strengthening" judicial independence as long as judges cannot judge independently for fear of repression and discrimination from the regime, or in training other officials in the methods they should apply were they to act in democracies. They might well know, but will still not be able to act accordingly because the logic of current regimes which centralize power does not allow this.

Fifth, if practitioners of DP do not wish to contest the assumption of rational actors, they must take seriously their autocratic counterparts' worries about opening up their polities and losing control. If "partners" really are considered partners, ways have to be sought through political dialogue to demonstrate this clearly enough so that mutual trust can take hold. The challenge is to identify areas where genuine improvements in governance are realistically feasible without cutting the regimes' lifelines. "Democratization," by contrast, implies a vital risk to the core interests of partner governments because by definition, it implies their farewell to the long-held monopoly of power. It is not only against the interest of Arab regimes to strive for democratization, but also against Western governments' interests: Asking Arab governments to cooperate in "democratization" means abolishing the partner and expect him to cooperate in the business— which is not a particularly realistic scenario. Therefore, donors would do better to avoid the term "democratization" altogether in any future strategies which aim at supporting political change.

This terminology creates exaggerated expectations within both Arab and Western societies which will fall back on Western governments' reputation and credibility when not lived up to. Instead, a more feasible course of action would be to seek areas of common ground where true achievements for social forces can be achieved without directly threatening the incumbents' positions. There is a feeling of a need for reform even among the most hesitant Arab rulers today. While autocrats' motives for acknowledging this may not always be noble, this fact does constitute a possible starting point for renewed intergovernmental relations. Both sides wish to avoid violent ruptures, and both sides acknowledge the need for change. The aim for donors in this context must be more modest, and, as Ottaway et al. (2002) put it, the commitment must be long term. The aim could be to contribute to convincing incumbents that a less repressed public sphere in which citizens can interact horizontally does not automatically result in violence or revolution against their regimes. While the Arab world is the world's most illiberal, this very fact also provides considerable space for concrete improvements for citizens' daily lives below the level of systemic transition.

For current research, the key challenge is to increase our knowledge of the causes for Arab authoritarianism. This topic has only recently become a core area of research on Middle East politics. Donor strategies, in their turn, should follow research and be ready to enter the "post-democratization era," take into account these causes, and develop new ideas in order to explicitly address them. They will have to elaborate realistic operationalizations of how the causes can be circumvented or ruled out. Such ideas need to start from present authoritarian conditions in recipient countries rather than from ideal-type images of liberal democracies. Rather than continuing the search for a blueprint or a one-size-fits-all concept of DP based on a random collection of elements of liberal democracy, a sound answer to the problems this chapter has discussed must start from a thorough analysis of currently incumbent regimes and the mechanisms that have so long kept them in power.

Notes

* The opinions, findings and conclusions expressed in this contribution are those of the author and do not necessarily reflect those of the institution the author is affiliated with. I am indebted to Sheila Carapico, Benoît Challand, Nader Fergany, Dietrich Jung, Maye Kassem, Daniela Pioppi, and Søren Schmidt for constructive criticism on previous versions of this paper and/ or for fruitful discussions on democracy promotion in the Arab world which helped me clarify my own views for the present contribution. Responsibility for all errors remains, of course, exclusively with myself.

1. They tend to hold that on the whole, current Arab political change is more adequately interpreted as a re-equilibration and adjustment of authoritarian rule to changed internal and external conditions (cf., e.g., Kassem, 2003; Kienle, 2001; Heydemann, 2002; Lust-Okar, 2004).

2. For more on the topic see Brumberg, 2002; Brownlee, 2001; Schlumberger, 2000a; Albrecht and Schlumberger, 2004; Schlumberger and El-Khazen, 2004, as well as many case studies on individual countries.

3. There is no space here to engage in discussions on the concept of political stability, its relation to durability and change, and its individual dimensions. For a detailed discussion and formalization, cf. Schlumberger (2004b).

4. The reasons for this difference most probably lie in the different methodology since *polity* looks a lot more at formal institutions—and obviously, Arab countries

have not reformed their formal political institutions in such a way that formal democratic institutions such as elections in Gulf countries, to give but one example, have been installed in many countries. However, this has not had any significant impact on real opportunities for participation or the level of individual rights that are guaranteed, not granted, by the respective regimes. By contrast, several authors have identified this as a process of "imitative institution building" (Albrecht and Schlumberger, 2004) of institutions that formally look like their democratic sisters, but fulfil fundamentally different functions from those in democratic settings. In reality, therefore, such institutions are "dictatorial institutions" that serve the "survival of dictatorships" (Ghandi and Przeworski, 2001).

5. Freedomhouse classifies countries as "democratic" if they reach a combined average value of civil and political rights of 2.5 or below. But also from a qualitative methodological view, it is erroneous to call the more liberal Arab countries either "democracies" or "semi-authoritarian" (Carothers, 2000; Ottaway, 2003). This is insofar misleading as all Arab political regimes today fulfil the entire range of definitional criteria of "authoritarianism" as defined by Linz (1964 and 1975) more than forty years ago and as used in comparative politics ever since. In fact, the addition of diminutive attributes to the "authoritarian" serves precisely these regimes in that it "halves" their authoritarian character, evokes the image of them being more amenable to DP, or somehow less "bad." This clearly runs counter to the scholarly desire to gain a more profound understanding of the working mechanisms of Arab regimes. "Semi-authoritarianism," at least when applied to Arab regimes, as does Ottaway with the Egyptian case, clearly is a misclassification. It is not surprising, therefore, that in her book, she cannot draw a clear distinction as to what makes "semi-authoritarian" regimes different from authoritarian regimes as defined by Linz. The only reference made to him is the hint that "Truly authoritarian regimes typically win elections by absurd majorities because they can proclaim whatever results they want" (Ottaway, 2003: 143; note 7). This criterion, wherever it may stem from, does not occur in the classical definition of authoritarianism and is therefore no way of distinguishing "semi-authoritarian regimes" from "truly" authoritarian ones.

6. This question is not only one of terminology, but also important for resulting policy recommendations. I shall get back to this point at the beginning of Reflecting on Challenges for Donors & Researchers.

7. This simple fact is supported by the empirical history of recent transitions: Among the several dozen systemic transitions to democracy that have taken place worldwide since the mid-1970s, there is not a single case where democratization was effectuated with the old regime elites remaining in power. It is naïve, therefore, to assume democratization to be a gradual thing that could somehow automatically take hold without major socio-political disruptions. Even Latin America's and Eastern Europe's "pacted transitions," where old elites were negotiated rather than thrown out of office, transition by definition requires democratic counter elites to the authoritarian regime to be strong enough to force incumbents out of office, and, once founding elections can be

held, requires all relevant political actors to accept the rules of the democratic game even in case of defeat. Democratization always goes along with a redistribution of power.

8. This has long been known among scholars, but is now also underlined by the findings of UNDP's third *Arab Human Development Report* (AHDR 3; UNDP, 2005). Policy-makers who feel they need to have an official document to support their positions now have unambiguous UN statements formulated by independent Arab scholars which they can easily refer to. The question today is thus not about an unclear state of affairs, but purely about the donors' political will to prioritize the support for democracy over other interests.

9. Broadly speaking, at least five different directions within this literature can be distinguished, all of which aim at explaining the above questions, but focus on different independent variables: (1) structuralist approaches, which draw on social structure, the relative distribution of power in society, or class conflict (e.g. Moore, 1966; Rueschemeyer, Stevens and Stevens, 1992; Vanhanen, 1997); (2) culturalist approaches, which emphasize norms and values as traduced through culture and civilization (most notably: Huntington, 1996 and 1984; Kedouri, 1992); (3) modernization-theoretically inspired and functionalist approaches, which focus on the level of socio-economic development as a prerequisite for democratization (e.g. Lipset, 1959 and 1994; Parsons, 1964, and a whole range of neo-modernization theoretical literature); (4) actor-centered explanations, which build on rational choice and the importance of actors behavior (Przeworski, 1986 and 1991; O'Donnell and Schmitter, 1986; Colomer, 2000); and (5) explanations that draw on international factors.

10. Carothers (2002) correctly criticizes donor strategies of democracy promotion and assumes they were built on what he calls "the transition paradigm." While I am not so sure whether any such paradigm ever existed, the main error of thought lies in the fact that he equates transitology as an academic (sub-) discipline with the truncated ideas donor agencies have taken from it and incorporated into policies. See also O'Donnell's (2002) "Partial Defense of an Evanescent Paradigm" in the subsequent issue of the *Journal of Democracy*.

11. The currently ongoing debate about the possible causes of the durability of authoritarianism in the Arab world would over-stretch the scope of this contribution. For this point, see Schlumberger (2005: 18–24 and 2004a: ch. 3 in greater detail).

12. To be precise: The initial goal was not always narrowed down to explaining merely processes of democratization, but systemic political change in general. Linz (1978), for instance, examines "the breakdown of democratic regimes," thus systemic change in the 'opposite' direction. Non-democratic transitions are discussed in Schlumberger (2002).

13. For an intelligent approach to this question, see Sayyid (1995). The most comprehensive treatment of civil society problems in the Arab world remains the two-volume study edited by Norton (1995 and 1996).

14. For instance, the five countries of the Caspian region (Uzbekistan, Kazakhstan, Azerbaijan, Turkmenistan and Kyrgyzstan), if taken as one region, score as poorly as or even worse than the average for Arab countries based on democracy

indicators (cf. Schlumberger, 2004a: ch. 2). In South and South-East Asia, countries like Burma, Brunei, and even Malaysia suffer from "freedom-deficits" (to borrow a term from UNDP's first *AHDR*, 2002a) as large as the ones found in Arab countries, and a number of African countries plus the Central American cases of Haiti and Cuba demonstrate that the persistence of non-democratic political rule is not a phenomenon restricted to one region only.

15. That is, if one wishes to apply the term of a "bourgeoisie" at all, given the fact that a large part of that social group has displayed little that matches with the Schumpeterian or Weberian entrepreneurial spirit these authors see as characteristic. Therefore, it is futile to expect large-scale business to become change agents for political liberalization or democratization.

16. Political regimes are not, of course, monolithic blocs but composed of a coalition of dominant social forces. In Arab countries today, this coalition can roughly be generalized as consisting of the top political elite, large private entrepreneurs, and the upper ranks of the military and security services. The latter have, over time, developed economic interests and are therefore no longer the purely military-political actor they were in the 1950s and 1960s. Yet, what they all share is their interest in maintaining power and prosperity. While these intra-regime constellations may shift and their preferred strategies of power maintenance may vary (hard-liners will argue for repression in the face of crises while soft-liners will advocate widening the bases of legitimacy through co-opting strategically important social segments), they are united in their desire to remain in power.

17. Examples of such outcomes would be the emergence of autonomous civil society organizations or the growing of uncontrolled spaces for societal organization beyond the state, independent judiciaries, undesired election results, and anything else that could endanger the regime's control over the political and economic process.

18. Note that this suggestion is neither exhaustive nor final. It serves here solely the purpose of distinguishing the broadest possible settings which practitioners of democracy promotion may encounter in different countries.

19. However, the attribute "semi-authoritarian" for Arab countries is a misnomer, as explained above (note 4).

References

Albrecht, Holger (2005) "Das Prinzip Hoffnung: Zivilgesellschaft im Vorderen Orient," in Deutsches Übersee-Institut (ed.): *Neues Jahrbuch Dritte Welt*, Opladen: Verlag für Sozialwissenschaften (2006).

Albrecht, Holger and Oliver Schlumberger (2004) " 'Waiting for Godot': Regime Change Without Democratization in the Middle East," *International Political Science Review*, 25 (4): 371–392.

Bratton, Michael and Nicolas Van de Walle (1994) "Patrimonial Regimes and Political Transition in Africa," *World Politics*, 46 (4): 453–89.

—— (1997) *Democratic Experiments in Africa: Regime Transitions in Comparative Perspective*, Cambridge: Cambridge University Press.

Brownlee, Jason (2001) "And yet they Persist: Explaining Survival and Transition in Neopatrimonial Regimes," *SCID*, 37 (3): 35–63.

Brouwer, Imco (2000) *US Civil Society Assistance to the Arab World. The Cases of Egypt and Palestine*, Florence: EUI [RSC Working Papers Series No. 05/2000].

Burnell, Peter (2004) "Democracy Promotion. The Elusive Quest for Grand Strategies," *International Politics and Society*, 4: 100–16.

Carapico, Sheila (2002) "Foreign Aid for Promoting Democracy in the Arab World," *Middle East Journal*, 56 (3): 379–95.

—— (2005) "Why Export Democracy to the Arab Mediterranean?" Paper presented to the 6thAnnual Mediterranean Social and Political Research Meeting organized by the Robert Schuman Centre, European University Institute, Montecatini Terme, March 16–20, 2005.

Carapico, Sheila and Abla Amawi (2005) "Democracy Promotion in the Arab Mediterranean," Workshop Description to the *6th Mediterranean Social and Political Research Meeting (MSPRM)* organized by the Robert Schuman Institute of Advanced Studies, European University Institute, at Montecatini Terme, 16–20 March.

Carothers, Thomas (2002) "The End of the Transition Paradigm," *Journal of Democracy*, 13 (1): 5–21.

—— (2000) "Struggling with Semi-Authoritarians," in Peter Burnell (ed.): *Democracy Assistance. International Co-Operation for Democratization*, London: Frank Cass.

Challand, Benoît (2005) "Benevolent Actors? International Donors and Civil Society Support for Palestinian NGOs," paper presented to the 6th Mediterranean Social and Political Research Meeting, European University Institute, Montecatini Terme, March 16–20, 2005.

Colomer, Joseph (2000) *Strategic Transitions. Game Theory and Democratization*, Baltimore: Johns Hopkins University Press.

Dahl, Robert (1971) *Polyarchy. Participation and Opposition*, New Haven, CT: Yale University Press.

Di Palma, Guiseppe (1990) *To Craft Democracies: An Essay on Democratic Transitions*, Berkeley: University of California Press.

Diamond, Larry, Juan Linz and Seymour Lipset (1988) *Democracy in Developing Countries, Vol. II: Africa*, Boulder: Lynne Rienner.

El-Khazen, Farid (2003) "Political Parties in Postwar Lebanon: Parties in Search of Partisans," *Middle East Journal*, 57 (4): 605–624.

Elsenhans, Harmut (1991) *Development and Underdevelopment. The History, Economics and Politics of North-South Relations*, New Delhi and London: Sage.

Freedomhouse (ed.): [annually, 1973–2004] *Freedom in the World*, New York: Freedomhouse.

Ghandi, Jennifer and Adam Przeworski (2001) "Dictatorial Institutions and the Survival of Dictators," Paper prepared for the Annual Meeting of the *American Political Science Association*, San Francisco, August 30—September 2, 2001.

Guazzone, Laura and Daniela Pioppi (2004) "Democratisation in the Arab World Revisited," *The International Spectator*, 4 (2004): 89–101.

Hammoudi, Abdellah (1997) *Master and Disciple: The Cultural Foundations of Moroccan Authoritarianism*, Chicago, ILL.: University of Chicago Press.

Heydemann, Stephen (2002) "La question de la démocratie dans les travaux sur le monde arabe," *Critique International*, 17 (2002): 45–62.

Hinnebusch, Raymond (2004) "The Viability of Authoritarian Rule in the Middle East: An Overview and Critique of Theory," accessed February 15, 2005 at: http://www.mafhoum.com/press6/ 176P51hinnebusch.htm#_edn1

Huntington, Samuel (1984) "Will More Countries Become Democratic?" *Political Science Quarterly*, 99 (2): 193—218.

—— (1996) *The Clash of Civilizations*, New York: Simon and Schuster.

Kassem, Maye (2003) *Egyptian Politics: The Dynamics of Authoritarian Rule*, Boulder, Co.: Lynne Rienner.

Kedouri, Elie (1992) *Islam and Arab Political Culture*, Washington, D.C.: The Washington Institute for Near East Policy.

Kienle, Eberhard (1998) "More than a Response to Islamism: The Political De-Liberalization of Egypt in the 1990s," *Middle East Journal* 52 (2): 219–235.

Kienle, Eberhard (2001) A Grand Delusion. Democracy and Economic Reform in Egypt, London: I.B. Taunis.

Lawson, Fred (2003) "Bahrain," in: Freedomhouse (ed.): *Countries at the Crossroads*, Washington, D.C.: Freedomhouse.

Lingnau, Hildegard (2003) "Zivilgesellschaft—Zur Problematik einer Wunschvorstellung der staatlichen Entwicklungszusammenarbeit," *Nord-Süd Aktuell*, 17 (2): 233–238.

Linz, Juan (1964) "An Authoritarian Regime: Spain," in Erik Allard and Yrjö Littunen (eds.): *Cleavages, Ideologies and Party Systems—Contributions to Comparative Political Sociology*, Helsinki: The Academic Bookstore [Transactions of the Westermarck Society No. X].

—— (1975) "Totalitarianism and Authoritarian Regimes," in N. Polsby and F. Greenstein (eds.): *Handbook of Political Science, Vol. III: Macro-Political Theory*, Reading, MA.: Addison Wesley.

—— (1978) "The Breakdown of Democratic Regimes. Crisis, Breakdown and Reequilibration," in Juan Linz and Alfred Stepan (eds.): *The Breakdown of Democratic Regimes*, Vol. 4, Baltimore: Johns Hopkins University Press.

Lipset, Seymour (1959) "Some Social Requisites of Democracy. Economic Development and Political Legitimacy," *American Political Science Review*, 53 (1): 69–105.

—— (1994) "The Social Requisites of Democracy Revisited," *American Sociological Review*, 59 (1): 1–22.

Lust-Okar, Ellen (2004) "Divided They Rule: The Management and Manipulation of Political Opposition," *Comparative Politics*, 36 (2) 139–156.

Maghraoui, Abdesslam (2002) "Depoliticization in Morocco," *Journal of Democracy*, 13 (4): 24–32.

Moore, Barrington (1966) *The Social Origins of Democracy and Dictatorship. Lord and Peasant in the Making of the Modern Society*, New York: Beacon Press.

Norton, Augustus and Farhad Kazemi (2004) "Middle Eastern Political Reform," in Foreign Policy Association (ed.): *Great Decisions 2004*, New York: Foreign Policy Association.

Norton, Augustus (ed.) (1995–96) *Civil Society in the Arab World*, 2 vols., Leiden: Brill.

O'Donnell, Guillermo and Philippe Schmitter (1986) *Transitions from Authoritarian Rule. Vol. IV: Tentative Conclusions About Uncertain Democracies*, Baltimore: Johns Hopkins UP.

O'Donnell, Guillermo (2002) "Partial Defense of an Evanescent Paradigm," Journal of Democracy, 13 (3): 6–12.

Ottaway, Marina (2003) *Democracy Challenged. The Rise of Semi-Authoritarianism*, Washington, D.C.: Carnegie Endowment.

Ottaway, Marina et al. (2002) "Democratic Mirage in the Middle East," *Policy Brief No. 20*, Washington, D.C.: Carnegie Endowment.

Parsons, Talcott (1964) "Evolutionary Universals in Society," *American Sociological Review*, 29 (1964): 339—357.

Perthes, Volker (2004) "Elite Change and Systems Maintenance," in Volker Perthes (ed.): *Arab Elites. Negotiating the Politics of Change*, Boulder, CO: Lynne Rienner.

Pioppi, Daniela (2004) "From Religious Charity to the Welfare State and Back. The Case of Islamic Endowments (waqfs) Revival in Egypt," *EUI Working Papers*, RSCAS No. 2004/34.

Przeworski, Adam (1991) *Democracy and the Market. Political and Economic Reform in Latin America and Eastern Europe*, Cambridge: Cambridge University Press.

—— (1986) "Some Problems in the Study of Transition to Democracy," in O'Donnell, Guillermo, Philippe Schmitter and Laurence Whitehead (eds.): *Transitions from Authoritarian Rule, Vol. III (Comparative Perspectives)*, Baltimore: John Hopkins University Press.

Putnam, Robert (with R. Leonardi and R. Nanetti) (1993) *Making Democracy Work: Civic Traditions in Modern Italy*, Princeton, NJ: Princeton University Press.

Rueschemeyer, Dietrich, Evelyne Stevens and John Stevens (1992) *Capitalist Development and Democracy*, Cambridge: Polity Press.

Sayyid, Mustapha K. (1995) "The Concept of Civil Society in the Arab World," in Rex Brynen, Bahgat Korany, and Paul Noble (eds.): *Political Liberalization and Democratization in the Arab World, Vol. I: Theory and Concepts* Boulder, CO: Lynne Rienner.

Schlumberger, Oliver (2000a) "The Arab Middle East and the Question of Democratization. Some Critical Remarks," *Democratization* 7 (4): 104–132.

—— (2000b) "Arab Political Economy and the EU's Mediterranean Policy: What Prospects for Development?" *New Political Economy*, 5 (2): 247–68.

—— (2002) *Transition in the Arab World: Guidelines for Comparison*, Florence: EUI [RSC Working Papers Series No. 22/2002].

—— (2004a) *Demokratie- und Governance-Defizite in den Ländern Nordafrikas und des Nahen Ostens. Ursachen, Veränderungstendenzen und Schlussfolgerungen für die Rolle der EZ* (Democracy- and Governance-Deficits in the Middle East and North Africa. Causes, Trends, and Implications for Development Co-Operation), unpublished ms., Bonn: German Development Institute.

—— (2004b) "Political Liberalization, Regime Stability, and Imitative Institution-Building: Towards a Formal Understanding", paper presented to the 5th annual Mediterranean Social and Political Research Meeting, organized by the Robert-Schuman-Centre for Advanced Studies, European University Institute, Montecatini Terme and Florence, 18–22 March 2004.

Schlumberger, Oliver (2005) "Promoting Democracy in Authoritarian Regimes. Dilemmas of Development Co-Operation in the Arab World," paper presented to the 6th Mediterranean Social and Political Research Meeting (MSPRM), organized by the Robert Schuman Centre, European University Institute, Montecatini Terme, March 16–20, 2005.

Schlumberger, Oliver and André Bank (2002) "Succession, Legitimacy and Regime Stability in Jordan," *Arab Studies Journal*, 10 (1): 50–72.

Schlumberger, Oliver and Farid El-Khazen (2004) "Dynamics of Stability," Workshop Description for WS 12, 5th Mediterranean Social and Political Research Meeting, Florence and Montecatini, March 24–28, 2004.

Tocqueville, Alexis de (1981) [1835] *De la démocratie en Amérique*, 2 vols., Paris: Flammarion.

UNDP (2002a) *Human Development Report: Deepening Democracy in a Fragmented World*, New York: Oxford University Press.

——(2002b) *Arab Human Development Report*, New York: UNDP.

——(2005) *Towards Freedom in the Arab World. Arab Human Development Report 2004*, New York: UNDP.

United States of America (2002) *The National Security Strategy of the United States of America, September 2002*, accessed on March 21, 2005 at www.whitehouse.gov/nsc/nss.html

Vanhanen, Tatu (1997) *The Process of Democratization. A Comparative Analysis of 170 Countries*, New York: Routledge.

World Bank (2003) *MENA Development Report. Better Governance for Development in the Middle East and North Africa. Enhancing Inclusiveness and Accountability*, Washington, DC.: World Bank.

3

Who's Afraid of Transnationalism? Arabism, Islamism, and the Prospects of Democratization in the Arab East

Thomas Scheffler

Introduction: Democratization, Boundaries, and Indirect Powers

All attempts to "democratize" the Middle East have to take into account that the idea of democracy is historically intertwined with the idea of numerically, territorially, and sometimes even culturally delimited political units: A political body that generates its vital decisions through *voting* procedures is well advised to know who exactly is entitled to vote and who is not. Some scholars have also argued that the political equality of all citizens, a cornerstone of democratic decision-making, is predicated upon a basic stock of substantial similarity (homogeneity) between them, be it based on common language and culture, shared historical experiences, customs, and beliefs, or on the citizens' social status (Heller, 1928; Schmitt, 1928: 227–234). Finally, "sovereignty" and "accountable governance" require an effective boundary shielding the state from interference of "indirect powers," that is, external or transnational actors that might try to influence a commonwealth's decision-making without being directly accountable for the results.

[handwritten note: Any Nation Building — External Players, and those E.B. will always attempt to gain.]

In European political thought, the concept of indirect power originated in the struggles between Church and State during the religious wars of the sixteenth and seventeenth centuries. Prominent Jesuit jurists, most notably Robert Bellarmine (1542–1621) and Francisco Suárez (1548–1617), conceded that the State was sovereign in temporal affairs, but that the Catholic Church, due to its superior spiritual and eschatological world mission, had a *potestas indirecta* (or *potestas directiva*) *in temporalibus*, entitling it to interfere in the temporal affairs of any Christian state for the sake of spiritual guidance. Thomas Hobbes (1588–1679) developed his concept of sovereign absolutist statehood in opposition to Bellarmine's theory (Hobbes, 1985: III, ch. 42). For Carl Schmitt (1888–1985), Hobbes's critique of the corrosive effect of indirect power on effective statehood constituted his pivotal and lasting contribution for later centuries—during which, according to Schmitt, the "old adversaries" of territorial state-building, for example, the indirect powers of the Church and other medieval non-state actors, were reappearing in modern shape: as societal associations, trade-unions, and ideological political parties (Schmitt, 1982: 26, 113, 116–18, 127, 130–32).

In the nineteenth and twentieth centuries, territorial statehood in the Middle East developed in the crossfire between two types of indirect power. On the one hand were the multifaceted attempts of Western powers to select, direct and, if necessary, obstruct local leaders—attempts that appeared in various historical and juridical disguises: as capitulation treaties, consular jurisdiction, international debt administration commissions, protectorates, treaties of friendship and alliance, high commissioners, policy advisors, missionaries, development agencies, covert intelligence operations, bribes, threats, sponsored opposition groups, and so on. On the other hand were regional pan-movements, such as pan-Islamism and pan-Arabism, which tried to counteract the intervention of foreign intruders by strengthening the unity of Arabs and Muslims across the political and social boundaries that divided them. Pan-Islamism and pan-Arabism were sometimes used as ideological resources for state-building, especially when a local ruler claimed a hegemonic role for his own country. Sultan Abdülhamid II (r. 1876–1909), for example, turned to the "politics of Pan-Islam" when the ideology of Ottomanism had failed to stabilize his empire (Landau, 1994: 36–72). King Faysal I of Iraq (r. 1921–33), facing the task of building, as a foreigner, a new state in a highly fragmented country, opted for making Iraq the pioneer and hegemon of Arab unity (Porath, 1984b). In these and other cases, however, both pan-Islamism and pan-Arabism frequently turned into a means of mobilizing the population of other Arab and Muslim countries against their own rulers.

It is this latter type of indirect power and its impact on the region's democratization with which this chapter deals. More precisely, it poses the question of whether these pan-ideologies must be seen as an obstacle to democratization in the region. According to the statistics of Freedom House, the countries of the Arab world, being predominantly inhabited by Arabs and Muslims, share one important characteristic that seems to promise them successful democratization: They are "monoethnic"—at least according to Freedom House, which classifies a state as "monoethnic" if more than two-thirds of its population belong to the same ethnic group (Karatnycky, 2002: 107). Freedom House claims that there are "noteworthy distinctions between monoethnic and multiethnic countries with regard to freedom and democracy" (107), the most important being that "a state with a dominant ethnic group is three times more likely to be Free than a multiethnic state" (110). Out of eighty-six countries that were considered "free" in the institution's annual survey for 2001, sixty-four were monoethnic, and among the 121 electoral democracies, seventy-nine were monoethnic. All in all, these numbers seem to confirm the old thesis that democratization is easier in homogeneous countries. In theory, thus, most Arab countries should have a reasonable chance to develop into successful democracies. Alas, this expectation is not confirmed by Freedom House's empirical finds, which rather show "a dramatic gap in the state of freedom and democracy between majority-Muslim countries—particularly the Arab states—and the rest of the world" (Karatnycky, 2002: 99).

One way to explain that paradox would be to assume that there are so many other causes for authoritarianism at work in the Arab East that the beneficial effects of ethnoreligious homogeneity, that is, Arab-Muslim majority, simply cannot work out. Another, rather complementary, approach, however, would be to assume that "monoethnicity" in itself is not always beneficial. For instance, an oversupply of similarities among neighbors might intensify their desire to develop new distinctions and social boundaries between them. The numerical dominance of a particular ethnic or religious group might also turn into an obstacle to state-building and democratization if it is not confined to one single territorial state. If similarities do not stop at the border, it is the border itself that will be contested or become permeable.

The kind of conflicts that may emerge from such a constellation will also depend on how the importance of political borders is perceived by the main actors: Nationalist pan-movements, for instance, usually invoke the existence of a kind of national meta-"substance" that is tragically dispersed into many political bodies and ought to be reassembled into a united body, namely, the nation-state. The resulting aversion against all boundaries dividing the "nation" may easily lead to violent irredentism and hegemonic wars. In the framework of Islam's *tawhid* theology, however, it has been much easier to reconcile the ideal of Muslim unity with political diversity. The meta-substance of the worldwide community of believers (*ummah*) is the *shariah*, and the unity of the ummah exists as long and in as far as the shariah remains what the term's etymology already suggests: the common "water hole" of its members, a fountain of normative and spiritual guidance for all. Certainly, this type of normative super-legality, too, may lead to conflict, especially when a local power-holder is accused of not respecting the shariah, but the aim usually is to correct or to replace the ruler, not to dissolve the state and join it to another one.

In the twentieth-century Arab world, however, both types of conflict overlapped: The regional state-system set up in the former Arab provinces of the Ottoman Empire after World War I was the work of European governments who were neither inspired by the shariah nor by the wishes of the local population and its leaders. Cutting across larger and older ethnic, religious, tribal, and linguistic affiliations, the new political boundaries reflected the strategic visions of non-Muslim and non-Arab powers that tried to control the region by divide-and-rule politics. Not surprisingly, the legitimacy of the new states was time and again contested by local elites and counterelites, and attempts to overcome the region's "artificial" fragmentation by larger pan-Arab political structures or to change the politics of a particular Arab state under the banner of pan-Arab unity were not a rare occurrence.

For pan-Arab ideologues, the struggle for Arab unity across the borders of the existing Arab states was justified by a common culture and a common past as well as by common political and economic necessities: The Arab language and the memory of a glorious Arabo-Islamic past seemed to be powerful facilitators of common action. Considering the region's notorious centrality in world politics and the frequency of external interventions caused by its geostrategic situation, a strong and united Arab commonwealth seemed to be the best way to ensure the independence and sovereignty of all Arabs. In addition, the unequal distribution of important economic resources such as fertile land, water, population, oil, and access to maritime transportation routes lent credence to the view that the social problems of the Arab world could only be solved in the overarching framework of a comprehensive pan-Arab solution.

In practical terms, the dream of a greater Arab commonwealth seemed to be much more than merely a castle in the air. After all, the Near East had been ruled by large imperial states for centuries, the last one being the Ottoman Empire, which had been dismantled by external powers after 1918. True, several Arab countries—most notably Iraq, Lebanon, Palestine, and Sudan—have considerable non-Arab and non-Muslim minorities, but many of these minorities also belong to one of the larger majorities of the region—Christian minorities like the Copts, Greek-Orthodox, Maronites, Melkites, and Jacobites being part of the Arab majority; non-Arabs like the Kurds being part of the Muslim majority.

The intensity of pan-Arab visions is indicated by the many attempts of Arab leaders to translate them into different schemes of political unity (Kienle, 1995; Mufti, 1996; Porath, 1984a, 1984b; Simon, 1974). The most important among them have been the Hashemite efforts to unite the Arab provinces of the former Ottoman Empire under the rule of their dynasty since 1916, King Abdallah of Jordan's "Greater Syria" schemes (1936–44), Nuri al-Said's scheme of Fertile Crescent unity (1943), the foundation of the Arab League (1944/45), the merger of Egypt and Syria into the United Arab Republic in 1958, followed by the establishment of the United Arab States, a loose federation between Egypt, Syria, and North Yemen (1958), as well as by a plethora of other initiatives, such as the unity talks between Egypt, Iraq, and Syria (1963–64), Egypt, Sudan, and Libya (1969), Egypt, Syria, and Libya (1971), Egypt and Libya (1972), Syria and Iraq (1978), and, finally, Syria and Libya (1980).

True, on the institutional level, most of these initiatives were short-lived and left no lasting results, but the obsession with repeating the ill-fated experience time and again points to an underlying psychological reality to which even the most pragmatic Arab statesman felt compelled to pay lip-service. Even the US-inspired Transitional Administrative Law for the State of Iraq, promulgated on March 8, 2004, while declaring Iraq "a country of many nationalities [*qawmiyyat*]," stipulates, at the same time, that "the Arab people [*shaab*] in it are an inseparable part of the Arab nation [*al-ummah al-arabiyyah*]" (TAL, art. 7 B).

Pan-Arabism and Democratization

For many of its critics, Pan-Arabism, and especially the Pan-Arabism of the 1950s and 1960s, had a rather negative effect on both state-building and democratization in the Near East. It was precisely the fact that Arab unity seemed to be so intuitively legitimate that led to the neglect of patient transnational institution-building and shifted attention to the premature question of who could become the "Bismarck" of the coming Pan-Arab commonwealth. Not surprisingly, the promotion of Arab unity became an amplifier of intra-Arab rivalry: While some leaders competed for the role of the most visible champion of the Arab cause by denouncing others as traitors and weaklings, others felt compelled to obstruct any initiative for inter-Arab cooperation because they were afraid it might be another veiled attempt to advance another leader's imperialist ambitions (Pfaff, 1970: 155).

In addition, the idea that there was only one single Arab nation and that all Arabs were brethren provided an easy excuse for frequent interventions in the domestic affairs of other Arab states by means of sponsoring militant local opposition groups, hostile radio propaganda, and, if need be, assassination attempts on other Arab leaders (Rubin, 2002: 150–67). The lasting result was a climate of mutual distrust between Arab governments that hampered their economic and military cooperation, blocked the development of effective transnational Arab networks and institutions, and facilitated the buildup of impressive local security apparatuses that hindered, in turn, the development of a vigorous civil society.

Under these circumstances, rhetorical hostility against Israel became the easiest and less contested way of expressing concern for Arab unity. But this form of negative integration had its price: Continuously invoking the hostile image of an external foe as the main problem of all Arabs and Muslims helped increase the budget of the Arab armies and became an easy tool to discredit political opponents as agents of Israel and postpone democratic reforms at home. It facilitated the militarization of Arab politics and helped undermine all attempts to integrate the region's non-Arab and non-Muslim minorities on a secure and long-term federal basis. In an overall climate of existential confrontation, monolithic unity of the greater "We"-group seemed to be the only way to survive and assert oneself. Political pluralism and federalism, however, appeared as the surest way to erosion, disintegration, and powerlessness. Last but not least, confrontation with Israel led time and again to real wars, which often ended in defeat, thus revealing to the Arab public that the Arab governments were unable to fulfill the most basic task effective contractual statehood is predicated upon, namely, to protect their citizens.

In hindsight, thus, the destructive power of pan-Arabism proved greater than its constructive one. Unable to shatter the individual Arab states, it disturbed and distorted their development, making them more authoritarian and distrustful against each other and, thus, blocking the way to greater transnational inter-Arab cooperation.

Western experts did not expect this state of affairs to last forever. "With each passing day," Richard Pfaff wrote in 1970, "existing political, economic, and social interests become more solidly cemented to the fragmented polity" of the Arab world (Pfaff, 1970:156), and

> as each particular Arab polity gains an historical depth of its own, as each develops its own peculiar social, economic, and political institutions, as each provides its own framework of identification and moral guidance, the

significance of Arab nationalism will surely wane. At that point, then, to be an 'Arab' will take on a meaning similar to being a member of the 'English-speaking world,' or will become as vacuous as the 'negritude' of Black Africa. (Pfaff, 1970: 167)

Anwar al-Sadat's journey to Jerusalem (1977) and the separate Egyptian-Israeli peace treaty (1979) that led to Egypt's temporary exclusion from the Arab League (1979–87) were the first indicators that the days of Pan-Arabism were over (Ajami, 1979) and that from now on Arab states would openly pursue their own interests and not the imperatives of the pan-Arab cause. Since the 1980s, a growing number of scholars has been arguing that the Arab states, in spite of their precarious and fragile origins, have established themselves for good against all kinds of pan-Arab challenges (Ben Dor, 1983; Halliday, 2004; Mufti, 1996; Owen, 1992; Yapp, 1991). Expanding state bureaucracies, armies, and security forces; the growth of the public sector, welfare politics, and agrarian reforms; oil revenues and external support have all helped expand the state's grip on local social interests and made large parts of the civil society dependent on government action. Some of the more optimistic authors even concluded that now that the region's states were finally transforming themselves into consolidated individual entities, they might also become mature enough to develop into liberal democracies (cf. Brynen et al., 1995).

Nevertheless, the specter of Middle Eastern transnationalism still seems to haunt Western policy advisors. In an open "memo" to the State Department's Under Secretary of State for Public Diplomacy, Karen P. Hughes, Robert Satloff, executive director of the Washington Institute for Near East Policy, came up with the following policy recommendation:

Banish the terms 'Arab world' and 'Muslim world' from America's diplomatic lexicon; be as country-specific as possible, in both word and deed. Radical Islamists want to erase borders and create a supranational world where the lines of demarcation run between the 'house of Islam' and the 'house of war.' Don't cede the battlefield to them without a fight. (Satloff, 2005)

Considering the many obituaries that have been published to announce the decline of Arabism (Ajami, 1979 and 1981; Dawisha, 2003) and even Islamism (Roy, 1992; Basbous, 2000; Kepel, 2000), this statement sounds rather surprising. It suggests that pan-Islamism and pan-Arabism might not be as dead as some of their critics wish them to be. How strong are they today? How are they interrelated? And how do they harmonize with the U.S.-led attempts to democratize the region after September 11?

Arabism and Islamism as an Obstacle
to Democratization?

The relationship between Arabism and Islamism in the Arab world may best be compared to a system of communicating tubes, in which movements in one part of the system affect the ups and downs in the other one. Both Arabism and Islamism draw their political energies from the same source: a widespread and emotionally deeply rooted aversion to foreign domination. This is a mental disposition that favors those movements which seem to be most successful in defying external enemies. In the 1950s and 1960s, the heyday of the national liberation struggle against European colonialism, Islamist groups were politically eclipsed by secularist national leaders like Gamal Abdel Nasser and the Baath Party. After the defeat of the secularist Arab regimes in 1967, however, Islamists slowly gained ground. After the demise of the Palestinian resistance movement in the 1970s and early 1980s, they evolved into the main protagonists in the struggle against foreign domination. From a resistance perspective, the successes of political Islam in toppling the Shah of Iran (1979), bombing the U.S. troops out of Lebanon (1983–84), forcing the Soviet occupation forces from Afghanistan (1979–89), and driving the U.S. humanitarian intervention forces from Somalia (1993–94) compared favorably with the humiliating defeat of the Arab armies in 1967, Sadat's readiness to conclude a separate peace with Israel, and the failure of the PLO and Syria in protecting Lebanon against the Israeli invasion of 1982. The massive return of Western troops to the Gulf region after the end of the Cold War and the dismantling of Iraq's secularist Baath regime in 2003 drew more and more former secularist nationalists into cooperation with Islamist networks. "The line between nationalism and the Islamic identity," Graham Fuller wrote in 2004, "is now nearly obliterated: Even non-Muslim Arabs generally identify with the broader Islamist-nationalist trend." (Fuller, 2004: 14).

In the short term, thus, both Arabism and Islamism have been competitors. Seen in a long-term perspective, however, they have been reinforcing each other. It was the nationalists who helped establish "the masses" (*al-jumhur*) and "the people" (*al-shaab*) as positive core concepts on the mental maps of Arab political thought. Without the impressive improvement of mass education under the nationalist reform regimes, the propaganda of text-based scripturalist fundamentalists would hardly have been as successful as they became after the 1970s. The symbiotic competition between Arabism and Islamism is not only apparent in the numerous personal crossovers between the two currents, but also in the ideological interpenetration between them: Due to the central role of Islam in Arab history and culture, even the most secularized versions of Arab nationalism have retained a strong Islamic coloring. Secular nationalist resistance movements like the Algerian FLN or al-Fatah used Islamic symbols and concepts like *jihad* and martyrdom to mobilize their followers (Johnson, 1982). Islamists, on the other hand, borrowed heavily from leftist and nationalist propaganda to get more attention (Halliday, 2004: 215). In a way, they were most successful where they transformed themselves into the vanguard of an ongoing national resistance struggle against foreign territorial occupation (Roy, 2004: 62–65), most notably in the cases of Hizballah and Hamas.

There are, however, several features that distinguish transnational Islamism from Pan-Arabism and contribute to its present success. First, the Islamists of the 1990s and 2000s have much more transnational media and societal networks at their disposal than the Arab nationalists of the 1940s, 1950s, and 1960s. In the mid-twentieth century, pan-Arabism still appealed to an imaginary Arab world that was mainly "integrated" by its linguistic and cultural similarities and a common adversity against European colonialism, but not by an overarching economic division of labor, by transnational mass migration, or exposure to the same mass media.

Much has changed since then: The oil revolution of the 1970s and 1980s boosted intra-Arab migration (Ibrahim, 1982) and put unprecedented sums of petrodollars at the disposal of Islamist propaganda. Cheap flight connections, mobile and satellite phones, the Internet, and electronic banking facilitate international communication and long-distance networking. Cinema, television, videos, and DVDs facilitate a much more intensive kind of visual propaganda. Satellite TV stations like al-Jazeerah, al-Manar, or al-Arabiyyah became powerful media to communicate the diversity as well as the unity of a transnational Arab audience. As a result of worldwide Muslim migration, family-, village-, and mosque-related networks now crisscross the globe. Emigration to Europe and America opened new public spaces for pan-Islamic activism beyond the control of Middle Eastern states ("Londonistan").

Second, Islamists have been much more society-oriented than Arab nationalists. Arab nationalism, ideologically indebted to European nationalist thought, was obsessed with the question of the nation-state as a source of anticolonial power. The existence of several Arab states, hence, was seen as something unnatural, as an artificial "balkanization," contrived by western imperialists and their local puppets. As a result, much political energy was wasted in struggling for larger political structures. The corresponding mode of politics was an elite-focused top-down approach that relied, its populist rhetoric notwithstanding, on military coups, military elites, authoritarian mass parties, and security services in order to control

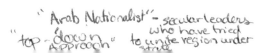
" Arab Nationalist" - secular leaders
who have tried
" top - down" to unite region under
Approach" state

and mobilize the population. On the level of symbolic politics it promoted identification with a few state leaders, such as Gamal Abdel Nasser, Hafiz al-Asad, Saddam Hussein, or Moammar al-Gadaffi, who were hailed as embodiments of the greater Arab cause.

Islamism, on the other hand, has invested much more energy in politics "from below" and a less centralized leadership structure, a method that was more in tune with the traditions of the Muslim ummah. As can be seen from the development of the Society of Muslim Brothers (*jamiyyat al-ikhwan al-muslimin*), founded in 1928, modern Islamist activism focused to a considerable degree on issues "below"—or, seen from a religious perspective, rather "above"—the level of the state, such as education, social charity, public morals, observance of public religious rituals, appropriate dress, food, prayers, and so on. This was a grassroots policy with a strong potential to link the individual to the issues of the broader community. Changing one's food and dress, growing a beard, wearing a headscarf, renouncing alcohol, attending Friday prayers, fasting at Ramadan, are, perhaps, tiresome, but they are things that every Muslim can do at little cost. For people who feel unable to change the "system" of their society, the experience of being able to change oneself or one's family, is an experience of personal empowerment and moral strength that finally may encourage them to engage themselves in greater activism in the larger society, too. As Hasan al-Banna (1906–49), the Brotherhood's founder, put it in a frequently quoted slogan: "Eject imperialism from your souls, and it will leave your lands" (Mitchell, 1993: 230).

While nationalism is essentially related to state-building, Islamism, thus, is essentially a man- and society-changing project—an approach that made it also more interested in knitting far-reaching societal networks across state borders. Already in the early 1950s, the Muslim Brotherhood, for instance, had a Section for Liaison with the Islamic World (*qism al-ittisal*), which ran nine sub-committees, seven of which dealt with different regions of the Muslim world: (1) North Africa; (2) Ethiopia, Somaliland, Nigeria, and Senegal; (3) Syria, Palestine, Lebanon, Jordan, and Iraq; (4) Saudi Arabia, Yemen, and the Gulf principalities; (5) Turkey, Iran, Pakistan, and Afghanistan; (6) India, Ceylon, Indonesia, Malaya, the Philippines, China and other parts of the Far East and Pacific Ocean; (7) Muslim minorities in America, the USSR, and Europe (Mitchell, 1993: 173).

It is true that several Arab nationalist movements, most notably the Baath Party, tried to set up branches in many Arab countries. However, these networks were often confined to rather small circles, and the early success of nationalist coups in the 1950s and 1960s diminished the need for systematic grassroots activism. The branches degenerated into instruments of governmental politics, most visibly in the rivalries between the pro-Iraqi and the pro-Syrian branches of the Baath Party in many Arab countries.

The society-centered approach of most Islamist groups also enabled them to adapt themselves quite flexibly to their specific national contexts without compromising their global, transnational mission. After all, Islam, its universalism notwithstanding, is not opposed to nations and, hence, is flexible enough to adapt to diverse local or national contexts. In fact, the ethnic and religious diversity of mankind is considered part of God's plan for at least three reasons.

Diversity is a way to increase human knowledge:

> O men, We created you from a male and female, and formed you into nations and tribes [*shuuban wa-qabaila*] that you may recognize each other [*li-taarafu*]. (Koran 49:13)

" understand "

It is also a way to encourage positive competition between groups:

> If God had pleased He could surely have made you one people (*ummatan wahidatan*). But he wished to try and test you by that which He gave you. So try to excel in good deeds. (Koran 5:48; see also 42:8, 49:13)

And it is, finally, one of God's means of correcting sinful peoples and replacing them, if need be, by others:

> And if God had not restrained some people (*nas*) through some others, monasteries, churches, synagogues and mosques, where the name of God is honored most, would have been razed. (22:40)
>
> O believers, any one of you who turns back on his faith (should remember) that God could verily bring (in your place) another people (*qaum*) whom He would love as they would love Him. (Koran 5:54)

Hence, transnationalism and particular local identities have never been seen as mutually exclusive. For centuries, Muslim scholars and Sufi orders cultivated far-reaching transnational networks (Voll 1994), while, at the same time, accepting local rulers as long as the latter ruled according to the provisions of the shariah. Most modern Islamists oppose the nation states of the Muslim world, not because they are independent states, but because they accuse them of being ruled without adherence to divine law. Therefore, the most urgent strategic problem for Islamists is not how to replace the existing Muslim states with a world Caliphate, but how to impose uniform standards of righteous behavior upon the Muslims living in them.

Only a few minority groups, among them the maverick "Caliph of Cologne," Metin Kaplan (b. 1952), and his Caliphate State group, and the transnational Hizb al-Tahrir (founded in 1952), are openly pursuing the restoration of the Caliphate. Speakers of other extremist groups, like al-Qaeda, sometimes deplore the absence of the Caliphate, but they do not discuss in public the practical steps that are required to achieve its restoration in the foreseeable future (International Crisis Group, 2005: 17). It is true that some al-Qaeda-affiliated websites have posted strategy papers on how to arrive at an Islamic world state (Ulph, 2005) and the Jordanian journalist Fouad Hussein recently described a secret, seven-phased plan to establish an Islamic Caliphate by the year 2020 (Musharbash, 2005). However, it is far from clear whether these scenarios have been officially endorsed by al-Qaeda's leadership and whether they indeed have guided the organization's policy.

Far more Islamist parties in the Arab world have, however, adapted their policies to the institutional framework of the states they are working in and participate in national and municipal elections, provided they are permitted to do so. This applies, for instance, to the Muslim Brotherhood in Egypt and its offshoots and affiliates in Jordan, Algeria, Lebanon, Palestine, Kuwait, Morocco, and Yemen; to the Justice and Development Party in Morocco (*Hizb al-adalah wa-l-tatawwur*); to Hizballah in Lebanon; and the Shiite parties in Iraq (Fuller, 2004; International Crisis Group, 2005).

Toward a Social-Democratization of Islamism?

The parallel mutations of political Islam in Turkey, from the Welfare Party (*Refah Partisi*, 1983–98) to the Virtue Party (*Fazilet Partisi*, 1997–2001), and finally to the conservative Justice and Development Party (*Adalet ve Kalkinma Partisi*, since 2001), has led to discussions about the potential of Islamist groups to transform themselves into a Muslim version of Europe's Christian Democratic Parties (Ibrahim, 2005; Kristianasen, 2003; see also the contribution of Ziya Öniş in this volume). However, as far as transnationalism is concerned, a comparison with the decline of internationalism in European socialism might also be helpful.

In 1907, the German sociologist Robert Michels (1876–1936) published a thought-provoking analysis of the decline of internationalism in the European workers' movement. In the First and Second International, he argued, the call to subject the national member parties to the imperatives of "international solidarity" and the "world revolution" was usually strongest among those members who were most in need of international support, namely, exiled politicians and small parties, most notably from Eastern and Southern Europe. Excluded from political participation at home, these groups were desperately looking for external support and a forum where they could speak out. Internationalism was weakest amongst the larger social-democratic parties of Western and Central Europe that had already gained some influence in their home countries, were working under more or less democratic conditions and, hence, had become increasingly receptive to the needs of their local electorates and their parliamentary coalition partners. Fervent internationalism, in other words, was a compensator for political marginalization at home. It could be expected to pale into insignificance the more the respective parties were able to participate in local power management. For Michels, the underlying socio-psychological mechanism was quite a simple one:

> The greater the industriousness someone invests in managing the special problems of factory inspection and commercial law, of the trading stamp system in the coop shops and the control of gas consumption in municipal street lighting—the greater one's difficulties to keep an eye on the domestic workers' movements as a whole, the less the time, energy, and feeling available for foreign politics. (Ladislaus Gumplowicz, as quoted in Michels, 1907: 223–24)

Are similar effects to be expected in the development of modern Islamist movements? The answer is: yes and no. Yes, there is, indeed, a strong correlation between political exclusion and transnationalism: Groups that are persecuted in their home countries will try to develop transnational networks and cultivate the concomitant ideologies. Yes, there is a correlation between the integration of Islamist groups into the national political institutions of their home countries and the pragmatic moderation of their politics. However, if one expects democratization to cause a subsequent decline of Islamist transnationalism, the answer is no. In contrast to the times of Robert Michels and the European politics he was writing about, democratic local politics in the twenty-first-century Middle East are unthinkable without a strong dose of transnational networking. The only question is: What kind of transnationalism?

Exclusion, Violence and Transnationalism

As one might expect from Michel's reasoning, one of the most powerful factors driving Islamists to expand and tighten their transnational links has been violence, most notably the oppression they were exposed to in their home countries and the armed insurgencies they were actively involved in.

As peace researcher John Paul Lederach stated after September 11, "Military action to destroy terror, will be like hitting a fully mature dandelion with a golf club" (Lederach, 2001); the surviving members of a persecuted group will be compelled to dissipate and look for shelter, support, and new recruits in other regions. "Killing" the dandelion, thus, will help spread its seeds. Even more important, however, is another pattern of violence-related dynamics: Violence has the tendency to generate transnational structures and networks that allow its continuation: Facing a far more powerful enemy, insurgents are in need of money, weapons, safe havens, and access to international mass media. Much of this will be provided abroad, by actors and networks beyond the control of the government the insurgents fight: by external sponsor states, private donors, diasporas, transnational arms- and drug-trafficking, and the like (Napoleoni, 2004). The fear of becoming too dependent on one single sponsor may, in turn, become a motive to look for additional ones. And in order to cover over the traces of these international connections, even more complex hyper-structures of global transnational networks may be needed.

The dialectics between violence and transnationalism have been particularly intense and self-perpetuating in the conflicts in which Muslim volunteers from many countries have been involved during the last decades, most notably in Afghanistan, Bosnia, Chechnya, Kashmir, and Iraq. In his book *Bin Ladin bi-la qinaa*, al-Jazeera correspondent Ahmad Zaydan claims that in 2001 al-Qaeda's training camps in Afghanistan hosted some 4,742 persons from fifteen states, among them about 1,660 North Africans (including 560 Algerians), 680 Saudis, 520 Sudanese, 480 Yemenites, 430 Palestinians, 270 Egyptians, 180 Filipinos, 80 Iraqis, 62 British, 35 Turks, 30 Americans, and eight French (Zaydan, 2003: 203). The life-changing experiences and cross-cultural friendships in these multinational troops made many of their members believe that they were the ummah in action, and led some of them to the conclusion that fighting and martyrdom on the battlefield constituted the most important way to transform the ummah from an abstract category into a living body. As Sheikh Abdullah Azzam (1941–89), one of the mentors of Osama bin-Laden, once put it:

> Indeed this small band of Arabs [in Afghanistan], whose number did not exceed a few hundred individuals, changed the tide of the battle, from an Islamic battle of one country, to an Islamic World Jihad movement, in which all races participated and all colors, languages and cultures met; yet they were one, their direction was one, their ranks were one and the goal was one: that the Word of Allah is raised [sic!] the highest and that this Deen [*din*; "religion"] is made [sic] victorious on the Earth. (Azzam, s.d.)

The Arab volunteers who returned from Afghanistan in the late 1980s helped spread that militant message in their home countries, as well as in the Arab and Muslim Diaspora in Europe and America—a process that might be repeated when the present Arab volunteers return from Iraq.

It is highly significant that nearly all cases of successful moderation of Islamist parties have occurred in countries which are currently not subjected to foreign occupation (Turkey, Morocco, Egypt, Jordan, Algeria). Several other countries—Lebanon, Palestine, and Iraq—are currently caught in an open-ended transition process between foreign occupation and independence, which is mirrored in the Janus-faced behavior of their Islamist parties. Hizballah and Hamas are parties that have been involved in long-term *jihadi* warfare, but are, at the same time, mass organizations with a broad and visible network of charitable NGOs and remarkable successes in local elections. The Shiite parties that participated in the January 30, 2005, elections in Iraq did so for several reasons, most notably in order to strengthen Shiite leverage in future Iraqi politics and to accelerate the withdrawal of U.S. troops. However, in the absence of a clear and trustworthy roadmap to the withdrawal of foreign troops, it is not unlikely that some of them might reconsider the option to take up arms. In all these cases, a durable moderation of political Islam would require an international solution to the territorial conflicts involved.

While participation in elections might moderate Islamist politics, it would be, however, quite unrealistic to expect that it might induce them to cut their transnational links and confine themselves to domestic and municipal problems.

First, considering the region's economic and geostrategic centrality for external powers and the frequency of external interventions, it would be unreasonable to expect that, of all actors involved, the region's Muslim and Arab inhabitants should be the only ones to leave the cultivation of larger intraregional and extra-regional ties to outside powers. After all, the longevity of authoritarian regimes in the Arab world is, not least, due to the fact that its authoritarian regimes have been backed by foreign powers. The war in Iraq in 2003, the U.S. Middle East Partnership Initiative (MEPI), launched in 2002, and the G-8 Broader Middle East Initiative are all attempts to change the region through transnational, direct and indirect intervention. To be sure, "all politics is local," but in a region as continually exposed to external interventions as the Middle East, transnational links will remain an important part of both democratic and authoritarian politics.

Second, times have changed since the days Robert Michels published his analysis on the decline of internationalism. In the late nineteenth and early twentieth centuries, the nation-state was arguably the most powerful and all-pervasive device to integrate Western societies into the world market. Industrial late-comers tried to protect their markets not only by imposing high tariff barriers and subsidies for non-competitive industries, but also by creating a nationalist state-centered political culture. In the age of globalization, there is no question of shielding the state from the impact of transnational economic and ideological powers. Countries that would try to isolate themselves from transnational migration, business relations, satellite TV, or the Internet would pay a heavy price in terms of international economic competitiveness.

All in all, there is no realistic choice between transnationalism and no transnationalism in the Arab world, but, at best, between alternative transnationalisms.

"White Arabism," the G-8, and the Anti-Globalization Movement

In March 2005, the Lebanese law professor and civil rights activist Chibli Mallat published a plea for what he called a "white Arabism:"

> The Arab nationalism that has prevailed since the Nasser revolution is increasingly being dubbed 'black Arabism' by those of us who do not want to abandon their yearning for closer integration between societies separated by arguably artificial colonial borders. Black Arabism, in this perception, is characteristically fascist, and is epitomized by the Baath systems in Iraq and Syria. Against it is put forward the need for 'White Arabism', which harks back to such figures as Saad Zaghlul in Egypt, Kamel Chadirchi in Iraq, and Kamal Jumblatt in Lebanon. At the core of the message is democratic, non-violent change at the top in these countries, with Arabism read as a liberal call that unifies people irrespective of their religion or sect: in Egypt, Copts and Muslims; in Lebanon, the various communities that form the country; in Iraq, Shi'ites and Sunnis. (Mallat, 2005)

The kind of "white Arabism" Mallat probably had in mind was an extended cooperation between civil society organizations working all over the MENA region—a transnational approach more or less in tune with the United Nations Development Program's (UNDP's) Arab Human Development Reports (2002, 2003, 2004) that had been authored by a team of experts from many Arab countries. In fact, a few months earlier, on September 5, 2004, some forty NGOs working in the Middle East and North Africa (MENA) region had met in Beirut and issued a programmatic declaration that proposed an agenda for international cooperation organized around "two immediate imperatives"—democracy and freedom—and "seven medium to long-term programs" for structural reform in the MENA region—citizenship equality and participation, rule of law, freedom of expression and organization, revision of education, employment, combating corruption, promotion of creative arts and culture and the enlargement of public space (text in *The Daily Star*, Beirut, September 25, 2004).

Although the declaration invoked the "antiauthoritarian" heritage of Abd al-Rahman al-Kawakibi (1849–1902), one of the Muslim forefathers of Pan-Arabism, it avoided carefully to talk about external enemies and foreign occupation—topics that had been dear to "Black Arabism." Instead, it focused on the possibilities to improve the living conditions of the region's inhabitants and confined itself to deplore in rather vague terms the violence that was haunting the region, mentioning a few local leaders (Saddam Hussein, Moammar al-Gadaffi, Ariel Sharon, and Omar al-Bashir) who should be brought to justice. According to the declaration's authors, the text was a response to the G-8 initiative "Partnership for Progress and a Common Future with the Region of the Broader Middle East and North Africa" that had been launched by the G-8 summit at Sea Island, Georgia, on June 9, 2004. It was written to be submitted to a follow-up conference of twenty-four Foreign Ministers from the G-8 and Arab countries at New York, on September 23–24, 2004 and meant to feed into the "Forum for the Future" that was set up after the Sea Island summit and held its first session in Rabat, on December 11, 2004, co-chaired by U.S. Secretary of State Colin Powell and Morocco's Foreign Minister Mohamed Benaissa.

The attempt to promote transnational civil cooperation in the MENA region through cooperation with the G-8 and the existing Arab governments has its limits, however. First, as a matter of fact, the most thriving part of civil society in the Arab world today are "Islamist" NGOs. Western experts have become increasingly disappointed about the anti-Western attitude of these organizations. Political scientist Sheri Berman, for example, after discussing the central role of Islamist associations in Egyptian society, concludes that "there is no reason to believe that civil society activity will have democratic, liberal, or even particularly laudable results" (Berman, 2003: 266) and that the increasing presence of Islamists in Arab civil society is allegedly a sign "not of benign liberalization, but rather of profound political failure, and . . . an incubator for illiberal radicalism" (257). Steven Cook, a fellow at the Council on Foreign Relations, argues that many NGOs in Arab countries are either affiliated to Islamists or are cooperating with authoritarian governments and calls the idea to spur democratization through civil society promotion one of the main erroneous assumptions that U.S. policy should abandon (Cook, 2005: 92–4).

Second, Israeli and American security agencies are increasingly targeting transnational Islamist charitable organizations, which are either accused of directly funding terrorist organizations or of helping those organizations to save money by relieving them from the burden to spend their funds for charitable purposes (Levitt, 2004).

Third, during the last years, another kind of transnationalism has developed in the Middle East, namely, a cooperation of Islamists with leftists and secularists in the framework of the antiwar and antiglobalization movement. Shortly after the Beirut meeting of G-8 oriented NGOs mentioned above, an "International Strategy Meeting" of the Anti-War and Anti-Globalization Movements was held in Beirut on September 17–19, 2004, which was attended by some 300 participants from fifty countries. The welcoming committee included Hizballah, the Lebanese Communist Party, and the Progressive Socialist Party of Druze leader Walid Jumblatt (Karmon, 2005). The meeting was the first antiglobalization meeting in which Hizballah was involved, but it was not the first meeting of its kind. Since 2002 three conferences of the antiwar and antiglobalization movement have been held in Cairo (December 17–19, 2002; December 13–14, 2003; March 24–27, 2005). They were attended, among others, by representatives of the Muslim Brotherhood, the Egyptian Communist Party, the Wasat Party, the Sadr movement in Iraq, Hamas, by the British Stop the War Coalition, by Attac, and by a number of Western leftists and pacifists, such as former Labour MPs George Galloway, Tony Benn, former U.S. Attorney General Ramsey Clark, the former UN Director of the Oil-for-food program, Hans von Sponeck, and former Algerian President Ahmed Ben Bella.

Obviously, there are currently two tendencies of global transnationalism facing each other in the post–Cold War world: a transnationalism "from above"—most visibly embodied in the G-8 and the Davos Economic Forum—and a transnationalism "from below"—most visibly embodied in the antiglobalization movement and the World Social Forum. It can come as no surprise, then, that transnationalism in the MENA region is developing similar tendencies. For critical observers, the mixed audience of the Cairo Conferences might easily appear as a purely negative coalition, united only by its opposition to U.S. politics. However, considering the immense social problems the Arab world is to face in the coming decades, there will be ample opportunities for a populist transnationalism of the "downtrodden of the earth" from all religions and faiths. At a time in which fanatic Jihadi Islamists of the al-Qaeda type demand that true Muslims should avoid any relation with Christians and Jews (see, e.g., Koran 3:118, 5:51), the transnational cooperation of Sunni and Shiite Islamists with Arab and European Leftists and Secularists is an encouraging sign.

References

Ajami, Fouad (1979) The End of Pan-Arabism, *Foreign Affairs* 57 (2): 355–73.

—— (1981) *The Arab Predicament: Arab Political Thought and Practice since 1967*, Cambridge: Cambridge University Press.

Azzam, Sheikh Abdullah (s.d.), Martyrs: The Building Blocks of Nations, online at: http://www.religioscope.com/info/doc/jihad/azzam_martyrs.htm.

Basbous, Antoine (2000) *L'Islamisme: une révolution avortée?*, Paris: Hachette.

Ben-Dor, Gabriel (1983) *State and Conflict in the Middle East*, New York: Praeger.

Berman, Sheri (2003) Islamism, Revolution, and Civil Society, *Perspectives on Politics* 1 (2): 257–72.

Brynen, Rex, Bahgat Koranyi, and Paul Noble (eds.) (1995–1998) *Political Liberalization and Democratization in the Arab World*, 2 vols., Boulder, Col.: Lynne Rienner.

Cook, Steven A. (2005) The Right Way to Promote Arab Reform, *Foreign Affairs* 84 (2): 91–102.

Dawisha, Adeed (2003) *Arab Nationalism in the Twentieth Century: From Triumph to Despair*, Princeton, NJ: Princeton University Press.

Fuller, Graham E. (2004) *Islamists in the Arab World: The Dance around Democracy*, Washington, DC: Carnegie Endowment for International Peace (Carnegie Papers, Middle East Series, N° 49, September).

Ibrahim, Saad Eddin (1982) *The New Arab Social Order: A Study of the Social Impact of Oil Wealth*, Boulder, CO: Westview.

—— (2005) Islam Can Vote, If We Let It, *International Herald Tribune*, May 24: 9.

Halliday, Fred (2004) *The Middle East in International Relations: Power, Politics, and Ideology*, Cambridge: Cambridge University Press.

Heller, Hermann (1928) Politische Demokratie und soziale Homogenität, *Politische Wissenschaft* 5: 35–47.

Hobbes, Thomas (1985) *Leviathan* [1651], ed. C.B. Macpherson, London: Penguin.

International Crisis Group (2005) *Understanding Islamism*, Brussels: International Crisis Group (Middle East/North Africa Report, N° 37, March 2).

Johnson, Nels (1982) *Islam and the Politics of Meaning in Palestinian Nationalism*, London: Kegan Paul International.

Karatnycky, Adrian (2002) Muslim Countries and the Democracy Gap, *Journal of Democracy* 13 (1): 99–112.

Karmon, Elie (2005) *Hizballah and the Antiglobalization Movement: A New Coalition?* Washington DC: The Washington Institute for Near East Policy (Policywatch, N° 949, January 27), online at: http://www.washingtoninstitute. org/templateC05.php?CID = 2244.

Kepel, Gilles (2000) *Jihad: expansion et déclin de l'islamisme*, Paris: Gallimard.

Kienle, Eberhard (1995) Arab Unity Schemes Revisited: Interest, Identity, and Policy in Syria and Egypt, *International Journal of Middle East Studies* 27 (1): 53–71.

Kristianasen, Wendy (2003) Une démocratie chrétienne version islamique, *Le Monde Diplomatique*, April: 23.

Landau, Jacob M. (1994) *The Politics of Pan-Islam: Ideology and Organization* [1990], Oxford: Clarendon Press.

Lederach, John Paul (2001), The Challenge of Terror: A Traveling Essay, *Changemakers Journal*, October, online at: http://www.changemakers.net/journal/01october/lederach.cfm.

Levitt, Matthew (2004) Charitable Organizations and Terrorist Financing: A War on Terror Status-Check, Paper presented at the workshop "The Dimensions of Terrorist Financing," University of Pittsburgh, March 19, online at: http://www.washingtoninstitute.org/templateC07.php?CID = 104.

Mallat, Chibli (2005) White Arabism, *bitterlemons* 8 (3): online at: http://www.bitterlemons-international.org/previous.php?opt = 1&id = 74#302.

Michels, Robert (1907) Die deutsche Sozialdemokratie im internationalen Verbande: Eine kritische Untersuchung, *Archiv für Sozialwissenschaft und Sozialpolitik*, 25: 148–231.

Mitchell, Richard P. (1993) *The Society of the Muslim Brothers* [1969], New York: Oxford University Press.

Mufti, Malik (1996) *Sovereign Creations: Pan-Arabism and Political Order in Syria and Iraq*, Ithaca and London: Cornell University Press.

Musharbash, Yassin (2005) "What al-Qaida Really Wants," *Spiegel online*, August 12, 2005, online at: http://service.spiegel.de/cache/international/0,1518, 369448,00html.

Napoleoni, Loretta (2004) *Terror Inc: Tracing the Money behind Global Terrorism* [2003], London: Penguin.

Owen, Roger (1992) *State, Power and Politics in the Making of the Modern Middle East*, London: Routledge.

Pfaff, Richard H. (1970) The Function of Arab Nationalism, *Comparative Politics* 2 (2): 147–67.

Porath, Yehoshua (1984a) Abdallah's Greater Syria Programme, *Middle Eastern Studies* 20 (2): 172–89.

—— (1984b) Nuri al-Sa'id's Arab Unity Programme, in *Middle Eastern Studies* 20 (4): 76–98.

Roy, Olivier (1992) *L'échec de l'islam politique*, Paris: Seuil.

—— (2004): *Globalised Islam: The Search for a New Ummah* [2002], London: Hurst.

Rubin, Barry (2002) *The Tragedy of the Middle East*, Cambridge, UK: Cambridge University Press.

Satloff, Robert (2005) Memo to: Karen P. Hughes, Re: The Mission of Public Diplomacy, *The Weekly Standard*, March 28, online at: http://www.weeklystandard.com/Content/Public/Articles/000/000/005/380tnujk.asp.

Schmitt, Carl (1928) *Verfassungslehre*, München and Leipzig: Duncker & Humblot.

—— (1982) *Der Leviathan in der Staatslehre des Thomas Hobbes: Sinn und Fehlschlag eines politischen Symbols* [1938], Köln: Hohenheim.

Simon, Reeva S. (1974) The Hashemite 'Conspiracy': Hashemite Unity Attempts, 1921–1958, *International Journal of Middle East Studies* 5: 314–27.

TAL (2004) *Law of Administration for the State of Iraq for the Transitional Period*, March 8, online at: http://www.cpa-iraq.org/government/TAL.html, Arab text at: http://www.iraqcoalition.org/arabic/government/TAL-arabic.html.

Ulph, Stephen (2005) "New Online Book Lays Out al-Qaeda's Military Strategy [Analysis of Abu Bakr Naji, Idarat al-Tawahhush, March 18, 2005], online at: http://www.jamestown.org/news_details-php?news_id = 100#.

Voll, John Obert (1994) Islam as a Special World-System, *Journal of World History* 5 (2): 213–26.

Yapp, Malcolm E. (1991) *The Near East since the First World War*, London: Longman.

Zaydan, Ahmad (2003) *Bin Ladin bila qinaa: Liqaat hazzarat nashraha Taliban* [Bin Ladin without Mask: Interviews that the Taliban prevented from being published], Beirut: al-Sharikah al-alamiyyah li-l-kitab.

4

Democratization and the New Arab Media

Jakob Skovgaard-Petersen

Introduction

What is the relationship between liberalization and democratization in the Arab world on the one hand, and the new Arab media, principally the new Arab satellite TV stations, on the other? This seems an understandable question to ask, and indeed it has often been raised, especially in recent years. Yet, related to great differences of opinion as to whether a genuine democratization is actually taking place, and what role U.S. foreign policy takes within this, the attitudes of journalists and scholars with respect to the democratizing influence of these new media have changed over time. From initial enthusiasm in the late 1990s, they shifted to a much more negative attitude after 2001, and toward strong skepticism in the middle of this decade.

The year 2006 marks the tenth anniversary of the foundation of the centerpiece of all this debate, the al-Jazeera channel, and that may serve as a useful occasion to sum up the discussion on the democratic impact of the new Arab media. What I am going to present here is a historical outline of this debate, followed by a summary of the positions taken with regard to the democratic impact of these media, and ending with some comments on the role of the new media in the Lebanese and Egyptian upheavals in spring 2005.

The Historical Evolution of the New Arab Media

It seems fair to attribute the rise of the new media to a combination of visionary and committed individuals and technical innovations. The advent of satellite-based newspaper distribution and editing in the 1980s and of satellite-based Arab broadcasting in the 1990s enabled newspapers and later TV stations to set up shop in Europe and from there reach the Arab world, thus at least partly avoiding the political constraints with which local Arab media have to struggle in individual Arab states.

The three London-based newspapers were the real pathbreakers: *Ash-Sharq al-Awsat* was a Saudi newspaper established in London already in 1978 but at that time flown to the various Arab capitals. *Al-Hayat* was an older Lebanese newspaper reestablished in London in 1986 and in 1991 fully taken over by the Saudi Prince Khalid ibn Sultan. The third important newspaper is *al-Quds al-Arabi*, which is focused on Palestine and said to be owned by Palestinians.

At that time, these international newspapers were occasionally barred from entering some of the Arab countries, but today this happens only very rarely. Scholars and journalists who work on the Middle East quickly took these newspapers to heart, as they were available, covered the whole region, and were generally more outspoken than the local newspapers. *Al-Hayat*, it could be argued, was the "print version" of al-Jazeera of the time, also in the sense that it became the outlet of choice for militant Islamist communiqués which were faxed to London, since Islamist groups were very well aware that *al-Hayat* was the newspaper of choice for both the Arab elite and international observers. It is actually somewhat surprising to note that the London-based press was not the object of special studies or debates about democratization, even though its emergence coincided with the fall of the Berlin Wall. Neither local activists nor Western governments and observers had too high hopes about swift democratic transitions, and the international newspapers were a much too narrow and elite-based phenomenon to be seen to herald general social change. Even today, while especially *al-Hayat* and *ash-Sharq al-Awsat* enjoy a good reputation for trustworthy and detached reporting, their distributional numbers in most Arab countries are low. This is partly because they sell at a higher price than the local press. According to the (perhaps somewhat low) estimates of William Rugh, in 2003 *ash-Sharq al-Awsat* had a circulation of 60,000, *al-Hayat* had 40,000, and *al-Quds al-Arabi* had just 15,000 (Rugh, 2004: 173), with most of the sales of the first two in the Arab Gulf. In comparison, big national newspapers like *al-Ahram* and *al-Akhbar* in Egypt have a circulation of more than half a million, and the Algerian *al-Khabar* sells some 400,000 copies (Rugh, 2004: 123).

The Emergence of Satellite TV

So it is only with the advent of satellite TV that we can talk about a mass phenomenon that is truly reshaping the Arab World. Again, the first important station, MBC, was founded in London in 1991 (but moved to Dubai in 1999). The Lebanese TV stations, fiercely competing with each other at home, were among the next to go on satellite in the mid-1990s. This caused people in neighboring Syria to begin buying dishes in order to follow the varied and professional programs of Lebanese providers. Today every Arab government has its own satellite TV channel, and there are more than one hundred channels in total.

It was with the establishment of al-Jazeera in 1996 as a full-time news channel in a direct and uninhibited style that the full potentialities of satellite television began to be realized by all. The American-British campaign against Iraq in 1998 and the broadcast of Saddam Hussein alive, along with many other controversial figures—including Israelis—told the Arab audiences that something entirely new had appeared.

There is no reason to recapitulate the al-Jazeera story here, as it is generally known (cf. Miles, 2005). Its attraction is due to an impressive array of correspondents and strong on-the-spot news, especially when it is allowed to report from conflict areas such as Afghanistan, Iraq, and Palestine. But it also includes daring political talkshows, with phone-in sessions and heated debates between political adversaries who have never been in the same room together before. All of this a far cry from conventional Arab state broadcasting which remains to this day under severe regime control.

Now, al-Jazeera has been emulated but not surpassed. Other private channels have taken up the challenge and copied various parts of the al-Jazeera programming. But according to a summer 2004 poll conducted by Shibley Telhami, in terms of news viewership al-Jazeera remains a distinct number one with 40–60 percent of the viewers (Telhami, 2004).

There are many competitors to al-Jazeera, but only two challengers, set up explicitly to dent its influence. The first of these is al-Arabiyya, launched in 2003 with Saudi money, and predictably tame when it comes to news from the Kingdom and the Gulf. Apart from a somewhat more restrained tone, one may argue that al-Arabiyya resembles al-Jazeera a good deal, and in Iraq, for instance, it has run into many of the same problems of political censorship. In my view, al-Arabiyya broadens, rather than dents, the al-Jazeera phenomenon, providing competition on news and angles very much along the lines of al-Jazeera.

This can hardly be said of the other challenger, al-Hurra, launched in February 2004 by the U.S. government. My own viewing of it has been limited ... so I rely here on the characterization of al-Hurra made by Lynch (2004). Al-Hurra means "The Free" and seems to reflect a conviction among U.S policy makers that anything coming from their government must by definition be free. But, rather like the old Arab state channels, it has been set up to provide the point of view of the political authorities and, if my impression is correct, like them, it is ignoring or diminishing perspectives that differ from its own. In the previously mentioned survey by Shibley Telhami, al-Hurra does not figure at all, not even as a channel of second choice (Telhami, 2004). At the time of writing, in May 2005, it did not pose any challenge to the predominant role of al-Jazeera at all.

The Debate on New Media and Democracy

Turning now to the debate on the new Arab media, as we have seen, it only took off after the appearance of al-Jazeera. By 1998, when books and journals began devoting space and time to the new media, it was no longer possible to ignore their impact, even if for a time, the novelty of the Internet took all the interest away from that "trivial old piece of furniture," the television. In much of these literature, the new press is left out, and those who do include it agree that television is by far the most important medium in the Arab world.

The first book-length treatment of the new Arab media that had grasped their influence as such was written by Jon Alterman in 1998. Alterman assumed that the new media would lead to a new relationship between state and media and that old modes of censorship would be rendered less efficient. In this way, more sophisticated and direct political debate in the media would gradually lead to greater pressure for accountability on the part of the politicians in power. Although Alterman was aware that Saudi Arabia, in particular, stood to gain from the commercialization of television and that new forms of state influence would gradually evolve, his book is basically a positive assessment of the new media as a democratizing tool, and the theme of the erosion of state power played well into the 1990s' expectation that an Arab civil society was about to grow forth and challenge the powers-that-be (Alterman, 1998). This optimistic line has been retained in much scholarship, and it is generally to be found in the *Transnational Broadcasting Studies*, the journal that since 1998 has been covering the field.

The positive evaluation of the democratic potential of the new media can be summed up in the following propositions:

- A bastion of the authoritarian state has fallen, and people are watching and discussing politics rather more daringly and assertively than the traditional Middle Eastern state would allow them to.
- Rulers no longer appear infallible and are pressured to explain and defend their policies, instead of just decreeing them.

- Oppositional movements and personalities are finally appearing on TV.
- The new media teach audiences a new culture of debate where dissent is legitimate.
- Competition makes the channels interested in what people would like to watch, and although there are tendencies toward populism, this still enforces a sense of individual autonomy and entitlement.

Now, especially with the new American engagement in the Middle East since 2001 and the generally vehement and negative coverage it has received by the Arab Satellite TV Stations, and by al-Jazeera in particular, more critical voices concerning the political role of these channels have also appeared. These critics are predominantly, but not solely, Americans or Arabs with links to American policy circles. They may concede that the new channels have certain positive effects, but they consider these effects exaggerated, and they object to other aspects of the new satellite stations. The critical positions should probably be divided into several camps:

- One camp points out that the new owners of the channels are very close to the Arab regimes, and are often personal allies. The structure of ownership is largely unchanged, and it is therefore only the means of control that have changed, in that political control has given way to economic control. This has especially been argued by Naomi Sakr (Sakr, 2001).
- Another camp emphasizes that, even if the new media can raise issues, they actually cannot pursue them. Issues stay in the media, and there are no vehicles to take them further in the political and legal realms. The political culture and the societal room of maneuvre to take the cases further is simply not in place. Indeed, an especially pessimistic view would consider al-Jazeera not a supporter of but a substitute for political action, an instrument for venting anger. The viewer is taught that injustice rules and that there is little he can do about it.
- Others criticize the elite character of the media, in terms of a special class not just of owners (billionaires) but also of viewers (who must be able to afford the dish and understand modern standard Arabic). Additionally, the poor strata of the populations are actually worse off, as talent and funds are drained from the national terrestrial programming and redirected toward the more prestigious satellite programs. The satellite channels, then, are only affordable for the rich, and clearly directed toward the well educated (Mansur, 1999: 37).
- In particular, it has been pointed out that the staff tend to be of a certain ideological persuasion (Nasserist or Islamist) and biased in this

direction. An article in the *New York Times* by Fuad Ajami, for instance, went so far as to proclaim Osama bin-Laden as the real star of al-Jazeera (Ajami, 2001).

- A more internal kind of criticism in the profession would see the satellite news channels as being much too concerned with conveying political opinions and too little with actual journalistic investigation.
- The Egyptian Mamoun Fandy contends that Arab culture has a strong preference for oral communication from trusted, significant others, and that this has served Arabs well under dictatorship, but may not be the right kind of critical attitude in the face a phenomenon like al-Jazeera (Fandy, 2000). He and others, such as Abdel Moneim Saeed of *al-Ahram*, have also pointed out that, especially since 2001, al-Jazeera has adopted a position not unlike the Nasserist media of the 1960s, where Arabs are sketched as ordinary, innocent people who are being exploited by conspiring imperialists and local rulers in collusion. This populist and mobilizing stand is uncritical toward crimes committed by Arabs, and paints political issues as a struggle between good and evil (Saeed, 2003). While it may thus be on the side of average Arabs, it is in fact quite patronizing toward them.

Media Change but No Political Change

Broadly speaking, I am inclined to agree with the optimists, who believe in the democratic potential of the new Arab media. It is not an automatic delivery of democracy, and regimes are still the major players in the field, but there is undeniably a new sense of the right to call governments to account, and the very way in which governments have responded to al-Jazeera—with pressure, protests, and possibly intentional bombings—does demonstrate that they are annoyed, and indeed frightened, by the new public exposure and their diminished control over public opinion. As a result, policies have been adjusted, and public opinion is being taken more into account.

Why, then, have the politicians not changed? Why is it that, after ten years of al-Jazeera, we have the same presidents and kings all around—or their sons—even if, as in the case of Syria, this has forced legislators to make constitutional amendments? This is an important question, but it should not be dealt with in isolation. The general question of why authoritarianism is so particularly resilient in the Middle East has been keenly discussed. The reasons usually advocated in this discussion are oil rents, systems of patronage, the isolation of regimes from their populations, the role of the military and the security apparatuses, and the international toleration of autocratic rule.

As for the issue of the media, we may conclude that even if there have been important developments here in terms of a challenge to the prevailing political systems, relatively free media in themselves are not enough to occasion democratic changes. Moreover, the authoritarian regimes have developed ways to ensure that public scrutiny and criticism and outrage in the media may stay just there—in the media—without being transformed into public or legal action. Countries such as Egypt have long had oppositional papers protesting against corruption, nepotism, failings of the courts, and so on, but these papers remain unimportant next to the state-run and state-subsidized mass media. And when court cases are actually initiated, they are often directed against these newspapers themselves for alleged slander, of which they may in fact be guilty in one or the other individual case. Critical media may be an important component of democratization, but in themselves they do not account for that much.

The question is, then, how the rise of critical pan-Arab media may play together with other factors on the ground, and what the sociopolitical environment must look like for any democratic developments to take place at all. To probe into that, I shall take a look at two events during the spring of 2005, the Lebanese political upheavals in February, March, and April, and the public protests in Egypt leading up to the popular referendum on the Constitutional amendment on May 25, 2005.

Public Protest and the Media: The Experiences in Lebanon and Egypt

The Lebanese Spring in 2005

Something happened in Lebanon during the spring of 2005. The assassination of former Prime Minister Rafiq al-Hariri on February 14, triggered the rise of an important oppositional movement that through public demonstrations and vigils at Hariri's grave forced the resignation of the government and the withdrawal of Syrian troops and led to protracted negotiations for an interim government to be in charge for the upcoming parliamentary elections in May–June 2005.

What role did the media play in these developments? Certainly a quite important one. Among the sophisticated and affluent Lebanese, mobile phones and the Internet were important means of communication for the opposition, and, at least to a certain extent, also for an opposition to the opposition, which had staged a number of demonstrations itself. But the reason for the success of the Lebanese opposition (as it is known in the Arab press) again has to do with factors other than media, or rather with facts of Lebanese political life, which have also structured the Lebanese media in a rather different way compared to all other Arab countries.

As is well known, Lebanon is an amalgamation of religious sects and groups, and since the time of the French Mandate (and to a certain extent even before), political power has been shared between the religious groups in a formalized and constitutional arrangement which includes the parliament, the military, and the ministries. In contrast to all other Arab countries, this means that the state itself is fairly weak, government is always a compromise, and there are a number of power holders within each sect competing with each other and making alliances across religious divides, and, to some extent, with outside forces as well.

What is currently known as the opposition has its basis in the Christian groups most dissatisfied with the post–civil-war settlement. During most of the 1990s, these groups would regularly organize demonstrations outside the ministry of justice or similar institutions to voice their protest against, for example, the imprisonment of the previous Christian militia leader Samir Geagea. Yet these groups were small and fairly unpopular in the public at large, basically due to their role in the civil war. The marginalized trend had its own minor outlets, including the Internet. The protest was there, then, but limited to a marginal group which was not allowed to reach broad audiences on a more permanent base.

With the Israeli withdrawal in 2000, other voices joined in calling for the retreat of the Syrian army. At that point, however, this position was still largely confined to the Christians, and although they had a foothold in Parliament with a group called Qurnet Shahwan—and a more important outlet with the newspaper *an-Nahar*—they were too few and too confined to sectarian groups to pose a real threat to Syria and its allies.

By the mid-1990s, new regulation of the television market in Lebanon left the country with a handful of influential stations, each affiliated to a powerful religio-political group. Affiliated to the Sunni religious community was Future TV, owned by Rafiq al-Hariri, the billionaire entrepreneur who was serving as prime minister at the time. Those who were in power, then, shared the airwaves among themselves. Hizballah, which took part in political life, but always in opposition, ran its own outfit, al-Manar. But the more marginalized Christian groups did not have a channel, as the two major channels, LBC and al-Murr, were affiliated to Christian politicians who were members of the circles in power. In 2001, however, Murr TV suddenly changed its direction and moved toward the previously marginalized Christian groups. This proved unacceptable to the Syrians and, with them, to the Lebanese power holders; Murr TV was summarily closed down by the authorities (Ahmed, 2002).

This cozy arrangement was disrupted in the fall of 2004, when the Syrians forced the Parliament to extend the presidency of Emile Lahoud, although he had served the maximum constitutional term. Hariri stepped down as Prime Minister and he and the Druze leader Walid Joumblatt moved toward the opposition. The Lebanese media were critical of the extension and fueled a deep-rooted anger in parts of the population. This anger erupted in full when Hariri was killed by a roadbomb in February 2005, and it was directed against the most likely culprits, the Syrians.

And now the media went along with the trend. The bewilderment and anger at the killing called for action, also in the media. So when the outburst of sorrow and anger at Hariri's grave united the Lebanese, or a great part of the Lebanese, in a political demonstration against the Syrian presence, it had full coverage by the national Lebanese TV stations, the Arab satellite channels, and the international media. Future TV led the way by calling for an international investigation of the assassination. This was a direct challenge to the pro-Syrian President and government. And there was no strong minister of information who could make this media coverage go away. Pluralistic media had turned into oppositional media.

After some wavering, Hizballah decided to distance itself from the anti-Syrian opposition at Martyr's Square. In March, it was able to rally a pro-Syrian demonstration matching the size of the anti-Syrian protest. Hizballah's al-Manar channel (along with its radio and newspaper) focused on this and other pro-Syrian statements and downplayed the coverage of Martyr's Square.

The anti-Syrian camp responded with an even larger demonstration on March 14, 2005, with an estimated one million Lebanese gathering in central Beirut. It was a standoff between the new opposition and a new opposition to the opposition. Both had a full range of media at their disposal. And the Arab satellites were covering both, siding, as did al-Hayat, with the anti-Syrian opposition. From initially being united in showing old footage of al-Hariri and Nasrallah as allies, Future TV and al-Manar were parting ways in their coverage of the competing demonstrations. Future TV was supported by its traditional rival, the big entertainment and news channel LBC1, with its many Christian viewers. Al-Manar, on the other hand, was joined by its competitor among the Shia, the pro-Syrian Amal movement, and the latter's NBN Network. And the political standoff continued.

Al-Hariri, then, was not only a former Prime Minister, he was also a media tycoon. And Hizballah is not only a sociopolitical and religious movement, it is also a media conglomerate. This interrelation allowed for the close connection between protest in the media and protest in the streets. In no Arab country other than Lebanon was such a varied, competitive and private media environment in place to respond to and further a popular political momentum.

The Egyptian Spring in 2005

The Egyptian media system

At first glance, though, Egypt may appear to be going down the same road. Numerous newspaper article and TV shows have presented Lebanon and Egypt as two examples of a more general turn toward democracy in the Arab World. Like Lebanon, Egypt is a country with a long constitutional and legal heritage, with a parliament, political parties, and an oppositional press. In contrast to Lebanon, the Egyptian population is, in terms of religion and ethnicity, much more homogenous. Regarding the democratic credentials of the country, however, it seems that appearances are deceiving; there is little indication of a genuine democratization in Egypt, and the media are not allowed to play a mobilizing role as in Lebanon. Although economic and political reforms have been announced since 1990, most observers would agree that, politically speaking, Egypt has actually moved away from democratization. In the 1990s, the country instead became more of a model of a de-liberalizing state (Kienle, 2001: 175–7).

Most observers would agree that the Mubarak government is an authoritarian regime with an all-powerful presidency, the secure dominance of one party (the National Democratic Party), a weak parliament, and an incomplete independence of the judiciary. It should be mentioned that Egypt experienced under President Nasser (1952–70) a populist single-party rule and before that, in the period from 1923 to 1952, a constitutional monarchy with a lively, liberal political public and party press, even if key state decisions were made by the British colonial authorities.

Egypt's media date back to the nineteenth century, and many of the country's famous writers were active in journalism during the liberal period until 1952 or as supporters of Nasser's regime in the 1960s. There are thus fond memories of earlier, more liberal phases. Another legacy of the period under Nasser is the strong social involvement of the press, as well as a mobilizing and patronizing attitude that seems to go along with it. The press and major publishing houses were nationalized in the late 1950s, but since the Sadat era, a new party press has been established, and independent newspapers can be published if they have a license. Radio and television have been set up by the state and remain under state control.

The media system, then, mirrors the political realities: there is near total state control of the audiovisual media and all the mass-circulation newspapers. But next to it there does exist an opposition press and private commercial magazines, and even the government press houses may have minor prestige publications with a fairly liberal stand and with some criticism of specific government actions. Most opinions can thus be voiced in Egypt, but real mass circulation is under fairly strict government control. And even the nongovernmental press can be cowed in a number of ways, including by limiting access to paper and ink, press accreditation, and finance. As in the case of Murr TV in Lebanon, the government had no difficulty closing down the party paper of the oppositional Labour Party in 2003 when it became too much of a nuisance (Rugh, 2004: 122).

There is no doubt, that the pan-Arab press, the Arab satellites, and the Internet have made their entrance, and the government is not in a position to influence any of those very much. So these are important sources of news for the well off and well educated. Yet press penetration is much lower than in many of the more affluent parts of the Arab World, and satellite dishes are not that widespread, especially in the countryside and in Upper Egypt. Compared to most other Arab countries, the Egyptian population is not so much involved in politics, and many Egyptians seem to find that what is on offer in the national media may have its flaws, but is still good enough for them.

The events of spring 2005

In the spring of 2005, Egypt, too, had its share of political turbulence. This is related to the fact that it was an election year, with both parliamentary and presidential elections scheduled for the fall. But it probably also reflects the weak economy, related popular discontent, and a sentiment in certain parts of the population that, given the new international focus on democracy and American commitment to a democratic Middle East, the time was ripe to challenge the regime and to press for democratic reforms.

This must have been the conviction of those few people who in December 2004 had the courage to break the ban on demonstrations. With yellow stickers saying *kifaya* ("enough") they protested against a new term for President Mubarak, or against the suspected passing on of the presidency to his son Gamal. Criticizing the President directly was entirely novel and perhaps so shocking that the authorities let them get away with it. Or else, and perhaps more likely, the regime viewed these people as being weak and politically unconnected, and it might have taken into account that the world media were covering the demonstrations.

In any case, nothing happened to the Kifaya movement, as it became known, and after another demonstration in February 2005, it even seemed that this tiny protest was having an impact. President Mubarak announced an amendment of the constitution in order to allow for multi-candidate competition in the upcoming presidential elections, instead of the previous procedure, a mere referendum on a candidate chosen by the parliament. Widely hailed as a step forward in Egypt's democratic reforms, and praised by the U.S. administration and the world press, it was now up to Parliament and negotiations with the opposition to find a precise formula for an amendment of article 76 of the constitution. The main oppositional force, the outlawed Muslim Brotherhood, indicated that it might vote for President Mubarak if that could lead to the official recognition of the movement. This would have been a major breakthrough, as the mutual withholding of recognition had been a major tool in the contestation between the regime and the Brotherhood (Awadi, 2004: 2). The rest of the opposition was quite skeptical about the government's reform intentions, as they were not really given a role in the formulation of the new article 76, and other relevant articles (such as art. 77, which mentions no limitation to the number of periods a president can stay in office) were not to be touched.

In late March 2005, new demonstrations erupted. On March 27, the Muslim Brotherhood announced its first demonstration for decades. Although announced, the security forces arrested 200 Brotherhood activists in the early morning, and cordons of soldiers scattered the demonstration into minor groups in several streets and squares in downtown Cairo. In contrast to previous decades, the Brotherhood is no longer talking about the implementation of the Sharia and the establishment of an Islamic state; *Islam* has been replaced with *islah* (reform). Judging from its publications and statements, this reflects a new and more liberal political thinking on the part of the Brotherhood. But the Islamic identity and slogans are still there, of course, and their absence at the demonstration and on the lips of their leaders mainly suggests that the Brotherhood has adopted a strategy of allying with the opposition in order to gain its rightful place on the political scene. Its slogans now tend to be less confrontational and offensive than those of the Kifaya movement.

The Kifaya Movement had already announced its own demonstrations in many Egyptian cities for March 30. No wonder, then, that the authorities could no longer allow these demonstrations, either; in Cairo they were driven into the headquarters of the Journalists' Union. Throughout April, the demonstrations continued, but remained inside public institutions, primarily universities. The students' movements which organized these demonstrations seemed to be dominated by people close to the Brotherhood, even if other forces joined in. Soon the security apparatus was also operating inside the campuses, and some students and teachers were arrested, especially in Upper Egypt. One more Kifaya demonstration, taking place in thirteen cities, was once again scuppered by the security forces.

The confrontation came to its head on May 4, 2005, when the Brotherhood succeeded in organizing a huge demonstration of perhaps some 70,000 participants which blocked central Cairo and led to clashes in a number of cities. This was the most daring challenge to the Egyptian regime for many years and a break with a long tradition of political acqui-escence. The response of the security forces was merciless: 1,500 members of the Brotherhood were arrested, and more arrests followed during May, including those of its most popular spokesman, Isam Aryan, and its head of organization, Mustafa Izzat. All of them were charged with belonging to an illegal organization and fomenting public disturbances. During May, other parts of civil society, including university teachers and judges, expressed their support for the organization and called for political reforms.

The press performance
It would have been easy enough to live in Egypt without discovering the political turbulence mentioned above. Indeed, this is probably what happened to most Egyptians. On certain days in Cairo, traffic would have seemed especially bad, and one would have noticed big concentrations of police, or the occasional banner. However, the demonstrations themselves were only reported in the international Arab (and Western) media, while very few local newspapers mentioned them. Even the oppositional news-papers did not cover the Kifaya demonstrations. The much bigger Muslim Brotherhood demonstrations were not mentioned on national news, but only dismissively and in small print in the press; in a tiny column on its front page the following day, the biggest daily, *al-Ahram*, spoke of the "arrest of 50 individuals for obstructing the traffic during demonstrations in Cairo" without mentioning the Brotherhood by name (*al-Ahram*: March 28, 2005).

Apart from a small paper sympathizing with the Brotherhood (the *Afaq Arabiyya*) and a minor newspaper giving coverage to the Kifaya movement (*al-Misri al-Yaum*), the two movements basically had their websites as their outlets, but had good connections to the international and Arab press. Calls for demonstrations, for instance, were primarily made by word of mouth and on the website of Kifaya, but often reported by the interna-tional Arab newspapers. Thus the modern Arab media, in the form of Internet, satellites, and international Arab newspapers, and the Western press were at the disposal of the challenging civil movements. By contrast, the traditional media, such as the big national newspapers and national radio and television, were firmly in the hands of the government and the National Democratic Party (NDP). The oppositional newspapers, finally, were wavering, as they seemed envious of the new social forces appearing. In their attitude toward the government and its proclaimed reforms, they were, however, skeptical right from the beginning.

On May 26, the referendum for the amendment of the Constitution was finally held. In dramatic headlines, the oppositional press called on people to stay home, whilst the government press and television and banners in the streets and from public buildings appealed for a vote to support democracy (or, revealingly, more often, to support President Mubarak). The Brotherhood and the Kifaya Movement had announced demonstrations to persuade people not to vote, but the Brotherhood retracted. The Kifaya Movement went ahead, though, although a dire warning was issued by the Minister of Interior the day before the elections. In two localities in Cairo, police broke up the tiny demonstrations and stood passively by as thugs affiliated to the NDP attacked the Kifaya demonstrators and even molested some female journalists. These attacks made headlines in the coverage of the election in the international press, the Arab press, and the Arab satellites during the day, but not in the Egyptian national media. *Al-Ahram* reported an overwhelming victory for the amendment, 82.8 percent and a voting turnout of 53 percent of the registered voters (*al-Ahram* May 27, 2005). The opposition judged it more likely that the turnout was below 20 percent. But although foreign and Arab media generally leaned toward the opposition's reading of the elections, this did not seem to build up any pressure inside or outside the country that would force the government to move in any direction of conciliation or even thinking seriously about forms of powersharing.

Conclusions

In a broader movement from authoritarianism to democratization, a number of factors, both in terms of structure and agency, must be in place. In this set of variables, the press and the media are only one component, albeit an important one. As remarked by Kienle on Egypt in the 1990s, you can actually have a liberalization of the press whilst a more general political de-liberalization, or curbing of other liberties, is taking place (Kienle, 2001: 177).

For democratization to take place, there is a need for social movements on the ground. The media have a role in mobilizing such movements and giving them a plausible and simultaneous understanding of the impasse and the course of action needed. To do this, a significant part of the media must be sufficiently independent to represent various strata and forces in the population and to consider the possibility of moving toward direct opposition if certain limits are reached.

The new transnational Arab media do seem to be sufficiently independent and committed to challenging the state-controlled media and their version of events in any single Arab country. If people wanted—and many people did—they could watch a balanced and committed coverage of the Egyptian referendum on May 26 and the parliamentary elections in Beirut on May 29 on the al-Jazeera and al-Arabiyya television channels. As with these channels' previous coverage of elections in Iraq and Palestine, for instance (not to mention the U.S. presidential elections of 2004), an interested viewer was also able to get a good impression of the issues at stake, the social bases and orientation of groups within the electorate, and indeed of the degrees of fraud and bullying. In the Beirut elections on May 29, 2005, correspondents were posted at different voting stations in different parts of the town and reported on the surprisingly low participation (28 percent) and asked people and experts about it. Clearly, al-Jazeera, al-Arabiyya and other pan-Arab satellite channels do educate viewers in the intricacies of elections and popular participation.

Our two examples of Lebanon and Egypt in the spring of 2005 are interesting, not only because they were parallel in time, but because in both cases a civil movement sprang up remarkably swiftly, supported by coverage by the international Arab media, and they were themselves quite astute at catering to these external media and employing the Internet. So a new alliance was established between the new media and the demonstrators.

There is also the interesting parallel of the marginalization of institutional politics. In both Egypt and Lebanon, the demonstrators had given up on the parliament, claiming that the parliament and the major domestic media were representing and serving the executive, and not the people. And, at least for a time, the parliamentarians were indeed also fairly contemptuous of the demonstrations.

The same may be said of the political parties. In Lebanon, political parties are traditionally weak and not very ideologically focused, with Hizballah as the most obvious exception. Politics are centered on leading figures (*zaim; pl. zuama*) and their religiously based constituencies. And even in the case where these figures are also heads of parties or movements (e.g. Walid Joumblatt and Nabih Berri), political authority rests with the leader who often even has inherited his position from his father. The civil protest erupted over the murder of such a political figure (Hariri) and arguably it also ended with the endorsement of Hariri's son Saad as the new *zaim* in the Beirut elections and the return of other *zuama* to the political scene, most notably Michel Aoun, who, since 1990, had been in exile in France. Still, the civil movement was arguing for a new direct involvement of the citizenry who wanted "to claim back Lebanon."

This desire for involvement was more pronounced in Egypt, where the political parties also seemed uneasy about the Kifaya Movement and their newspapers abstained from covering its demonstrations. Although the opposition parties maintained an unusual unanimity in their criticism of the constitutional amendment and managed to form a united front, they have long been satellites of the authoritarian system, and their popular bases remain weak. In both Egypt and Lebanon, then, the new civil movements did not spring out of the existing oppositional parties. Rather, they erupted out of frustration with the whole political scene and as an alternative to the existing oppositional forces, which were seen as either co-opted by the government or politically inefficient. There was a longing for a whole new system, including serious constitutional amendments.

What the Lebanese and Egyptian experience have in common, then, is a new kind of politics. Turning their back on both the political power and the institutional opposition, new civil groups with an advanced political awareness have opted for new kinds of political action. This goes beyond demonstrating to include sporting badges, slogans, dress, colors and other "civilian" items which are eminently suited for launching these movements in the media and in public consciousness, not to mention the vigils at the grave of Hariri, and on June 8, 2005, at the grave of Saad Zaghlul, one of the founding fathers of modern Egypt, and at the place where the attacks against women took place. In both cases, we have seen that the government was unprepared for this sort of media-savvy challenge and responded clumsily, thereby proving the points of the challenge.

However, turning to the question of political results, this is where the similarities end. The success of the opposition in Lebanon must be ascribed to the composition of the political scene, with many power centers, important links to outside forces, the unpopularity of the Syrians and their representatives, and the international isolation of Syria as well as the aggressive U.S. policy toward it. For years, Rafiq al-Hariri had cooperated with the Syrians and had been derided by the intelligentsia for his self-serving political schemes and the political weight of his media and business conglomerate. A kind of Lebanese Berlusconi, he was an unlikely icon for a democratization movement. But even if he was merely pursuing his own goals, the political setup in Lebanon allowed other tycoons and established leading families (*zuama*) to do the same. The political landscape had been divided into fiefs, and so had the airwaves. Owned by and allied with the political elite, the Lebanese media were still representing competing factions and interests in society. And as some of these forces coalesced into a new oppositional front, directed against the Syrians and their allies, the media went along with them and supported the oppositional mobilization.

In Egypt, on the other hand, the civil forces were formally unrecognized and could be targeted by the security system whenever it saw it fit. The Kifaya group was growing, but still small (as of May 31, 2005,

6,293 members had signed up on its website www.harakamasria.com). The Muslim Brotherhood was undoubtedly very large, but still formally illegal and also a divisive force in the opposition, as most of the parties rejected its religiously based ideology. The Egyptian media were overwhelmingly under the control of the government and did not really represent competing political forces. Other media were allowed, but the really forceful ones—national television and radio and mass-circulation newspapers— were under full regime control. Interestingly, the Kifaya movement and the Muslim Brotherhood had a voice in and were sympathetically covered by the Arab satellite channels and on the Internet, but they only excelled in their implementation of new media, which might be good for conveying information and representing an organization, but perhaps not for local mobilization, as the penetration of these media is weak and they are utilized in a more individualistic manner.

It seems, then, that the pan-Arab media have their limitations when it comes to local mobilization, as opposed to mobilization on pan-Arab issues. On the local level in national politics, local media maintain a strong influence and seem to remain much more capable of popular mobilization. Some degree of coalescence of local and pan-Arab media is needed to create that effect. On the other hand, it also seems clear that pan-Arab media have an important role to play in democracy education, in teaching civil participation, electoral procedures, and a sense of entitlement. It is an interesting question whether, even in Egypt, the sudden emergence of the Kifaya movement, or the new democratic reform orientation of the Muslim Brotherhood, might not have been inspired, or at least furthered, by a new consensus on pluralism, democratic dialogue, and popular participation that, after all, is the professed point of departure of several of the new pan-Arab newspapers and satellite stations.

References

Ahmed, Assya (2002) "The Closing of Murr TV," www.tbsjournal.com fall 2002 issue.

Ajami, Fuad (2001) "What the Muslim World is Watching," *New York Times Magazine*, November 18, 2001, reprinted in www.tbsjournal.com spring 2002 issue.

Alterman, Jon (1998) *New Media, New Politics?* Washington DC: Washington Institute of Near East Policy.

Al-Awadi, Hisham (2004) *In Pursuit of Legitimacy. The Muslim Brothers and Mubarak, 198–* London: I. B. Tauris.

Fandy, Mamoun (2000) "Information Technology, Trust and Social Change in the Arab World," *Middle East Journal*, 54 (3): 378–94.

Kienle, Eberhard (2001) *A Grand Delusion. Democracy and Economic Reform in Egypt*, London: I. B. Tauris.

Lynch, Marc (2004) "America and the Arab Media Environment," in William Rugh (ed.): *Engaging the Arab and Muslim Worlds through Public Diplomacy*, Washington: Public Diplomacy Council.

Mansour, Khaled (1999) "Pan-Arab Media: Talk Shows for the Elite," *Middle East Insight* 14 (2): 37.

Miles, Hugh (2005) *Al-Jazeera. How Arab TV News Challenges America*, London: Grove Press.

Rugh, William (2004) *Arab Mass Media. Newspapers, Radio and Television in Arab Politics*, Westport and London: Praeger.

Saeed, Abdel Moneim (2003) *The Arab Satellites—Some Necessary Observations!* www.tbsjournal.com, winter 2003 issue.

Sakr, Naomi (2001) *Satellite Realms: Transnational Television, Globalization and the Middle East*, New York and London: I.B. Tauris.

Telhami, Shibley (2004), under: http://www.bsos.umd.edu/SADAT/pub/.

Part II

Case Studies

5

The Political Economy of Islam and Democracy in Turkey: From the Welfare Party to the AKP*

Ziya Öniş

Introduction

The Kemalist or the republican model of modernization in twentieth-century Turkey had a number of important achievements to its credit.[1] It was able to accomplish significant industrialization and economic development. Through its hyper-secularism, it was able to exclude the alternative, the Islamic political order, in a predominantly Muslim society. Certainly, the progressively more moderate course that the Islamists have been adopting in Turkey in recent years reflects, in part, the impact of the Kemalist modernization project, with its strong emphasis on the principle of secularism. Within the broad parameters of this modernization project, Turkey was able to make a transition to a democratic political order in the immediate postwar period. The key institutions of representative democracy have been established, and despite periodic breakdowns and military interludes, parliamentary democracy has remained the norm throughout the postwar period. In comparative terms, this constitutes a considerable achievement judged by the standards of countries in other parts of the world notably in Latin America, East Asia, and Eastern Europe, which are at similar stages of economic development.

By the 1990s, however, the Turkish model of modernization had reached a certain impasse. On the economic front, development had occurred over time, but the pace of development was not enough to produce a dramatic increase in living standards that would produce rapid convergence to Western European norms over a short space of time. Turkey experienced a dualistic pattern of economic growth involving a coexistence of rich regions with substantial pockets of poverty in the presence of rapid population growth. On the political front, the existing democratic order increasingly failed to accommodate societal demands for greater recognition and participation. The combination of nationalism and secularist ideology on which the Kemalist modernization project was based effectively excluded significant segments of Turkish society from active engagement in the formal political space. A rigid interpretation of the principles of secularism and national identity limited its capacity to incorporate the demands of groups that wished an extension of the boundaries of the political space on the grounds of religious and ethnic identity. Hence, by the end of the 1990s, Turkish modernization was confronted with two major challenges. First, there was a need to reform the "soft state" in the economic realm so that economic development could proceed more rapidly and equitably without costly crises and interruptions. Second, there was a demand to reform the "hard state" in the political realm to create a space for political opening for those groups that favored an extension of religious freedoms or the practice of their minority rights within the broad parameters of a secular and unitary nation state.

In the Kemalist modernization project, modernization and Westernization were largely synonymous terms. In this context, developing close relations with Europe was a natural counterpart to the broader project of Westernization. Indeed, Turkey was one of the countries that tried to involve itself in the formal process of European integration right from its formative stages, becoming an associate member in 1963. The depth of the relationship that developed during the period 1963–99, until the time when Turkey was formally recognized as a candidate for full membership, should not be underestimated. Important trade and investment links were forged over time between Turkey and the Community culminating with the signing of the Customs Union Agreement, which became effective at the end of 1995. There is no doubt that the strong links that developed in the economic realm had a counterpart in the political sphere. The ultimate interest of Turkish elites in full membership of the Community also had a conditioning effect on Turkish democracy. Arguably, the presence of the European anchor was one of the factors that kept the periodic military interludes in Turkey short by Latin American standards. Nevertheless, a central point to emphasize is that the kind of relationship that developed between Turkey and Europe over the 1963–99 period was not sufficiently deep or powerful enough to make a dramatic impact on the Turkish economy or Turkish democracy.

There is no doubt that the stronger signals provided by the EU in recent years and a more credible set of incentives in the direction of full membership have played a key role in helping to transform the Turkish political system. It is not external actors alone, but a complex interplay of domestic and external influences which have been shaping this process of transformation which in many ways is an ongoing and incomplete process. Thus this chapter has two interrelated objectives. The first goal is to highlight the paradoxical role of the Justice and Development Party (the AKP), a party with Islamist roots, in Turkey's recent transformation and Europeanization process. The second goal is to use the recent Turkish experience to shed light on the broader question concerning the possibilities of transforming an Islamist political movement into a party that embraces the norms of liberal democracy. A central claim in this context is that this kind of transformation is possible and the norms of liberal democracy can be firmly entrenched in a predominantly Muslim society. However, this outcome is context specific, being conditional upon the coexistence and the interplay over time of a number of favorable internal and external processes.[2]

Is Political Islam Compatible with Liberal Democracy? The Relevance of the Turkish Experience

The question of whether political Islam is compatible with liberal democracy has considerable practical relevance not only for societies with Muslim populations, but also for the future of the international economic and political order, particularly in the post-9/11 global context. The empirical observation that the vast majority of countries in the Middle East and the Islamic world in general are ruled by authoritarian regimes, which are rather impervious to the kind of democratic currents that affected much of Latin America, Eastern Europe, and East Asia following the end of the Cold War, also appeared to raise deep questions concerning the compatibility of political Islam and liberal democracy. Turkey, as a secular and democratic state with a predominantly Muslim population appeared to be a rather unique case in the Islamic world. Nevertheless, Turkey's own democratic deficits limited its ability to play the kind of role model that could be effective in the process of political liberalization in Arab or other Muslim societies. More recently, however, the kind of political and economic transformation that Turkey has been undergoing has also helped to raise the credibility and the international appeal of the Turkish experience. Hence, it is now much more meaningful to talk about the relevance of the Turkish experience to the rest of the Muslim world than perhaps a decade or so ago.

Given the increasing international relevance of the Turkish experience, what are some of the key lessons that can be derived from this particular national and historical context? Certainly, one key lesson is that a secular political order is a precondition for liberal democracy. There is no way that liberal democracy can take root in a Muslim society without a strong commitment on the part of the political elites to the principle of a secular political order and firm constitutional safeguards that prevent the violation of the secular character of the state. In spite of its limitations, one of the achievements of the Kemalist state in Turkey has been to prevent the alternative of an "Islamic state" (based on Islamic Law) right from the beginning. The process of top-down implementation of the secularist ideology has also triggered a process of long-term social and political change. As a consequence, by the 1990s, even the most authoritarian-looking versions of political Islam in Turkey, such as the Welfare Party (the RP) in the 1990s, were moderate by the standards of other Muslim societies, and the goal of establishing an Islamic state enjoyed marginal political support by society at large.[3]

Yet another striking lesson is the long-term impact of the democratization process on the behavior of key political actors. Democratization over time necessarily involves a learning process, and Islamists in Turkey have not been immune to this process.[4] Indeed, scholars of Christian democracy in Western Europe have identified a similar learning process in this region, whereby a largely authoritarian political movement has been transformed and has progressively embraced liberal democratic norms in the process of trying to construct broad electoral coalitions within the boundaries of parliamentary democracy (Kalyvas, 1996). Islamist political actors have also experienced a similar and often painful learning experience, which has increasingly altered their basic perception of what was permissible in a democratic environment given the nature of domestic and external constraints. What is interesting is that this learning process has helped instigate a "virtuous circle" over time, whereby the Islamists have learned not so much how to respond reactively to the democratization process, but have become a pro-active force contributing to the process of further democratic deepening.

A third major lesson that one can derive from the Turkish experience is the importance of economic transformation that also helps to produce a substantial middle class of entrepreneurs and educated professionals. If political Islam is primarily a movement oriented toward mobilizing the interests of the underclass of urban marginals and rural poor, the so-called losers of the globalization process, it is more likely to adopt a radical posture. If in contrast, it is a movement based on a cross-class electoral coalition which includes a significant proportion of the winners of globalization, it is more likely to orient itself in a more moderate direction. Clearly, the

Turkish experience of economic development over time and more specifically the process of neoliberal restructuring, in spite of its shortcomings, over the past two decades have led to the development of a kind of conservative middle class or bourgeoisie component which represents a significant moderating force in the Turkish context. Moving in a moderate direction and accommodating the precepts of a secular regime do not necessarily mean, however, that the norms of liberal democracy will be embraced. Certainly, one can refer to the Malaysian example, where a flourishing bourgeoisie has been making a major contribution to economic development without undermining the authoritarian political foundations of the existing regime. Hence, the rise of an economically successful and influential middle class could be considered as a necessary but not a sufficient condition for the entrenchment of liberal democracy.

Yet another lesson concerns the importance of the role of the intellectuals and civil society organizations. There is no doubt that civil society started to flourish in Turkey during the 1990s and a wide variety of groups started to voice their claims against the limitations of the existing political order. Similarly, intellectuals from the "secularist" and "Islamist" components of society have emerged as key sources of criticism against the existing democratic order. Hence, democratization in Turkey, especially in the 1990s, is strongly rooted in the domestic sphere, and pressures have been building from below for the transformation of the Turkish state and the nature of the democratic regime.[5]

Finally, however, there is no doubt that the EU anchor has been extremely important in terms of helping to soften the underlying secular-versus-Islam divide in Turkish society. In this context, one should emphasize both the long-term impact of Europeanization and Westernization on Turkish democracy and the more recent impact of stronger signals in the direction of full membership, which have radically altered the incentive structure for key political actors and have helped to reshape the Islamists more than anybody else in the process. However, the very significance of this point raises certain questions concerning the broader applicability of the Turkish experience to the Arab Middle East, for example, where the EU may become increasingly active in the future whereas the transformation process, depending on a weaker set of incentives, may fall considerably short of full-membership requirements.

Transformation of Islamist Politics in Turkey: The Interplay of Domestic and External Dynamics

The Islamist movement has been radically transformed in Turkey over the course of the past decade. By 1995, The Welfare Party (the RP) had emerged as a key political force in Turkish politics, following its major electoral victories in the main metropolitan areas of Istanbul and Ankara during the municipal elections of March 1994. The rise of the RP continued in the general elections of December 1995. The party captured more votes than any of the established political parties and was able to form a coalition government as the major coalition partner.[6] Whilst the RP was moderate by the standards of most Islamist political movements and was a coalition of a diverse set of interests and tendencies, it nevertheless had certain authoritarian leanings. Its authoritarian bias originated from the fact that it was willing to work within the parameters of a democratic political order and yet considerable doubts were raised in the public mind considering the degree of respect the party had for a pluralistic political order. It appeared that the party conceived of democracy in rather instrumental terms in their quest to transform the Turkish state and Turkish society toward a more Islamist direction. In the economic sphere, their underlying model was one of hyper-populism based on heavy interventionism of the state in line with their popular conception of the "just order" (adil düzen). In the sphere of foreign policy, their approach involved a marked anti-European dimension in addition to being strongly opposed to the state of Israel. The main thrust of their foreign policy appeared to be the development of strong relations with other Muslim countries, with a clear focus on the Arab Middle East and North Africa.

What is interesting is that this kind of vision has encountered serious setbacks and reversals during the course of the past decade. Certainly, developments in domestic politics had a key role to play in this process. The authoritarian leanings of the party faced serious resistance from both the secular establishment and the society at large. The "post-modern" military intervention of February 28, 1997, resulting in the collapse of the RP-led coalition government in June 1997 and culminating in the process resulting in the closure of the party by the beginning of the following year itself, was an authoritarian move. Nevertheless, it signaled what was broadly permissible within a secular political environment reflecting the preferences of large segments of the Turkish state and Turkish society.

The Islamists undoubtedly underwent a serious learning process during this episode. The RP's successor, the Virtue Party (the FP) was a political party with much more moderate political force compared with its predecessor. Increasingly, the emphasis shifted to the extension of religious freedoms within the boundaries of the existing secular order. The FP was much more market friendly in its approach to economic policy and much more supportive of developing close relations with the EU. However, even this particular political party could not escape closure, which, in part, reflected the authoritarian bias of the Turkish state. The outcome of this decision was to generate a massive internal debate within the party between the "modernizers" and the "traditionalists," resulting in fragmentation. The result was the emergence of two separate political parties, with the modernizers constituting the backbone of the newly founded AKP. Looking back, it is interesting that the degree of intraparty debate was much stronger in the late 1990s in the FP compared to the leader-dominated mainstream parties of the center-right and the center-left.

State policies and disciplines were not alone in triggering off a process of fragmentation and transformation. Certainly, a discursive change in the approach of Islamist intellectuals and civil society organizations were also evident, swinging the pendulum in the direction of "modernizers." Key civil society organizations such as the major religious-conservative business association, Independent Industrialists and Businessmen's Association (MÜSİAD), that had been at the backbone of the RP and represented a moderating force within the movement, experienced a significant change in outlook by the end of the decade. Reports of the more recent MÜSİAD era placed much more emphasis on the theme of democratization, extension of the realms of civil and human rights, and integration with Europe (MÜSİAD, 2000). Similarly, the discourse of Islamist intellectuals in Turkey has been undergoing a parallel transformation leading to their increasing embracement of the values and norms of liberal democracy.[7]

This naturally brings us to the importance of the EU, which increasingly played a key role in shaping the preferences of the key political actors, including the Islamists, long before the critical Helsinki decision of December 1999. It is interesting that even the RP, when it came to office, accepted operating within the boundaries of the newly signed Customs Union Agreement with the EU. Certainly, the RP's successors were much more positive in their attitudes toward the EU, increasingly seeing the EU as a necessary safeguard against the established secularist state elites and as a vehicle to consolidate their position in Turkish society. Hence, any account that leaves out the role of the EU is likely to provide a highly incomplete and misleading interpretation of the transformation of Islamist politics in the Turkish context.[8]

The Transformative Impact of the EU:
The Post-Helsinki Context

Turkey's relations with the EU took a radically different turn following the Helsinki Summit of 1999. The fact that Turkey was given formal candidate status at Helsinki had a dramatic impact in terms of increasing the credibility of EU conditionality in the minds of both the policy-making elites and the public at large. The improved mix of incentives and conditions, in turn, was instrumental in accelerating the reform process both in the economic and in the political spheres. Consequently, Turkey was able to experience an unprecedented degree of democratic opening over a relatively short period of time, notably during the course of the 2002–04 period. These set of reforms, though by no means complete, have set off a process whereby Turkey has been able to make significant progress in terms of consolidating its democracy and accomplishing a genuinely open, pluralistic, and multicultural political order.

Reforms have been particularly striking in key areas such as human rights, protection of minorities, improvement of the judicial system and the role of the military. Within the broad area of human rights, significant progress has been achieved with respect to the fight against torture and ill-treatment in prisons, the freedom of expression and the freedom of peaceful assembly and association. Within the domain of minority protection, important strides have been made in terms of extending cultural rights for the Kurds, as well as non-Muslim minorities. More recently, changes have been taking place which have the potential of radically altering the military-civilian balance in Turkish society.[9]

The fact that the membership option became far more credible after 1999 contributed to a process whereby the pro-reform or the pro-EU coalition became increasingly stronger and more vocal in Turkish politics. The pro-EU coalition, meaning groups in Turkish society which not only favored EU membership as an abstract idea in itself but also displayed a strong commitment to undertaking reform, had already gathered momentum during the course of the 1990s. Civil-society organizations rather than political parties have emerged as the forerunners of the pro-EU coalition, and within civil society itself, business-based civil-society organizations have played a particularly active role.[10]

After the Helsinki decision, civil initiatives have become much more pronounced. Indeed, the very base of the pro-EU coalition has become increasingly broad and includes key segments of the state bureaucracy. The Europeanization process in Turkey during the 1990s produced a rift between state and business elites. It created major divisions within the Turkish state itself, helping to tilt the balance in favor of the pro-EU coalition. It is quite striking that the main agents of the political order, namely political parties, have joined the queue with a certain time lag. One of the paradoxical features of the Turkish experience after 1999 was that the coalition government in power during the 1999–02 era, dominated by two highly nationalistic parties on the left and the right of the political spectrum, was actually quite lukewarm in its approach toward the EU-related reform agenda.[11] Nevertheless, given the magnetism of the EU, the coalition government was not able to swim against the tide and ironically it was responsible for some of the most far-reaching reforms in Turkish history.[12] It was only after the elections of November 2002, however, that the dominant political force of the new era, the Justice and Development Party (the AKP), was able to take over the leadership role in the pro-EU coalition.

The dynamic process initiated by the Helsinki decision also helped to diminish the power and resilience of the Euro-skeptic elements or, stated somewhat differently the anti-EU coalition in Turkish society. The terms Euro-skeptic and anti-EU coalition convey a specific meaning in the Turkish context. They refer to those segments of the state, society, or the party system that are not against the idea of EU membership in principle, but are nevertheless against the implementation of key components of the Copenhagen criteria (such as education and broadcasting in Kurdish language) on the grounds that such reforms would undermine national sovereignty, leading to the break-up of the Turkish state.[13]

In retrospect, a series of unexpected shocks have helped this reform process to occur at a more accelerated speed than would otherwise have been the case. For example, the major economic crises that Turkey experienced in November 2000 and in February 2001 had an unintended consequence in terms of changing the balance of power quite drastically in favor of the pro-EU coalition.[14] The magnitude of the crises, which created a massive wave of unemployment and bankruptcies and hit all sections of society, rendered the potential material benefits of EU membership all the more attractive.[15] Furthermore, following the economic crises, both key domestic economic actors and the international financial community placed even greater emphasis than before on the need for a permanent EU anchor as opposed to simply relying on temporary IMF discipline for establishing durable economic growth and avoiding future financial crises. Consequently, the behavior of market participants increasingly depended on the country's ability to undertake EU-related reforms, both on the economic and political fronts. It was perhaps ironic that the periodic reports of key international banks or financial institutions focused on political developments and the implementation of the political component of the Copenhagen criteria as a means of interpreting the current state of the Turkish economy and conveying information to potential investors. In this kind of environment, key elements of the anti-EU coalition found themselves in a highly defensive position.

The next key turning point in this dynamic process was the War on Iraq. Previously the military-security establishment in Turkey, a key segment of the anti-EU coalition, being rather unreceptive to some key political reforms proposed by the EU, had often perceived the United

States-Israel-Turkey triangle as an alternative axis to the EU.[16] However, the deterioration of relations with the United States following the failure of the Turkish Parliament to endorse the decision involving the passage of American troops across the Turkish border to Iraq helped to weaken significantly, if not to undermine completely, the long-standing strategic alliance linking Turkey to the United States. Turkey's decision to abstain from the war effort and also not to allow the passage of American troops across her border had the unintended repercussion of bringing Turkey closer to Europe and notably to the position held by the core Franco-German alliance.[17]

With the United States firmly based in the Middle East, the military was no longer in a position to intervene in Northern Iraq on the grounds that this posed a major security threat. This chain of events had the impact of changing the balance of power in Turkish politics in favor of civilian elements. This, in turn, paved the way for a number of important changes centering on the status of the military in Turkish politics involving limitations of the powers of the National Security Council and controls over defense expenditures.[18] The military-security establishment has been undergoing a learning process during the recent era, like other key actors in Turkish politics. As a result of this, it has been progressively shedding its hard-liner posture and adopting a more favorable pro-European stance. This is clearly a novel phenomenon and has also been very much in evidence in the relatively passive or neutral approach that the military elites have adopted with respect to Cyprus, a position that stands in sharp contrast to their heavily nationalistic attitude in the past. At this point, it might be too early to conclude that the military has undergone a complete transformation. Certainly, there is a strong line of continuity with the past, notably with respect to the single-minded commitment to the principle of secularism. Furthermore, developments concerning the Kurdish and Cyprus issues continue to be approached with considerable caution and reservations. In spite of these qualifications, it is fair to say that the military in Turkey has been changing in such a way that it no longer makes sense to place it firmly within the Euro-skeptic camp.

It is perhaps not that surprising that these dramatic and unexpected set of developments in Turkey's domestic front have helped to add another dimension to post-Helsinki dynamics. Opinions in Europe regarding Turkish membership have started to change. In the same way that the pro-EU coalition has been strengthening in Turkey, the pro-Turkey coalition in Europe has also been gathering momentum. Key elements of European society which have historically viewed Turkey's membership negatively for quite different reasons ranging from claims of cultural incompatibility to failure to conform to democratic norms have gradually become more receptive to the idea of its membership. Hence, one can detect the development of a virtuous circle whereby more powerful and credible signals from the EU have helped to accelerate the reform process in Turkey. The very pace and intensity of the reform effort, in turn, have helped to reshape elite opinion in Europe toward the desirability of Turkey's membership.

The AKP and Its Rise to Electoral Dominance: The Underlying Determinants

The extraordinary electoral success of the AKP in the November 2002 general elections, following a decade of political instability under successive coalition governments, represented a major turning point in Turkey's political and economic trajectory. Economic bases of this success and interrelated hypotheses are advanced to explain this phenomenon.

First, the party has been extremely successful in constituting a cross-class electoral alliance, incorporating into its orbit both winners and losers from the neoliberal globalization process. Business support, notably from small and medium-sized business units falling under the umbrella of a major nation-wide business association, constitutes a crucial element of the AKP's electoral support. Second, the strong track record of the AKP's predecessors, the Welfare and the Virtue Parties (the RP and the FP respectively) at the level of the municipal governments is another element of key importance. Third, the failures of the conventional or established parties of either the center-right or the center-left in achieving sustained and equitable growth, avoiding costly financial crises and tackling the problem of pervasive corruption have also paved the way for the party's unprecedented electoral success in the recent era.

In spite of its Islamist roots and a natural association in terms of its leadership and core bases of political support with the Welfare and the Virtue Parties, the AKP has nevertheless managed to present itself as a new face with a claim to the very center of Turkish politics. Consequently, it has been able to construct a much broader electoral coalition judged by the standards of two major predecessors.

Whilst explaining the rise of the AKP is an interesting issue in itself, an even more interesting question is whether the party will be able to consolidate its power and establish itself as a hegemonic force in Turkish politics, at least during the next decade. Clearly, a satisfactory answer to this question requires a systematic and critical analysis of the AKP government's performance, notably in the economic realm. Our assessment in this context is quite favorable, though with certain reservations. Although it might be too early to provide a full-scale assessment, the evidence to date suggests that the AKP is unlikely to experience a serious setback by the time of the next general elections.[19]

There is no doubt that the 2001 economic crisis, the deepest crisis that Turkey has experienced in its recent history, with negative repercussions on all segments of Turkish society, rich and poor, educated and noneducated, urban and rural, had a devastating impact on the electoral fortunes of established political parties in Turkey. Clearly, the three parties that experienced major setbacks with a dramatic collapse in their electoral support were the parties that made up the coalition government that came into office following the April 1999 elections and were ironically though somewhat unintentionally responsible for some of the major economic and political reforms that Turkey has experienced in recent years. The leading member of the coalition government, the Democratic Left Party (the DSP) led by Bülent Ecevit, experienced a total collapse. Similarly, the Nationalist Action Party (the MHP) and the Motherland Party (the ANAP) also experienced dramatic declines in their bases of electoral support. Indeed, none of the three members of the coalition government could even pass the ten percent threshold in the November 2002 elections, which meant that they were effectively excluded from participation in parliamentary politics after 1999. Yet another political party that was not in government in the 1999–2002 era, but nevertheless a major political force throughout the 1990s, namely the True Path Party (the DYP), also experienced a deep setback and was relegated to the sidelines. Clearly, large segments of the Turkish electorate demonstrated deep dissatisfaction with established political parties on both the right and the left of the political spectrum. Center-left parties were penalized for failing to protect the interests of the poor and the underprivileged. The center-right parties suffered, in addition, from their association with widespread corruption.

Hence, the AKP as a new force in Turkish politics capitalized on the failures of conventional political parties. The AKP managed to present itself to wide segments of Turkish society as a progressive force that could come to terms with the positive aspect of economic globalization based on active participation and competition in the global market. At the same time, the AKP's approach involved a serious concern with social justice issues concerning both the distribution of material benefits as well as the extension of individual rights and freedoms. Compared to its rivals, the party appeared to be forward-looking and reformist in its approach, aiming to come to grips with the forces of globalization, meaning capitalizing on the material benefits of globalization whilst aiming to correct some of its negative consequences at the same time. Indeed, in certain respects, the AKP appeared to be more of a European-style social democratic party of the third way, compared to its main rival in the November 2002 elections, the

Republican People's Party (the CHP). With its emphasis on the benefits of the market, the need to reform the state in the direction of a post-developmental regulatory state, its concern with social justice issues, its commitment to multiculturalism and extension of religious freedoms and its transnationalism as exemplified by its commitment to EU membership and the associated set of reforms more than any other political party in recent Turkish society, the AKP projected the image of a political party of the third way more so than the CHP, which appeared much more inward-oriented and in certain respects far more conservative judged by the standards of European-style third-way politics.[20]

The CHP has capitalized on the benefit of the doubt of not being in government or even in Parliament during the 1999–2002 era. In some ways, in spite of its long history, it was also a partially new face that the voters could turn to in the face of their deep dissatisfaction with the principal parties in office. Nevertheless, the CHP leadership, in spite of the recruitment of the former Minister of State for the Economy, Kemal Derviş, failed to overcome its heavily nationalistic, statist and inward-looking orientation. Furthermore, the party's single-minded adherence to a rather strict and rigid version of secularism contributed to alienating it from important segments of the Turkish society that favored an extension of religious rights and freedoms within the boundaries of a secular state. Hence, the traditionalism, the lack of adaptability, and the relative lack of concern of the CHP with economic issues constituted some of the key factors that clearly helped to enhance the AKP's electoral fortunes, with the gap between the parties widening even further in the municipal elections of November 2004. Stated somewhat differently, the AKP has clearly benefited from the absence of a powerful and vocal opposition and this very absence of a genuine alternative from either the right or the left of the political spectrum with a capacity to adapt itself to changing circumstances and the new parameters within which Turkish politics operates may help to accentuate the dominance of the AKP even further during the course of the next few years.[21]

The Turkish Alternative to Christian Democracy? The AKP and Its Contribution to the Process of Democratic Consolidation

The emergence of the Justice and Development Party (the AKP) as the dominant force in Turkish politics in the elections of November 2002 represented yet another landmark in Turkey-EU relations.[22] From a comparative perspective, what rendered the AKP experiment interesting was that it was a new party with strong Islamist roots but nevertheless far more moderate and centrist in terms of outlook compared with its predecessors. Even more interesting was the fact that the party presented itself as an active and vocal supporter of EU membership. Indeed, the party in office pursued the EU-related reform agenda with a far greater degree of consistency and commitment than the previous coalition government. It is fair to argue, therefore, that the AKP established itself as the dominant component of the pro-EU coalition after November 2002. The degree of commitment displayed by the party to the EU-related reform agenda was also important in terms of contributing toward the development of a sizable pro-Turkey coalition within the European Union itself.

The AKP itself is a strange, hybrid political formation. The fact that key leaders of the party, as well as its core electoral support, have been associated with the Islamist parties of the past resulted in considerable skepticism on the part of the secular segments of the Turkish state and society, as well as the broader international community in the immediate aftermath of the elections of November 2002. Nevertheless, it became quite clear after a while that the party was far more moderate in outlook judged by the standards of its predecessors. From a social-science perspective, it is hard to locate the party on the conventional left-right political axis. There is no doubt that a strong conservative streak exists in the party's make-up, with a major emphasis on religion, morals, and the need to preserve traditional values. The conservatism of the party manifests itself rather vividly in issues relating to women's rights and gender equality. Indeed, the party describes itself as being "conservative democrats," identifying a close affinity with the development of their Christian democratic counterparts in Western Europe.[23] Furthermore, the electoral base of the party is made of a cross-class coalition that includes small- and medium-sized enterprises as significant beneficiaries of the neoliberal globalization process. The fact that business is an important component of the party's electoral base is another attribute that naturally leads many commentators to interpret the party as a party of the center-right.

At the same time, however, it is possible to identify certain parallels between the AKP and the third-way-style European social democratic parties in Europe, given the party's apparent commitment to the principles and values of multiculturalism, social justice, and a properly regulated market economy.[24] A benign view of the AKP is that it is a party committed to multiculturalism, at least in the narrow sense that one of its objectives is to extend the boundaries of religious freedom and encourage religious diversity as opposed to challenging the notion of secularism itself. At the same time, the party appears to pay more attention to social justice and the plight of the poorest compared with its rivals, although what it can actually accomplish in this sphere is severely limited by the financial disciplines imposed through the IMF program that the country has been applying in recent years. It is also important to take into account that social democratic parties of the recent vintage are typically based on a cross-class electoral alliance of which small- and medium-sized businesses constitute a key component.

What is striking in the present context is that the AKP has effectively captured the ground which was previously occupied by both the center-right and the center-left parties in Turkish politics. There is no doubt that the major economic crisis that Turkey experienced had a devastating impact on the electoral fortunes of the established political parties. Hence, the AKP as a novel hybrid formation with a cross-class electoral appeal, representing a unique synthesis of reformism and conservatism, was able to capitalize on the failures of the previous parties in office. In office, the party has been able to consolidate its power and popularity even further, both in domestic and international circles, by displaying a mixture of pragmatism in implementing fiscal discipline and economic reforms, and radicalism in implementing the EU-related political reforms. The result has been a mixture of economic recovery and a further opening of the political space for democratic participation in Turkey. Admittedly, the favorable pattern described had started earlier, but the AKP, by accelerating the momentum of this process, has been able to capture much of the credit in a way that increasingly enhanced its electoral dominance while marginalizing the opposition parties of both the right and the left in the process.

In addition to important initiatives undertaken on the economic and the democratization fronts, the AKP government displayed a significant shift in foreign-policy behavior away from a hard-line nationalistic stance toward a more balanced and pragmatic approach. This was clearly evident in the government approach to the Cyprus problem which has constituted a long-standing obstacle to Turkey's aspirations for EU membership. The AKP government was effectively the first government that welcomed a compromise solution which would bring the dispute to a peaceful conclusion. Similar forms of balanced foreign-policy behavior were displayed with respect to the Iraq War and relations with the United States, as well as relations with Israel and the Arab World. Relations with all neighboring countries continued to improve. Clearly, Turkey during this period, in line with the process of democratization at home, started to make a transition from a coercive to a benign regional power, effectively countering the criticisms that Turkey would be more of a security liability than a security asset for Europe in the process.

Putting the AKP experiment in a broader context, what is striking is that Turkey's Islamic identity had been identified as a source of difference, providing an argument for exclusion from the EU. The typical line of argument, based on a Huntington-style, strong East-versus-West dichotomy, was that Turkey's true Islamic identity would be lost through the process of closer integration with Europe. The recent experience stands in sharp contrast with this line of reasoning in the sense that a party with a moderate Islamist orientation has been the key political force in bringing secular Turkey closer to the center of the European project. Indeed, one is able to uncover an underlying paradox here: the moderate Islamists in Turkey have seen the importance of EU membership for Turkey as a means of consolidating and solidifying their own position against possible threats from the hyper-secularism of the established state elites as well as key sections of Turkish society, helping to expand the boundaries of religious freedoms in the process. Hence, European integration in a rather unexpected fashion became a mechanism for preserving Turkey's Islamic identity and making it more compatible with a secular, democratic, and pluralistic political order.

Having gone through a process of radical reforms and having experienced the paradoxical era of the early years of the AKP government, it is perhaps safer to claim that Turkish synthesis of secularism and democracy in a predominantly Muslim setting can offer a credible alternative for the rest of the Muslim world. An obvious qualification is called for in the sense that the secularism-versus-Islam divide and the debate involving the boundaries of secularism are far from being settled issues in Turkey. Moreover, in spite of the AKP's alleged moderate credentials, there is still the major problem of trust in Turkish society, and significant elements both within the state and the society at large continue to view the party's moderate image with considerable suspicion. Indeed, any attempts to advance identity claims such as the wearing of headscarves by women in public spaces generates major tension and resistance, as a consequence of which the government has by and large relegated these issues to the background in order to avoid serious conflict.[25] Certainly, the AKP's own commitment to multiculturalism is open to serious criticism, given that the party has so far not been too receptive to the idea of extending religious rights to Christian minorities or putting an end to the domination of state-organized religious practice in Turkey. Perhaps, it is fair to say that, in spite of certain initial reservations, the international community has been far more receptive to the AKP government, whereas serious divisions continue to exist within the domestic sphere.

What is also crucial in this context is that, while the EU attaches a very high priority to secularism, it does not offer a single blueprint for concrete practice. Indeed, within the EU there is a variety of national models concerning the translation of the principle of secularism to actual implementation. Hence, the EU has helped to push Islamists in Turkey into a more moderate dimension by restricting the space within which they could operate. However, this does not mean that EU membership alone will be able to completely resolve the secularism-Islam divide in the Turkish context. One would expect that this issue is likely to be an important and lively source of public debate and contestation both in Turkey and in Europe over the coming years. All these observations suggest that there is a need for further democratization in Turkey in terms of extending the realm of religious freedoms. This, in turn, depends on Turkey's ability to develop and agree upon compromise solutions in the sphere of domestic politics without necessarily hoping for a blueprint to arrive from the EU. The headscarf issue is clearly a good example of a long-standing dispute that awaits a compromise solution. The fact that the AKP government has so far been able to continuously postpone the issue does not mean that the issue itself has become irrelevant.

The Political Economy of the AKP's Future: The Challenges Ahead

By the end of 2004, the position of the AKP as the dominant force in Turkish politics appeared to be secure for the foreseeable future. The decision of the European Council in December to start off the process of accession negotiations with Turkey by October 2005 was clearly a favorable development that helped to bolster the AKP's fortunes in both the economic and the political realms. There is no doubt that a major setback on the EU front in December 2004 could have easily triggered a vicious circle of negative reactions in financial markets, leading to a serious downturn on the economic front, which would quite easily undermine the comfortable majority of the AKP government long before the onset of the new elections.

In spite of these developments, however, it would be premature to predict that the unchallenged position of the AKP represents a kind of medium- or long-term equilibrium in Turkish politics. A number of developments on both the domestic and external fronts could result in a reversal of the benign scenario for the AKP based on the experience of the 2002–04 period. Certainly, a crucial consideration in this context is the performance of the Turkish economy. If the Turkish economy is able to grow at rates of six to seven percent per annum over the course of several years, then this will help to contain the serious distributional conflicts that have been part and parcel of the Turkish political economy. Clearly, this kind of high-growth scenario is based on large inflows of foreign direct investment (FDI) and significant improvements in savings, investment and productivity performance in the domestic sphere. Whilst the investment climate has improved in recent years as a result of the government's strong commitment to fiscal discipline and broadly favorable developments on the EU front, there is nothing inevitable about the high FDI-growth scenario, especially in an environment of intense international competition for FDI flows.

A low-growth scenario, however, could seriously upset the benign equilibrium, with potentially negative political consequences. One should take into account the fact that the period of accession negotiations with the EU, which are likely to last over a period of at least a decade, are likely to entail costly adjustments in terms of restructuring the agricultural sector and the implementation of tight regulations among others, in line with the EU norms. Hitherto, Turkish public opinion has been strongly in favor of EU membership, primarily because of the material benefits that are likely to arise from this process. In a slow-growth environment, the nature of the adjustment process in the new era of accession negotiations may undermine the enthusiasm of key sections of Turkish society both within and outside the business community for the already protracted process of EU membership. The outcome of this process could be a radical revitalization of the nationalistic and Euro-skeptic bloc in Turkey in the course of the next few years. Indeed, the political contest in Turkey during the new era is likely to be between the different segments of the center-right, involving the "Muslim Democrats" and the nationalists in an environment where European-style social democracy is largely nonexistent. Signs that the electoral contest in Turkey is already moving in such a direction were already evident during the municipal elections of March 2004, which marked a notable improvement in the electoral fortunes of two nationalistically and Euro-skeptically inclined parties, the MHP and the DYP.

Rural poverty and unemployment, especially youth unemployment, are the two key issues which are likely to present a formidable challenge to the AKP in the new era. The recovery process in terms of growth that Turkey has experienced in the aftermath of the 2001 crisis has so far not been translated into an improvement in employment figures. In a slow-growth environment, the possibility of growth without employment is likely to be an even stronger possibility, which effectively means that large segments of society will look out for alternative avenues to express their political grievances. The Euro-skeptic parties will present themselves as the natural alternative to the AKP. Further strengthening of such parties, in turn, may emerge as a serious threat to the on-going process of democratic consolidation and economic reforms in Turkey. Similar conjectures are possible in the case of small- and medium-sized business, which has been a major electoral backbone of the AKP in recent years. As emphasized before, such enterprises have been less receptive to the somewhat tight IMF disciplines than large conglomerates. If the economy continues on a high growth path, small businesses are also likely to share in the benefits of this process, and a possible distributional conflict between small and large business units will be avoided. In a less dynamic economic environment, however, small- and medium-sized business may also start to look for alternative avenues of representation.

All these considerations highlight the fact that the AKP itself is a broad coalition. The very success of the "Muslim Democrats" in 2002 and 2004 was based on their ability to forge a broad electoral coalition that brought together many diverse and potentially conflicting elements of Turkish society. The danger is that, if things start to go wrong in the economy or in external relations, the result could be a serious fragmentation of this coalition. We should also take into account the fact that the AKP, during its early years, effectively avoided tackling the kind of thorny issues, such as lifting the existing ban on the entry of girls with headscarves into universities, which would have satisfied its core supporters but nevertheless would have generated serious resistance from the secular establishment. The AKP government has largely avoided such issues on the grounds that the economy and relations with the EU were the more immediate problem areas to be tackled. The more sensitive and divisive issues relating to Islamic symbols and identity could be safely postponed to a future date. In this manner, the party leadership no doubt wanted to avoid the fate of their predecessors, the Welfare Party and the Virtue Party, both of which faced closure on the grounds that they violated the secular character of the Turkish Constitution.

What is obvious from this discussion is that the fault lines that separate Islamists and secularists in Turkish society have not disappeared. Indeed, whenever the AKP government tried to push sensitive identity-based issues on the policy agenda, the outcome was serious resistance and conflict with the secular political establishment.[26] So far, the approach of the government has been quite pragmatic. While trying to pay lip service to its core supporters, it has been remarkably tactful in avoiding a confrontation on issues that their core supporters regard as central items of the agenda on human-rights grounds. Yet, a skeptic might argue that the AKP will not be able to postpone such issues forever. Otherwise, this core group, which is less than ten percent of the electorate, would increasingly feel alienated and search for alternative avenues of political expression. The natural but not the only alternative is the "Happiness Party" (Saadet), which represents the linear descendent of the Erbakan-style "National Outlook Movement" (Milli Görüş). This party could only capture some 2.5 percent of the vote in November 2002. However, its electoral fortunes may improve if many of the disgruntled supporters of the AKP see it as the natural alternative. Another possibility is that nationalist parties may capture some of these shifting votes, as indeed was the case in the April elections of 1999 with the ultra-nationalist, the MHP, gaining ground at the expense of the Virtue Party. The MHP with its particular brand of nationalism and Euro-skepticism on the one hand and its religious conservatism on the other could well emerge as the most serious rival of the AKP in an environment where various components of the AKP's underlying coalition feel dissatisfied for a rather different set of reasons and feel the need to shift their political preferences in novel directions.

Turning to a different realm, one should not discard the possibility that external developments can play a disequilibriating role with potentially negative consequences for the AKP's electoral fortunes. Significant progress has been made in relations with the EU in recent years, and Turkey is step by step approaching the goals that are a prerequisite for full membership. Nonetheless, even an optimistic assessment needs to take into account that Turkey's path toward EU membership continues to be an uphill struggle. Considerable division exists within the EU over the question of Turkish membership, in spite of the pace and depth of the reform process of the recent era, the kind of division which has largely been absent in the accession process of the new members from Central and Eastern Europe. Stated somewhat differently, the EU continues to send relatively ambiguous signals to Turkey, which renders the job of a government committed toward the implementation of EU-related reforms all the more difficult. Added to this, the Cyprus dispute continues to be a serious hurdle on the path to EU membership, and given the asymmetric incentives provided by the EU to the key actors concerned, it is unlikely to be resolved in a smooth manner in the near future. Finally, the instability in Northern Iraq and deteriorating relations with the United States continue to present formidable challenges. All these considerations suggest that the extraordinary success of the "Muslim Democrats" in the past few years does not necessarily represent a stable equilibrium, given the fragile domestic and external context of Turkish politics.

Returning to the Theme of Political Islam and Democracy: Concluding Observations

The central message of this essay is that an Islamist political movement can transform into a party promoting Western integration and liberal democracy. At the same time, there is nothing inevitable about the emergence and consolidation of liberal democracy in a predominantly Muslim setting. The historical context matters, and the outcome depends on the intersection of a combination of forces both domestic and external. The specific experience of Turkey provides a good example of how liberal democracy can take root and flourish as an example of a secular state in a predominantly Muslim setting, with the qualification that liberal democracy is still in the process of being consolidated in Turkey. In retrospect, several factors have contributed to the emergence of this benign outcome in a specific historical setting.

The constitutional order of the modern Republic with its strong commitment and arguably authoritarian interpretation of secularism was important in the first instance in terms of excluding the radical alternative of an Islamic state right from the very beginning. The principle of a secular political order is a precondition for a liberal democratic order, although the boundaries and the implementation of secularism in everyday life constitutes an area for political contestation. The Kemalist nation-building project in Turkey with its hyper-secularism made a positive contribution by helping to define the boundaries within which the Islamists could operate, although it also played a repressive role in terms of restricting the boundaries of political participation.

Representative democracy, in spite of its shortcomings, has been the norm in Turkey during the course of the postwar period. Hence, there is no doubt that the Islamists in Turkey have experienced a learning process. The democratic order has helped to shape the demands of the Islamists in a more moderate direction, as they realized that compromise solutions were vital for their effectiveness and survival within the boundaries of the secular process. Indeed, the learning process accelerated and flourished particularly in the aftermath of the "February 28 Process" or the postmodern coup that effectively led to the collapse of the coalition government led by the Welfare Party in June 1997 and the subsequent closure of the Welfare Party. This rapid learning process was arguably at the heart of not only the AKP's electoral success but also its ability to consolidate its position in Turkish politics after assuming power in November 2002. Indeed, a kind of virtuous cycle appears to have emerged in Turkey in recent years with the democratization process leading to the democratization of the Islamists themselves and then the Islamists, in turn, ironically taking up a key role in the further democratization and Europeanization of the Turkish political system.

Turning to the economic realm, the emergence of a significant middle class or "counter-elite" within the Islamist movement including intellectuals, businessmen, and highly educated professionals, who themselves benefited from the process of globalization and neoliberal economic restructuring, clearly helped to tilt the balance in a moderate direction. Clearly, the objective of this new bourgeoisie was to enlarge the boundaries of freedom and political participation as well as achieving an improved social status and greater access to state resources. A head-on clash with the secular establishment was clearly not in their interests. Turkey's empirical realities lend strong support to the observation that the emergence of a strong middle class is a crucial precondition for the emergence of liberal democracy.

Finally, the EU has played and is likely to continue to play a critical role in making Islam and liberal democracy compatible in the Turkish setting. The role of the EU has been particularly striking in reshaping the outlook of the Islamists in Turkey who increasingly saw the EU as a necessary safe-guard for protecting their own identity against the secular state establishment in recent years. Consequently, the Islamists or more recently the Muslim Democrats have become the most vocal element of the pro-reform or the pro-EU coalition in Turkey. The prospect of EU membership helped to provide a common project for different elements of Turkish society and as a result helped to soften the fundamental secular-Islamist divide in Turkish society. One would guess that in the absence of such a powerful external anchor as the credible prospect of EU membership, the domestic factors would play a moderating role without necessarily leading to the consolidation and deepening of liberal democracy.

Highlighting the importance of contextual changes inevitably implies that it would be misleading to think of the Turkish example as a "model" that can easily be transplanted to the Arab Middle East. It is equally wrong to argue that the Turkish experience holds no relevance for the Arab Middle East given that the elites in these countries for a variety of histori-cal reasons, including the Ottoman legacy of imperial rule, the way that secularism has been put into practice during the modern Republican era, and Turkey's single-minded orientation toward the West, have tended to distance themselves from and lacked any kind of enthusiasm for the "Turkish model" (Taşpınar, 2003). Considering that both Turkey and the region as a whole are in flux, undergoing a process of deep-seated trans-formation, past perceptions may provide a limited guide to future devel-opments.

We may conjecture that the relevance of the Turkish experience as an example as opposed to an exportable model would depend on both the nature and speed of the political liberalization process in the Middle East region, as well as Turkey's own performance in the spheres of economic and political reforms resulting in a smooth transition to EU membership. Certainly, the more enclosed and authoritarian regimes of the Middle East and Central Asia are likely to visualize the Turkish experience as an existential threat and are likely to distance themselves from this ongoing experiment as much as possible. In contrast, regimes which are in the process of being liberalized are likely to be more receptive to the Turkish experience. Interestingly, therefore, the greater the degree of democratization in the region, the greater will be the relevance of the Turkish experience, which will help to contribute to the economic development and democratization of the region even further. Added to this, the fact that the recent "Europeanization" of Turkish foreign policy has resulted in a more balanced foreign policy behavior toward Israel and the Arab States is also likely to increase the receptivity of the policy makers and intellectuals to the ongoing transformation process that Turkey has been experiencing.

Notes

* A first draft of this chapter was presented at the Workshop on "Democratization and Development. New Political Strategies in the Middle East" at the Danish Institute for International Studies (DIIS) held in Copenhagen, Denmark, April 2005. The author would like to thank Dietrich Jung, Thomas Scheffler and other participants at the workshop for their valuable comments.

1. On the "Kemalist" or the "Republican" model of modernization in Turkey, see Mardin (1994) and Bozdoğan and Kasaba (1997).
2. The contribution of Ayoob (2004 b) is particularly telling in this context.
3. For evidence, see Çarkoğlu and Toprak(2000).
4. For further elaboration, see Heper (1997) and Öniş (2001).
5. On the nature of civil society activism and the role of the intellectuals, see Keyman and Içduygu (2005) and Göle (1994).
6. The RP has generated significant literature. See amongst others Öniş (1997) and Yavuz (2003).
7. See in this context the important study by Dağı (2004).
8. See in this context Öniş (2001) and Tanıyıcı (2003).
9. For the details of the reform initiatives see Aydin and Keyman (2004).
10. Perhaps the most influential organization in this respect was TÜSİAD, the association that represented the interests of big business in Turkey. TÜSİAD published a report outlining a blueprint for democratic reforms, notably with respect to the extension of minority rights in 1997, which generated considerable controversy and generated critical reaction from key sections of the state establishment. See Tanör (1997). Other major business associations such as MÜSİAD, representative of "Islamic Business" in Turkey, followed TÜSİAD's lead toward the end of the decade. See MÜSİAD (2000).
11. The parties concerned were left-nationalist the Democratic Left Party (the DSP) and the ultra-nationalist The Nationalist Action Party (the MHP).
12. A fair assessment has to point out that the minor member of the coalition government, the Motherland Party (the ANAP), was quite vocal in its support

of the reform process. This particular party could, therefore, be considered the first major political party in Turkey during the recent era that actually established itself as an active member of the pro-EU coalition.

13. On the nature and depth of Euro-skepticism in Turkish society, see Avci (2004) and Yilmaz (2004). The term "soft Euro-skeptics" is a better characterization of the dominant form of Euro-skepticism in the Turkish setting. These elements are quite receptive to the idea of Turkey's integration with Europe on the grounds of modernization and Westernization, yet what they actually desire is a form of integration on their own terms, which essentially means integration without reform.

14. On the origins and nature of the economic crises in 2000 and 2001, see the collection of essays in Öniş and Rubin (2003).

15. Opinion polls indicate that 74 percent of the Turkish public are in favor of EU membership. The main motivation for this appears to be pragmatic considerations relating to higher living standards. For evidence, see Çarkoğlu (2003).

16. "The Sèvres Syndrome" is an appropriate way to characterize the behavior of the state elites that formed a key component of the Euro-skeptic coalition. This was based on a fear, historically conditioned by the memories of the post-World War environment that Turkey found itself in, that some of the key political reforms imposed by the EU would necessarily undermine the essential unity, leading to the break-up of the Turkish state. For a good discussion of this issue see Kirişçi (1999).

17. For a further elaboration of this argument, see Öniş and Yilmaz (2005).

18. For the details of this process see Aydin and Keyman (2004).

19. These have to take place in November 2007 at the latest.

20. On the role of the AKP in Turkey's recent Europeanization and democratization experience, see Ayoob (2004 a) and Keyder (2004), Öniş and Keyman, (2003).

21. On the nature of the Turkish party system and the principal characteristics of the political parties involved see the articles in Heper an Rubin (2002).

22. On the elections of November 2002 and the rise of the AKP, see Öniş and Keyman (2003), Çarkoğlu (2002), Insel (2003) and Mecham (2004).

23. On the ideological make-up of the AKP and the concept of "conservative democracy" see Akdoğan (1995).

24. For a detailed elaboration of this point see Keyman and Öniş (2004).

25. The only exception to this has been the introduction of the higher education bill, an important element of which was the extension of the opportunities offered to religious secondary schools during May 2004. However, this proposal was shelved following fierce resistance.

26. A good example of such an episode was the proposed extension of rights for the graduates of religious secondary schools, "Imam Hatip Liseleri," in terms of their ability to attend universities. This particular component of the proposed Higher Education Bill caused considerable havoc. As a result, the government withdrew this proposal to avoid further instability and conflict.

References

Akdoğan, Yalçın (2005) "AK Parti ve Muhafazakar Demokrasi," available at http://www.akparti.org.tr/muhazafakar.doc.

Avci, Gamze (2004) "Turkish Political Parties and the EU Discourse in the Post-Helsinki Period: A Case of Europeanization," in Mehmet Uğur and Nergis Canefe (eds.), *Turkey and European Integration: Accession Prospects and Issues,* London and New York: Routledge.

Aydin, Senem and Fuat Keyman (2004) "European Integration and the Transformation of Turkish Democracy," *Centre for European Policy Studies, EU-Turkey Working Papers,* No. 2, August.

Ayoob, Mohammed (2004 a) "Turkey's Multiple Paradoxes," *Orbis,* 48 (Summer): 451–463.

—— (2004 b) "Political Islam: Image and Reality," *World Policy Journal,* 21 (3): 1–14.

Bozdoğan, Sibel and Reşat Kasaba (eds.) (1997) *Rethinking Modernity and National Identity in Turkey,* Seattle, University of Washington Press.

Çarkoğlu, Ali (2002) "Turkey's November 2002 Elections: A New Beginning?" *Middle East Review of International Affairs,* 6 (4) Available at http://meria. idc.ac.il/

—— (2003) "Who Wants Full Membership? Characteristics of Turkish Public Support for EU Membership," in Ali Çarkoğlu and Barry Rubin (eds.): *Turkey and European Union: Domestic Politics, Economic Integration and International Dynamics,* London: Frank Cass Publishers.

Daği, Ihsan (2004) "Rethinking Human Rights, Democracy and the West: Post-Islamist Intellectuals in Turkey," *Critique: Critical Middle Eastern Studies,* 13 (2): 135–151.

Göle, Nilüfer (1994) "Towards an Autonomization of Politics and Civil Society in Turkey," in Metin Heper and Ahmet Evin, (eds.): *Politics in the Third Turkish Republic,* Boulder Co: Westview.

Heper, Metin (1997) "Islam and Democracy in Turkey: Towards a Reconciliation?" *The Middle East Journal,* 51 (January): 31–45.

Heper, Metin and Barry Rubin (2002) *Political Parties in Turkey,* London: Frank Cass.

Insel, Ahmet (2003) "The AKP and Normalizing Democracy In Turkey," *South Atlantic Quarterly,* 102: 293–308.

Kalyvas, Stathis N. (1996) *The Rise of Christian Democracy in Europe,* Ithaca: Cornell University Press.

Keyder, Çağlar (2004) "The Turkish Bell Jar," *New Left Review,* 28: 65–84.

Keyman, Fuat and Ahmet Içduygu (2005) *Citizenship in a Globalizing World: European Questions and Turkish Experiences,* London: Routledge.

Keyman, Fuat and Ziya Öniş (2004) "Globalization and Social Democracy in the European Periphery: Paradoxes of the Turkish Experience," available at: http://home.ku.edu.tr/~zonis/publications.htm.

Kirişci, Kemal (1999) "Turkey," in Stelios Starvidis, Theodore Couloumbis, Thanos Veremis and Neville Waites, *The Foreign Policies of the European Union's*

Mediterranean States and Applicant Countries in the 1990s, London: Macmillan Press.

Mardin, Şerif (1994) *Türk Moderleşmesi*, İstanbul: İletisim Yayınları.

Mecham, R. Quinn (2004) "From the Ashes of Virtue, A Promise of Light: The Transformation of Political Islam in Turkey," *Third World Quarterly*, 25 (2): 339–358.

MÜSİAD (2000) *Anayasa Reformu ve Yönetimin Demokratikleşmesi*, Istanbul: Müstakil Sanayici ve İşadamları Derneği.

Öniş, Ziya (1997) "The Political Economy of Islamic Resurgence in Turkey: The Rise of the Welfare Party in Perspective," *Third World Quarterly*, 18 (4): 743–766.

——(2001) "Political Islam at the Crossroads: From Hegemony to Co-Existence," *Contemporary Politics*, 7 (4): 281–298.

Öniş, Ziya and Fuat Keyman (2003) "A New Path Emerges," *Journal of Democracy*, 14 (2): 95–108.

Öniş, Ziya and Barry Rubin (2003) *The Turkish Economy in Crisis*, London: Frank Cass Publishers.

Öniş, Ziya and Şuhnaz Yilmaz (2005) "Turkey-EU-US Triangle in Perspective: Transformation or Continuity?" *The Middle East Journal*, 59 (2): 265–284.

Taniyici, Şaban (2003) "Transformation of Political Islam in Turkey: Islamist Welfare Party's Pro-EU Turn," *Party Politics*, 9 (4): 463–483.

Tanör, Bülent (2004) *Perspectives on Democratisation in Turkey*, TÜSİAD Reports, TY/171/1997 available at: http://www.tusiad.org/english/rapor/demokratik/index.html.

Taşpınar, Ömer (2003) "An Uneven Fit? The Turkish Model and the Arab World." *Brookings Institution, Us Policy Towards the Islamic World*, Analysis Paper, No. 5, available at: http://www.brookings.edu/printme.wbs?page = /fp/saban/analysis/taspinar20030801.htm.

Yavuz, Hakan (2003) *Islamic Political Identity in Turkey*, New York: Oxford University Press.

Yilmaz, Hakan (2004) "Euro-skepticism in Turkey," paper presented at the Johns Hopkins University Bologna Center, Second Pan-European Conference, Bologna, Italy, 24–26 June.

6

"Democratization" Reforms as a Means of Stabilizing Authoritarian Rule in Contemporary Egypt

Maye Kassem

Introduction

Over the last few years, several reform initiatives have been implemented in the Egyptian political landscape, including, the May 2005 amendment to Article 76 of the Egyptian constitution, which replaced the one-candidate referendum system of presidential selection by a multicandidate system of presidential election. Is this a sign that Egypt is in fact moving toward democracy? The purpose of this chapter is to arrive at an answer to this question by examining the Egyptian political arena and assessing these more recent developments.

The analysis will lead to a rather bleak conclusion. This chapter will illustrate why the political reforms that have been taking place over the last few years ultimately appear to be tactics primarily intended to stabilize and reinforce the survival of authoritarian rule rather than being carried out in order to create genuine liberalization and democracy in contemporary Egypt. After presenting the historical background of Egypt's presidential regime, I will analyze these "new reforms" by looking more closely at four particular cases that at first glance appear to be first steps toward more democracy.

The Historical Context of Presidential Rule in Egypt

Since the coup d'état of July 1952, the creation of the republic in June 1953, and Nasser's subsequent gain of control of the presidency in November 1954, the emergent political structures in Egypt can be characterized as being dominated by one major feature: an overwhelmingly powerful presidency essentially devoid of checks and balances. As Egypt's longest-serving president, Hosni Mubarak (1981–present), has shrewdly utilized and built upon his predecessors' system of governance. As vice-president at the time of Sadat's assassination, Mubarak's ascent to the presidency was straightforward. In contrast to his predecessors, the new president was not confronted with any particular power struggle at the start of his tenure in office. What Mubarak faced, however, was arguably something more challenging to the system of personal rule, namely, ideological, socioeconomic, and political disillusionment in Egypt. The 1967 war, which ended with Israel's occupation of Egyptian, Syrian, and Jordanian territories, ended the illusion of Arab power, nationalism, and unity. Sadat's peace treaty with Israel reinforced this and, consequently, isolated Egypt from the rest of the Arab world, as well as creating voices of dissent within the country. Nasser's socialist experiment with a centrally planned economy left the country in debt. Sadat's attempt at economic restructuring (*Infitah*) did little to help address the problem. In fact, when Sadat became President, he inherited a debt that had been calculated at five billion USD. With the introduction of *Infitah*—which produced a consumption boom that failed to stimulate investment in productive or export-orientated industries—this debt multiplied to a robust 30 USD in 1981 (see Ibrahim, 1996: 141).

Furthermore, President Mubarak inherited a newly constructed multiparty arena that could potentially challenge the existence of the personal authoritarian system. On the surface, Mubarak did not appear particularly concerned at the latter prospect. During his first few years in power, the new president portrayed himself as a prominent advocate of democracy. Stating that "democracy is the best guarantee of our future" and that he "had no wish to monopolize decision-making," the president went so far as to declare his disapproval of long-term presidential rule (public address, April 1982). As he stated in 1984, "I do not conceal from you the fact that I believe that the assumption of the office of the president by any one of us should not exceed two terms." Furthermore, he went on to pledge that "I will be the first President to whom this rule shall apply" (BBC SWB, June 26, 1984). Sadat had also initially proclaimed his disdain for long-term presidential rule. He even went as far as to implement a two-term limitation in Article 77 of the 1971 constitution, although this was duly amended in 1980 so that he could enter his third term, as a result of which there has been no formal limitation on presidential terms since then. As in the case of his predecessor, Mubarak went on to exceed two terms, and in September 2005 he started his fifth term in office. Moreover, the president's views on democracy soon changed after consolidating power. As he argued in 1987, democracy could not be achieved "overnight" (Mubarak interview, cf. Owen, 1994: 189). The president's revised argument was based on the view that, as a developing country, Egypt's priority was economic development. As he stated, "if we cease economic activity and grant freedom . . . we consequently place people in an unstable state" (BBC SWB, February 15, 1987). In this regard, Mubarak's change of view indicated that the then new president initially projected the image of being an advocate of democracy in order to legitimize his position and consolidate his power. Over twenty years later, it seems that through a series of reforms and changes that have taken place over the last few years, the President is attempting to portray himself as a democratic advocate once again.

New Millennium: New Reforms

The new millennium has brought some interesting changes within the Egyptian political arena. These changes have included reforms ranging from changes in legislative elections procedures (2000), internal restructuring within the National Democratic Party NDP(2001/2), the creation of a National Council for Human Rights (announced in June 2003, established in January 2004), and, a proposed revision of the prevailing presidential referendum procedures (March 2005). On the surface, it would appear that, with the new millennium, Egypt was entering a new era of reform and liberalization. On closer examination, however, the application of such reforms appears at best contentious.

Legislative Election Reforms in 2000

The Supreme Constitutional Court (SCC) ruled on July 8, 2000, that free elections could be better realized if full judicial supervision was implemented during legislative elections. The government tried to justify its position on the grounds of practical considerations, namely "that there were not enough judges to oversee the balloting process in all polling stations and, secondly, that judiciary monitoring was a formal supervisory capacity that did not require the actual presence of judges at the polling stations" (*Al-Ahram Weekly*, August 31–September 6, 2000). In response to the government's argument, the SCC justified its ruling by noting that the judiciary's supervision of the election process was necessary because the judiciary is an impartial entity. Moreover, it added that judicial "supervision must be sustentative rather than merely formal or professed" if citizens are to "choose their representatives in a safe and confident environment"

(*Al-Ahram Weekly*, August 31–September 6, 2000). As a consequence, "any excuse on the grounds that practical considerations stand against the application of the constitution's provisions is not acceptable, because constitutional requirements cannot be parleyed by excuses" (*Al-Ahram Weekly*, August 31–September 6, 2000). In regard to such a verdict and the equally powerful comments of the SCC, the government was left with little room for maneuver. Ignoring the ruling of the nation's highest court would have undermined respect for the rule of law that had been utilized as a main legitimization tool for the President's rule. As constitutional law professor Mohammed Merghani points out, "the government complied with the Constitutional Court's decision and saved itself from any embarrassment that might have arisen from other options" (cf. *Al-Ahram Weekly*, July 20–26, 2000). Interestingly, following the 2000 elections, the President stated "I took steps to place the electoral process under the supervision of the judiciary after listening for many years to opinions on how to promote confidence in the voting process and freedom of choice" (cf. *Al-Ahram Weekly* November 16–22, 2000). The President's statement acknowledged the positive role which judicial participation in the electoral process can produce. Yet, contrary to producing "confidence in the voting process and freedom of choice," the implementation of new electoral rules expanding the role of the judiciary produced new forms of constraining tactics previously unfamiliar to the majority of Egyptian voters.

Early indications that the new electoral framework was to face disparate resistance are detected in view of the Ministry of Interior's increasingly prominent role during the elections. On one level, the fact that the Ministry of Interior maintained its customary control over registered voter lists meant that certain obstructions and disruptions continued. The obstruction of an independent or opposition candidate's access to their constituency's voter list, for example, remained a common occurrence. More significantly perhaps was the rise in police interference outside polling stations, since the presence of members of the judiciary in polling stations meant that the rigging of ballot papers on election days became a more difficult process in comparison to the previous elections. It is in this context that the Interior Ministry increased its obstructive tactics outside polling stations, thus preventing voters from entering the polling station while the bewildered judges sat inside empty stations. In one reported case a judge presiding over the elections in the Qalyoubian village of Nay left the polling station to see why with so much noise outside there were no voters inside. Having discovered that the police, who were officially placed outside to protect the polling station, were serving an additional role of blocking voter entry, the judge demanded that they move aside so that voters could enter. The response of the officer in charge told him that "judges were only responsible for the ballot box inside and had no authority outside the polling station" (cf. *Al-Ahram Weekly*, November 16–22, 2000). Indeed, the Egyptian Organization for Human Rights (EOHR) noted in its 2000 electoral report the prevailing "pattern of preventing voters from casting their ballots," focusing in particular on the constituencies of Maadi and Basatin whereby it noted that "only buses packed with NDP supporters were permitted to reach the polling stations" (*Al-Ahram Weekly*, November 16–22, 2000).

Preventing voters from entering the polling station is a blatant form of obstruction and abuse of the electoral process in itself. However, the violent clashes that emerged as a consequence of such tactics between the security apparatus and the voters contributed an additional dimension to the 2000 elections that in previous elections may have also existed, but on a less widespread scale. Indeed, the electoral death toll of less than ten people in the 2000 elections is lower than that of the 1995 elections, which witnessed fifty-one nationwide deaths. However, the difference is the cause of the deaths. In the 1995 elections, most of the electoral fatalities were largely a consequence of "feuds within the confines of personality-based politics which are more easily begun and harder to contain" (Lande 1977, cf. Kassem, 1999). In other words, electoral violence until the 2000 elections was predominantly confined to conflict between competing candidates and their personal groups of supporters. This is a pattern that is not unusual in developing systems in which political parties are weak. The 2000 legislative elections brought violence stemming from the state targeting and confronting its citizens using the most blatant tactics. This fact is confirmed by one independent report that noted that while "violence between their candidates and supporters decreased, the violence from security forces against voters increased" (Ouda, el-Borai, and Saada, 2000: 75). In fact, "approximately 80 percent of the killings and injuries resulted from bullets or tear gas fired by security forces and not through rival fighting" (75).

Sameh Ashour, a member of the Nasserist opposition, commented prior to the elections that the court ruling could be considered a step forward toward achieving fair elections. However, he predicted that attempts by the government to avoid the application of the new ruling in the elections would lead "to a catastrophe that would endanger the stability of the state and society" (*Al-Ahram Weekly* July 13–19, 2000). In hindsight, the new tactics adopted by the regime to comply with the new rules of the SCC touched these fears and illustrated that, regardless of the implementation of political reforms on paper, it would appear that the regime has little intention of applying them in practice if they are perceived to threaten its own monopoly of power.

Restructuring the NDP

With the move toward a multiparty arena President Sadat created the NDP in 1978 to replace Nasser's single-party, the Arab Socialist Union (ASU). The NDP, like the ASU, was not only created by a President, but also was, and continues to be, headed by the President. Although other parties were also "encouraged" to emerge by President Sadat, the majority of ASU parliamentarians and senior party members swiftly converted to the President's NDP regardless of the alternatives that were being offered by the new "opposition" parties. Given the President's preeminent position in the political arena, it is not surprising that the majority of these individuals preferred to maintain their allegiance to the party headed by the President. One of the most significant aspects of the NDP has been the fact that it has systematically occupied no less than three-quarters of the seats in the Egyptian legislature even though it lacks a clear ideological stand. Its program, for example, is formally based upon the principles of promoting democracy and "fostering Egypt's affiliation to the Arab world, [and] venerating ... economic liberalization that encourages private investment" (*Al-Ahram Weekly*, October 12–18, 1995).

On closer analysis, however, it seems a deliberate tactic to leave the party's ideology vague and open to interpretation. As Hinnebusch points out, while the party was, by the end of the Sadat era, cleared of left-wing elements and had thus become established "firmly to the centre-right," the vagueness of its program meant that the party would be able to "accommodate a fairly heterogeneous spectrum of political attitudes" (Hinnebusch, 1985: 161). This flexibility in turn means that the President and his government can adopt any policy decision without appearing to be compromising the party's "official" standing.

In view of the NDP's overwhelming domination of the Egyptian legislature, the party is surprisingly structured along very simplistic lines. In terms of financial resources, for example, its main capital is the 20 million LE (Egyptian Pounds, approximately four million USD) that was raised by Sadat in the 1970s. The proceeds of this investment continue to be used to finance the party and its developmental projects. In addition to its bulk capital, the party also receives an annual subsidy of approximately 250,000 LE from the sale of its official publications, including its daily newspaper, *Mayo*. Another source of income is an annual grant of 100,000 LE from the Consultative (*Shura*) Council—an amount that is distributed to all legalized political parties in Egypt. The party's other known source of income is derived from the annual 2 LE subscription fee of its alleged two million members.

Yet in the absence of a compelling ideology, autonomous access to the state's resources or even independent, charismatic party leaders, the NDP has systematically occupied no less than three-quarters of the seats in the Egyptian legislature largely due to the patronage of the President and the enormous power and state resources at his disposal (see Kassem, 1999). However, it seems that by January 2001 the regime had decided that the NDP was in need of some reinvigorating reforms. The reasons behind such a decision can be linked to several factors. On one level, the outcome of the October-November 2000 legislative elections brought to light the overall unpopularity of NDP candidates and publicly embarrassed the regime in the process. In fact, even with wide-scale police interference, particularly in preventing voters from entering the polling stations to vote, only 172 (39 percent) of the officially nominated NDP candidates were elected. The saving grace for the NDP was the fact that "another 181 'NDP-independents'—members who had run in the elections despite not having received the party's nomination—won seats and subsequently rejoined the party. In addition, 35 actual independents joined the NDP after winning their seats, topping off the party's current 88 percent parliamentary majority—a margin comfortably above the two-thirds needed to pass legislation and rubber stamp the president's decisions" (Brownlee, 2002: 9).

On another level, reforming the NDP was seen within Egyptian political circles as a mechanism with which to establish the President's youngest son, Gamal, within the formal political structure. This perception seemed further validated, as will be discussed later, when the young Mubarak was given a prominent position in the new party structure. On the formal level, however, reforming the NDP was justified by the President on the basis that such a move would not only "prepare the new, young generations [so they will be capable] of filling the current political void," but also, and more significantly, that such reforms would "promote democratization in the sense of reinforcing political pluralism and stimulating participation in political life" (cf. Al-Ahram Weekly online, Issue No. 595, July 18–24, 2002).

The NDP reforms on paper do indeed appear to signify the start of democratic restructuring within the party itself. To begin with (and following the recommendations of a nine-member committee and a four-member subcommittee), the first of its two stages of reforms took place. This first stage, which was introduced in June 2001, entailed the creation of a "party primaries" system of selection for members intending to run for municipal and legislative levels of election. This, put simply, meant that in contrast to previous mechanisms of selection whereby the top party leaders personally nominated and approved official candidates to run for elections, the new system theoretically opened the way so that "holders of internal party posts were able to vote in electoral caucuses on their preferred nominees" (Brownlee, 2002: 10).

Evidence to suggest that, in practice, the new reform did little to widen the sphere of participation within the party was reflected in the June 2001 *Shura* (Consultative) Council elections, in which party leadership "interfered in the nomination by ordering voters to cast their ballot in support of more conservative candidates" (El- Tarouty, 2004: 68). As such, it is noted that "the party primaries did not by any means depend on the will of party members who had for the first time acquired the right to vote for their official candidates" (68). Instead, it continued to maintain its centralized, personalized mechanisms of control with little regard for the application of its own reform policies. In fact, the widespread failure of the primaries for both the *Shura* and, later, municipal council elections led Gamal Mubarak to admit in the summer of 2002 that "in some cases, members were forced by the party's leaders at central and local levels to choose certain candidates," but argued that "young people should not feel despair" at this predicament (*Al-Ahram Weekly*, online, July 18–24, 2002).

The second stage of the NDP's reforms took place in September the same year during the party's Eighth Congress. The main reforms adopted there focused predominately on restructuring the General Secretariat branch of the party. The General Secretariat, whose fourteen members, including President Mubarak, constitute the highest ranking officials within the party, was until then largely immune from almost any form of change, including in its membership composition. The removal of Yusef Wali by President Mubarak from his post as General Secretariat—a post he had held since 1984—and his replacement by Safwat al-Sherif, another long-serving minister and member of the general Secretariat, could hardly be perceived as an indication of fundamental reform within the highest level of the party.

More importantly, however, has been the creation of new appointments and positions within the General Secretariat, most notably the creation of the Policies Secretariat, which subsequently saw the expansion of the General Secretariat membership to twenty individuals, one of whom is Gamal Mubarak as the presidentially appointed head of the Policies Secretariat. While the nature of various other committees and sub-committees linked to the party's internal restructuring is beyond the scope of this chapter, it is sufficient to note that the main drive behind the internal reforms does not appear to be an attempt to "promote democratization" as the President had earlier stated. Rather, reforming the structure of the General Secretariat appears to be a move intended to curtail the powers of the incumbent "old-guard" members by indirectly moving some of their responsibilities and authority. Hence, although most of the "old guard" have not been stripped of their formal posts, the role of the Policies Secretariat since its creation, for example, is to direct party policies and potential legislation (with the assistance of six newly created affiliated committees representing Economic Affairs, Education, Health, Foreign Affairs, Youth and Women).

This evidently implies some overlap between the role of the Policies Secretariat and that of the various ministries representing these sectors. Even the creation of the two less-prominent Secretariats—the Membership Secretariat and the Financial and Administrative Secretariat—indicate this to be the case. As one author notes, "According to Article 50 in the party's by-law, the Membership Secretariat is responsible for gathering information about party members . . . [gathering] such information used to be [the role] of the Organization Secretariat, headed by Kamal El-Shazly [a member of the old guard]" (El-Tarouty, 2004: 76). Similarly, "when the Treasury Secretariat was replaced by the new Financial and Administrative Affairs Secretariat, [Zakariya] Azimi became its head. The Treasury Secretary used to report to Kamal El Shazly in his capacity as Organization Secretary; instead, the newly formed Secretariat . . . reports to the Secretary General" (El-Tarouty, 2004: 77). While the application of such tactics suggest perhaps a move toward a more balanced distribution of power at the highest level, opposition members, such as members of the *Kifya* movement, and respected political analysts argue that these moves are simply tactical maneuvers intended to discreetly replace one set of individuals with another. Moreover, the June 2004 cabinet reshuffle, which saw the incorporation of various young, Western-educated new ministers into the political landscape seems to reinforce this view. As one author notes:

"Critics and boosters alike noted that a slew of new ministers are fixtures in the retinue of Mubarak's son Gamal, head of the NDP's very influential Policies Secretariat. They include the McGill educated prime minister, Ahmed Nazif, Industry Minister Rashid Mohamed Rashi (CEO of Unilever Egypt), Tourism Minister Ahmed El-Maghrabi (CEO of the French tourism group Accor). . . and the purported economic whiz kid Mahmoud Mohieddine who leads the newly created Investment Ministry." (El-Ghobashy, February 2, 2005).

Finally, it should also be pointed out that the ideological platform of the NDP was barely touched during the reforms. As such, the party continues to maintain its vague centrist position whilst continuing to derive its legitimacy from the 1952 "revolution" and its formal identification with both the Nasser and Sadat eras. While the NDP's new literature does pledge to "uphold democracy and the rule of law, pluralism and freedom of expression," this aspect is rendered obsolete in view of the fact that "the new program left untouched the matter of . . . the emergency laws and made no mention whatsoever of the peaceful rotation of power" (*Al-Ahram Weekly* online, September19–25, 2002).

On this basis, the fact that there seems to be little indication on the practical level to confirm genuine reforms within the NDP can perhaps be better understood on the basis of the internal philosophy of the party in the Mubarak era. In the words of one senior NDP member, "Since I filled my position in the party in 1984 one of the philosophies of the NDP was that when we are calm *(nahda'a)*, the opposition parties will be calm (*tahda'a*) and when we are active (*nanshat*), the opposition parties will also be active and if they become active they might turn against us" (cf. El-Tarouty, 2004: 39). In this regard, it seems optimistic to have expected the NDP reforms to have produced any significant democratic changes that would potentially transform it into an autonomous, institutionalized entity, since such a reform would have serious repercussions with regard to the powers of the presidency over it and hence over the legislature. In other words, genuine reform within the party would challenge the very nature of the political status quo, and this would contradict the fundamental objective of the regime: to stay in power.

The National Council for Human Rights, the Issue of Human Rights, and the Permanent State of Emergency

In May 2003, the government announced its decision to establish the National Council on Human Rights (NCHR). By June 2003, the council's legislation had passed through parliament and by January 2004 its membership and composition had been finalized and announced to the world. According to Law 94/2003 on the NCHR, the council would be formally affiliated to the *Shura* (Consultative) council (since a national human rights commission could not, according to international law, be affiliated to the president). In addition, it would be based in Cairo, be state funded and consist of a chairman, deputy and twenty-five members, all of whom would be appointed by the *Shura* council. In order to enhance the council's legitimacy, the *Shura* chose to appoint twenty-seven of the most prominent political, diplomatic and academic elite in Egypt. As Stacher points.

> Former UN secretary-general Boutros Boutros-Ghali is the council's chairman, while international lawyer and acclaimed Islamist thinker Ahmad Kamil Abul-Magd became deputy. The additional twenty-five council members . . .[include]. . . Osama al-Ghazali Harb, editor of al-Ahram's international affairs quarterly, al-Siyasa al-Dawliyga, . . . former ambassador and NDP MP Mostafa al-Fiqi . . . Hossam Badrawy, a NDP MP and Gamal Mubarak associate . . . popular Wafdist MP, Monir Fakhry 'Abd

al-Nor . . . Lawyer and women's rights activist, Mona Zolfiqar . . . Nasirist press syndicate head, Galal Arif . . .[as well as] Bahay al-Din Hassan, the director of the Cairo Institute for Human Rights Studies (CIHRS) and Hafiz Abu Sa'ada, the director of the Egyptian Organization for Human Rights (EOHR). (Stacher, 2005)

At first glance, it would appear that the government of Egypt was finally becoming more responsive to both domestic and international pressures with regard to the issue of human rights. After all, prior to the establishment of the NCHR, the only two governmental offices that dealt with human rights in Egypt were the prosecutor-general's office, which is formally empowered to investigate cases of abuse and the ministry of foreign affairs, whose role is limited to responding to allegations of abuse on behalf of the government. As such, the NCHR appeared as a positive development in the Egyptian political sphere, and in response to the cynics who viewed its establishment as a tool to serve the government, one member declared: "We [the council members] are influential figures in society. None of us can gamble on our careers to justify government policy" (El-Fiqi, 2004). It should be pointed out, however, that as illustrious as the council and its appointees may appear, the council was not embodied with any formal powers. Rather, according to Law 94/2003, the council's role is "to serve as an advisory and consultative body" for the government (Stacher, 2005). Hence with no powers to make government agencies accountable to it, "inconvenient council advice can be legally ignored or shelved." As such, the formal role of the NCHR cannot really "extend beyond requesting cooperation from governmental agencies and recommending cases for prosecution" to the office of prosecutor-general (Stacher, 2005).

Furthermore, as a consultative entity with no formal powers of its own, the NCHR is rendered powerless in the face of other more pressing constraints within the political arena. It is difficult for any human rights entity to function, for example, when faced with a political system that has depended upon twenty-three years of continuous emergency rule for purposes of political containment and control. Emergency laws, after all, allow a range of censorship over political activity that can range from the monitoring of political activity to the limiting of political expression. Furthermore, individuals can be arrested solely on the basis of suspicion of political crimes, and the gathering of five or more people or the distribution of any political literature without government authorization gives the government the right to arrest all those involved. With regard to the judiciary, there are several reasons why the imposition of a state of emergency proves useful to the regime as a means of limiting judiciary intervention.

On one level, under a state of emergency, the fifty-five days' limit on holding an accused person in custody for questioning can be extended indefinitely without a formal court hearing. More importantly, the role of the judiciary can be completely overlooked as a consequence of the 1966 law of the Military Judiciary, which states that "the President of the Republic has the right to refer to the military judiciary any crime which is punishable under the Penal Code or under any other law" (CFHRLA, 1995: 4).

This means that the President is given a virtual *carte blanche* to detain and prosecute civilians in military courts regardless of whether their activity endangers fundamental interests. It is worth noting that once a military court has passed its verdict, there is no appeal, even in the case where a civilian is condemned to death. This is in direct contradiction to standard judiciary procedure whereby a civilian is permitted to appeal to Egypt's Supreme Court of Appeal. In this regard, the prevalence of emergency rule is also significant because it limits the role of the judiciary and further contributes to the consolidation of authoritarian power.

According to Article 148 of the constitution, the president can declare a state of emergency for a "limited period" and upon the approval of the Assembly. Since the assassination of Sadat, Egypt has remained under a "state of emergency" because the president requests (and is granted) an extension every three years to combat the threats of violence and terrorism. Based on this view, the official argument has tended to follow the lines that emergency rule acts as "an indispensable deterrent . . . and guard . . . against the criminal forces who are still intent on seizing all possible opportunities to incite unrest and hit national interests" (*Al-Ahram Weekly*, March 2–8, 2000). The fact that emergency law is utilized for political reasons, as opposed to security, is evident on several levels. On one level, the application of emergency law has made it difficult, if not impossible, for political parties to function and interact outside of their own offices. It allows the security forces to arrest individuals who plan to partake in legitimate activities such as legislative or syndicate elections. Indicative of this, prior to the 1995 legislative elections, the security services arrested fifty-four prominent Muslim Brotherhood leaders to preempt their electoral participation in legislative elections. Placed in front of a military court, the fifty-four men were sentenced to between three and five years in prison with hard labor. Largely as a consequence of this, only one Islamist-orientated participant, Ali Sayid Fath al-Bab won a parliamentary seat in 1995.

A similar pattern emerged before the 2000 elections. A new group of twenty Islamists were arrested and accused in 1999 with "working to revive the outlawed Muslim Brotherhood" (*Cairo Times*, November 23–29,

2000). As in the case of the earlier group, these Brotherhood-affiliated individuals comprised prominent professional figures in the legal, medical, engineering, and academic spheres. In November 2000, the military tribunal had passed sentences of between three and five years imprisonment for fifteen of the accused. As one reporter noted, "mass Brotherhood trials have become something of an election-year tradition in Egypt" (*Bairo Times*, November 23–29, 2000). Indeed, this observation does appear to ring true. Preparations for the forthcoming legislative elections in October 2005 appear to be already taking place as ten members of the Brotherhood were arrested in January 2005 in the delta town of Zagazig following what was allegedly a quarrel between the members and state security personnel. Essam al-Erian, a prominent Brotherhood leader and himself one of the members arrested and imprisoned in the pre-1995 election round-up pointed out to the press that this most recent crackdown "was a warning from the government in advance of approaching parliamentary elections" (El-Hamalay and Summer, 2005). By early May 2005, al-Erian was arrested along with 200 other Brotherhood members and by the middle of the same month, mass round-ups had taken place across the country, which resulted in the arrest of over 2,000 Islamists, including most of their electoral candidates during the 2000 legislative elections.

While all these cases involved Islamists, the timing of the arrests and the fact they were not charged with terrorist-related or violent acts reflects the political benefits the regime incurs by the application of emergency rule. By applying emergency rule and using military courts to, put civilians on trial, the regime has become further empowered at the expense of the judiciary and it has increased the government's reliance on the coercive apparatus. It is not wholly unexpected that the dependence on emergency law has seen the power of the police expand considerably, as they are granted a virtual *carte blanche* for the arrest and detention of suspected political activists, regardless of whether or not they fit the description of a "terrorist." Furthermore, amendments of Law 109/1971 to Law 116/1981 expanded police responsibility from "safeguarding public security" to include the vaguely termed "public order" (Ouda, el-Borai, and Saada 2001: 25). Backed by such powers, it is not surprising to find that there are an estimated 12,000–15,000 political prisoners currently marking time in Egyptian prisons. In its quest to thwart potential challengers, regime dependence on the coercive state apparatus continues to expand and, in turn, so do the cases of human rights abuse.

The most recent indication of regime dependence on coercion and lack of regard for human rights was reflected in the events that immediately followed the bombing of the Taba Hilton, which killed thirty-four people on October 7, 2004. According to the Ministry of Interior, the bombing was carried out by nine people, their leader being a 25-year-old Palestinian microbus driver who lived in the North Sinai town of al-Arish. At the time, only two fugitives remained, as the other suspects had either been killed or captured by the security forces. In efforts to capture the two fugitives, the Egyptian security forces applied its logic of wholesale repression on the inhabitants of the two towns in which the suspects had allegedly lived: al-Arish and the neighboring town of al-Sheikh Zawyd. The logic behind this move was that "if the bombers resided there, the town's population has answers" (Stacher, 2005). According to the independently run EOHR, approximately 2,500 people had been arrested by mid-November (Human Rights Watch Vol. 17, No. 3 (E): 16).

More alarmingly than the massive dawn raids, arrests and torture of detainees was the arrest of family members, including women and children, "to secure surrender of wanted persons" (Human Rights Watch, Vol. 17, No. 3 (E): 17). In other words, the security forces were using innocent people as hostages. In response to the Human Rights Watch report, in which Joe Stork, the director of HRW Middle East and North Africa division, described the police tactics as "lawless behavior . . . on a scale not seen since the 1990s" (Lindsey, 2005: 9). The Egyptian Foreign Ministry argued that the fact that HRW "prepares reports like this, based on field visits, and the release of the report in Cairo, are the strongest evidence of Egypt's openness and transparency in human rights matters" (9). On the basis of this logic, the government seemed to be arguing that by not covering up such abuse is in itself a sign of its political progress.

More importantly, one of the most prominent indications that the Egyptian government's current "reform" initiatives are simply a façade not intended to implement genuine reform is the fact that the NCHR, which it so eagerly introduced to both national and international audiences as evidence of its commitment to human rights, did absolutely nothing with regard to investigating the al-Arish abuse. As one disappointed member of the NCHR publicly explained, "some [NCHR] members demanded that they hold a meeting for the victims and families and Egyptian NGOs, but there was not enough support to hold these hearings. . . . The secretariat said there wasn't the quorum to make such a decision." As the same member admitted, "the council failed to meet its responsibility" (Bahey Eddin Hassan, NCHR member, cf. Lindsey, 2005). The discrepancy between the adoption of an NCHR and the actual reality which renders such an entity powerless and largely in the face of continued governmental human rights abuses is yet again an indication of the façade of reforms within Egypt's formal political landscape.

Revising Procedures for Presidential Selection or the
Proposal to Amend Article 76 of the Egyptian Constitution

During a speech at Meunifiya University in his home town of Meunifiya on February 26, 2005, President Mubarak announced to a stunned audience that Article 76 of the 1971 Egyptian constitution would be amended to allow for direct multicandidate presidential elections in time for the September 2005 presidential election. As it stood to this day, the president was officially instated by referendum. The legislature (People's Assembly) is responsible for this presidential nomination. Once nominated, the candidate is required to obtain two-thirds of the votes of the People's Assembly before being "referred to the citizens for a plebiscite" (Article 76). The issue of referendum has, since Nasser's rule, been significant for two main reasons. First, since the Assembly can only refer one person to a national plebiscite, the president does not compete for his position with other candidates. Second, and related to the first, there are no sectors in society that formally support an opponent to the president. This means that formally the president acquires office not on majority-based support, but on near unanimous support and thus absolute *legal* legitimacy. The details of amendment were formalized at very short notice because in the tradition of personalized rule, only those closest to the president were even informed of the president's decision prior to the February 26 announcement. The amendment, which swiftly passed through the consultative council on May 8, 2005, and later, the People's Assembly on May 10, 2005, is predictably structured in a manner that will make it very difficult to actually challenge the political status quo. The amendment was subsequently referred to a public referendum on May 25, 2005, and in keeping with traditional custom, the referendum was approved by 83 percent of the 16.4 million eligible voters whom the government claims had participated in the referendum.

As it stands, the amendment of Article 76 limits presidential nominations to members of the politburo. In addition, the party in question is required to have been established for a period of five years and that its members occupy no less than five percent of the seats in the People's Assembly (23 seats) and five percent of the Shura Council (nine seats). However, according to the amendment, these restrictions will not be applied until the next presidential elections of 2011 and thereafter, presumably to save face in the international arena, since no one opposition party occupies any such number of seats in the incumbent parliament—in fact the total number of incumbent opposition party members in the People's Assembly combined for the current 2000–2005 term is only nineteen. According to the new amendment, independent candidates are also permitted to run as presidential candidates, yet the conditions appear to be even more constraining. To be eligible, an independent candidate is required to acquire 250 signatures of support from various elected officials. Of these signatures, sixty-five must come from elected members of the People's Assembly, twenty-five must come from elected Shura Council members, and 140 signatures must be obtained from ten elected officials (local council members) representing fourteen different governates.

It is worth noting that the President's NDP controls 98.5 percent of the local council seats in the country's twenty-six governates. As such, it would be virtually impossible for an independent candidate to have been eligible for nomination in the September 2005 presidential elections, especially since according to the new amendment, these conditions, unlike those for party nominees were already in effect. It seems rather apparent that these conditions are intended to deter potential Muslim Brotherhood members from participating, since as an "illegal" entity, their members have tended to compete as "independents" in the electoral arena. Therefore, in the Assembly of 2000–2005, there were seventeen "independents" who in reality were Brotherhood members. As mentioned in the previous section, the fact that thousands of Muslim Brotherhood members were arrested prior to and shortly following the amendment reinforces the assumption that the regime is leaving little to chance for either the Presidential elections of September 2005 or indeed the legislative elections that will follow in November 2005.

Put simply, while the President announced in his speech that the amendments are intended "to give the opportunity to political parties to enter the presidential elections and give guarantees that allow more than one candidate to be put forward to the presidency for people to choose among them freely" (Reuters, February 26, 2005) the conditions of the amendment suggest that, realistically, apart from the incumbent president it seems virtually impossible for other potential candidates to compete within the framework of such constraints. Not surprisingly, some opposition members have been voicing their discontent at both the nature and degree of amendments. As Refaat Said, President of the Tagammu party voiced in the party's mouthpiece al-Ahali: "The decision represents a positive step on the path of resistance towards realizing democracy, but it needs more developments and changes to other sections of the constitution to guarantee the realization of reform" (Al-Ahali, February 27, 2005).

Indeed, one can argue that the entire constitution needs an overhaul since one indication of the power imbalance between the three branches of government, for example, is the constitution's preoccupation with the president's role and functions in comparison to the legislative and judiciary branches. As one report highlights, out of the constitution's 55 articles dealing with the three branches of government "the president is recognized by thirty-five articles (63 percent), the ministers by four (2 percent), the judiciary by four (2 percent) and the legislative branch with its two subdivisions by fourteen (25 percent)" (Ouda, el-Borai, and Saada, 2001: 21). As such, once in office, the president retains, for example, the authority to promulgate as well as object to laws (Article 112). The president's power to rule by decree (Article 147), declare a state of emergency (Article 148), and appoint and dismiss the entire cabinet (Article 141) is also constitutionally preserved. In addition, the power to draft the budget of the state (Article 115) and formulate the state's general policy (Article 138) reinforces the formal powers of the president over the legislature. While the constitution empowers the legislature to query and dispute presidential authority, such powers are rendered ineffective by the president's authority to bypass it and call a referendum of the people (Article 152). Thus, for example, if the Assembly decides to use its constitutional prerogative to withdraw its vote of confidence from the cabinet (Article 126), the president can refuse to endorse the decision (Article 127) and is legally entitled to take the matter to a public referendum. The importance of the legislature for the president cannot be underestimated. Controlling the legislature ensures that there are no formal challenges to the presidency. It appears that this will also be the case following the anticipated amendments. Furthermore, presidential control over the legislature ensures the president's monopoly of policy making remains unhindered since approximately 80 percent of all bills initiated since the time of Nasser until the present originate from the executive. In fact, in the legislative year of 2004, over 90 percent of bills came from the executive (Morsi, 2005). In other words, the executive grip over the "multi-party" legislature appears to be as tight as, if not tighter than, under the socialist one-party system of Nasser's Egypt.

It should also be noted that the constitution continues to preserve the president's right to dissolve the People's Assembly if deemed "necessary" and "after a referendum of the people" (Article 136). This presidential safety valve carries enormous implications for the conduct of legislative members and the balance of power between MPs and the president. This means that should the legislature decide to take on a bigger role than supporting and formalizing presidential legislation, the president can resort to a referendum, dissolve it, and call for new elections. The undemocratic nature of electoral competition, as we have touched upon earlier, ensures that the vast majority of opponents and independent-minded legislators are denied both entry and reentry to the Assembly.

The president's constitutional grip on other political and state institutions is also preserved through the implementation of several laws. Whereas the

1971 constitution guaranteed "the independence and immunity" of the judiciary (Article 65), the president is empowered with presiding over a Supreme Council that "shall supervise the affairs of the judiciary organization" (Article 173). Furthermore, the subsequent implementation of Law 46/1972 reinforces presidential control over the judiciary due to his powers of appointment and promotion. According to this law, the president's powers extend to appointing and promoting judges as well as appointing the public prosecutor. It should also be noted that the president determines the salaries and overall budget of the judiciary body. In addition, as supreme commander of the armed forces (Article 150) and supreme chief of the police (Article 184), the president's powers of appointment and fiscal control remained as apparent within the military and police as during Nasser's time. Put simply, the 1971 constitution legally enshrines the preeminent position of the president over other government and state institutions in contemporary Egypt. It combines legal prerogatives with personal political judgment and enables the president to remain unchallenged at the apex of the governance.

In view of such powers and the potential constraints that are expected to accompany the amendments to Article 76 of the constitution, it is worth noting the arrest of Ayman Nour, a prominent opposition MP. Nour was arrested on January 30, 2005, outside the People's Assembly a few minutes before his parliamentary immunity was lifted. This move in itself was a direct breach of Article 99 of the constitution, which states that, "except in cases of *flagrante delicato*, no member of the People's Assembly shall be subject to a criminal prosecution without the permission of the Assembly." The purpose of Article 99 is that, in order to carry out their roles unhindered, members of the legislature are provided with parliamentary immunity from criminal and non-civil procedures unless the Assembly authorizes its removal. While in some cases the Assembly has found genuine justification to lift a legislator's immunity, the motivations for doing so can also be clearly political, as the case of Nour indicates. As the outspoken independent thinking head of the newly established opposition party, Al-Ghad, Nour can be regarded as one of the most charismatic and astute politicians in contemporary Egypt.

As a successful and wealthy lawyer, Nour entered the People's Assembly at the age of 30 in 1995 representing the working class constituency of Bab al-Sharqiya in Cairo. According to Nour, senior NDP officials approached him more than once during 1997–98 to convince him to join the NDP. Nour resisted governmental co-option on the basis that, "like Talaat Harb [Egyptian nationalist figure of the early twentieth century], decent businessmen should have integrity and not join the NDP" (Nour, 2002). Nour's arrest and forty-five days' detention was based on the allegations made by the State Security prosecutor that the official application for Al-Ghad's party license contained forged documents, even though it had already been submitted and approved by the government's Political Parties Committee in October 2004.

The questionable nature of Nour's arrest was also reflected in the unusually fast manner in which it took place. As one press article points out: "On 28 January, State Security notified the prosecutor-general of the charges, who in turn, informed the justice minister and the head of parliament the same night. The following morning, the People's Assembly was quickly convened to discuss lifting Nour's immunity . . . the parliamentary meeting was unscheduled and most opposition and independent MPs had not been notified" (Lindsey, 2005: 9). According to one report, Nour's unexpected and swift arrest is linked to a meeting he had with Madeleine Albright during her brief visit to Cairo a couple of days earlier in which "Nour appeared to backtrack on a deal with the government promising not to oppose Mubarak's candidacy in exchange for the Ghad party license" (El-Ghobashy: February 2, 2005).

Indications that there is merit to this argument can be detected on two levels: First, Nour's arrest and alleged forging of documents means that he is facing criminal charges. What this means is that if found guilty, Nour would have a criminal record and subsequently be ineligible to run for the presidency. On another level, while in detention, Nour announced his decision to run as a presidential candidate once the constitutional amendment is in place. This announcement indicates Nour's attempt to show that his arrest and the alleged charges have reinforced his determination to challenge the president as opposed to being cornered into submission. In short, while the amendment to Article 76 of the constitution reflects a much needed move away from the selection of the Egyptian President via referendum, the amendment still imposes various constraints that will make it difficult for any potential candidate to challenge the incumbent president.

The Ayman Nour case—which currently remains in progress—is a reflection of the fact that the regime is applying its legal and coercive tactics to prevent potentially viable candidates (as opposed to opposition personalities who are also aiming to present themselves as candidates but possess a minimal base of public support, such as the controversial feminist Dr. Nawal Al-Saadawi) from participating, even though the new rules of conduct will make it virtually impossible for Nour to secure formal nomination anyway. In other words, the idea of even a theoretical challenge is not acceptable within the arena of reform. Furthermore, the powers of the Presidency remain constitutionally protected and as such, regardless of the person occupying the Presidency, the biased nature of the system remains the same, thus rendering the reform to Article 76 rather futile.

Conclusion

When we examine Egypt's post-1952 political system, one of the most important characteristics to be observed is that the political transformations over the last five decades actually represent the continuation of authoritarian rule despite visible structural reforms. Nevertheless, there is little doubt that some observers appear to view these reforms in a positive light. As Boutros Boutros Ghali, head of the NCHR, exclaimed with regard to President Mubarak's proposal to amend Article 76 of the constitution, "This is an important step towards supporting the march of democracy and embodies a good faith response from (the President) to the demands and heartbeat of the Egyptian street" (*Misr al Yom*, February 27, 2005). Ismail Serag Eddin, Director of the Alexandria Library went even further to declare that: "The decision reflects the President's concern to realize democracy and his desire for reform" (*Misr al Yom*, January 27, 2005). Perhaps it is on this basis that the regime has indeed succeeded in its so-called reforms, since this is precisely the intended purpose of its endeavors: such policies are intended to provide an indication that reform toward "democratization" is progressing in order to bolster international support, dilute opposition unity and in some instances, recruit new social groups of supporters into the regime's co-optation network. In doing so, these strategies have, more importantly helped to reinforce and stabilize an authoritarian regime struggling for survival in both a national and an international environment in which it has long outstayed its welcome.

References

Abdel-Fattah, Nabil (2000) "A time to judge," *Al-Ahram Weekly* (August 10–16).

Abdel-Latif, Omayman (1999) "No partners in power," *Al-Ahram Weekly* (December 23–29).

—— (2002) "Changing from within," *Al-Ahram Weekly Online* (September 19–25).

Abou al-Maged, Nadia (2000) "Tempered jubilation," *Al-Ahram Weekly* (July 13–19).

Benin, Joel (2005) "Popular Social Movements and the Future of Egyptian Politics," *Middle East Report Online*, (March 10).

Brownlee, Jason (2002) "The Decline of Pluralism in Mubarak's Egypt," in *Journal of Democracy* 13 (4): 6–14.

Centre for Human Rights Legal Aid (1995) *Military Courts in Egypt: Courts Without Safeguards, Judges Without Immunity and Defendants Without Rights*, Cairo: CHRLA.

Dawoud, Khalid (2000) "Necessary precautions," *Al-Ahram Weekly* (November 16–22).

Essam al-Din, Gamal (2000) "Three more years of emergency," *Al-Ahram Weekly* (March 2–8).

—— (2002a) "Reinvigorating the ruling," *Al-Ahram Weekly Online* (December 5–11).

—— (2002b) "Shake-up of NDP," *Al-Ahram Weekly Online* (September 19–25).

—— (2002c)"Reforming the NDP," *Al-Ahram Weekly Online* (July 18–24).

—— (2005) "Devil in the Details," *Al-Ahram Weekly* (March 3–9).

El-Fiqi, Mustafa (2004) NCHR member, quoted from the roundtable discussion on "Houman Rights in Egypt," the American University in Cairo, March 7 [AN. Reordering of the references has been done in accordance with the guidelines of the Chicago Manual of Style. Trust this is acceptable.]

El-Ghobasy, Mona (2001a) "Echoes of shock," *Cairo Times* (May 31–June 6).

—— (2001b) "Public enemy no. 1," *Cairo Times* (February 22–28).

—— (2002) "With all deliberate speed," *Cairo Times* (June 6–12).

—— (2005) "Egypt Looks Ahead to Portentous Year," *Middle East Report Online* (February 2).

El-Hamalay Hossam and Said Summer (2005) "Arrests for All," *Cairo Magazine* (February).

Hinnebsuch, Raymond (1985) *Egyptian Politics under Sadat: The Post-Populist Development of an Authoritarian Modernising State*, Cambridge: Cambridge University Press.

Howeidy, Amira (2000a) "Destitute but determined," *Al-Ahram Weekly* (August 3–9).

—— (2000b) "Registering the aftershocks," *Al-Ahram Weekly* (November 16–22).

Ibrahim, Saad Eddin (1996) *Democracy and Egypt*, Cairo: The American University in Cairo Press.

Kassem, Maye (1999) *In the Guise of Democracy*, London: Ithaca Press.

—— (2004) *Egyptian Politics: The Dynamics of Authoritarian Rule*, Boulder and London: Lynne Rienner.

Lande, C.H. (1977) "The Dyadic Basis of Clientelism," in S.W Schmidt, J.C. Scott, C. Lande and L.Guasti (eds.) *Friends, Followers and Factions: A Reader in Political* Clientalism, Berkeley, Los Angeles and London: University of California Press.

Lindsey Ursula (2005) "Party Decapitated: Is the government going after Al-Ghad Party," *Cairo Magazine* (February).

Morsi, Mohammed, parliamentary specialist, interview with author, March 14, 2005, Cairo.

Nor, Ayman, Member of Parliament. Interview with author, March 28, 2002, Cairo.

Ouda, Jihad, Negad el-Borai, and Hafez Abu Saada (2000) *A Door onto the Desert: Egyptian Legislative Elections of 200*, Cairo: United Group and Friedrich Naumann Foundation.

Owen, Roger (1994) "Socio-economic Change and Political Mobilization: the case of Egypt," in Ghassan Salame (ed.): *Democracy without Democrats? The Renewal of Politics in the Muslim World*, London: I.B. Tauris.

President Mubarak Interview, *al-Ahram Weekly* (October 25–31, 2001).

"Presidential Public Address." Ministry of Information and State Information Service, Cairo (April 1982).

"Presidential Public Address." Ministry of Information and State Information Service Cairo: (May 1, 1998).

Shehab, Shaden (2000) "Missing the point," *Al-Ahram Weekly* (July 20–26).

Shiller, Norbert (2000) "Beaten at the polls," *Cairo Times* (November 16–22).

Stacher, Joshua, (2005) "Rhetorical Acrobatics and Reputations: Egypt's National Council for Human Rights", *Middle East Report* 235, under: http://www.merip.org.

El-Tarouty, Safinaz (2004) *Institutionlization and Reform: The Case of the National Democratic Party in Egypt*, M.A Thesis, Cairo: The American University in Cairo.

7

State and Market in Syria: The Politics of Economic Liberalization

Søren Schmidt

Introduction

According to a recent World Bank Publication, the current labor force in the Middle East totals some 104 million workers. This figure is expected to reach 146 million by 2010 and 185 million by 2020. Given this expansion, the economies of the region will need to create some 80 million new jobs in the next two decades. With unemployment now at about 15 percent, the more ambitious goal of absorbing unemployed workers in addition to the new entrants implies the need to create close to 100 million jobs by 2020, a doubling of the current level of employment (World Bank, 2004).

The future fate of the region will very much depend on the ability of its economies to rise to this huge challenge. Despite the activities of the private sector having grown steadily since the mid-1980s and at present largely surpassing the activities of the public sector, a dismal picture of Middle Eastern economies has prevailed. Manufacturing industries, which are crucial in any employment and economic-growth strategy, are very underdeveloped and basically geared to the limited domestic markets of the region. Total exports of manufactured goods from the Middle East (including Iran) do not exceed the exports of a small European country like Finland.

Syria is no exception to this general trend.[1] In taking Syria's economic liberalization as an example, this chapter attempts to identify why these policies have not increased the productive capacities of the country, created new jobs or resulted in sustainable economic growth. In theoretical terms, I claim that markets are nested in economic and political institutions, which ultimately are based on the way the state is configured. This configuration of the state is more than a question of the distribution of power (democracy), but also involves the more structural problematique of the ability of the state to function as a third party, that is, providing the neutral institutional framework for societal interaction. In this regard, the specific outlook, inclinations and social basis of state rulers and the fiscal foundation of the state are of equal importance.[2]

First, I will provide brief theoretical reflections on the relationship between states and market economies, as well as posing the question as to which factors influence the state's ability to provide the right institutions for a thriving market economy. In order to substantiate my claims I will then analyze the historical development of state-building in Syria. Within this analysis, the above-mentioned elements of state configuration may provide an explanation for the dismal development results of Syria's economic liberalization policies. After solidifying the historical analysis by providing a number of empirical case studies on state-economy relations in Syria, I finally draw some conclusions with respect to development strategies for Syria and EU policies toward the country.

State and Market Economy

The strength of a society may be defined as its ability to devise beneficial cooperation arrangements for its citizens. The particular difficulty of such arrangements is that they take place under conditions of distributive conflicts (Poulsen, 2004).[3] Institutions—understood as accepted patterns, rules and norms of behavior—are social constructs which play a crucial role in transforming antagonistic distributional relationships into agonistic relationships (Mouffe, 2004: 27).[4] Market relations depend in particular on the existence of institutions which dispense information, prevent cheating, provide public goods, define and enforce property rights, provide macroeconomic conditions, facilitate exchange with external markets and financial intermediation, and a host of other micro- as well as macroeconomic functions (Stiglitz, 1989).

Some of these institutions may be characterized as social institutions developed over long periods of time without (and sometime in spite of) the involvement of the state. But as economies develop in complexity and sophistication, formalized state institutions, including the effective means of rule and decision enforcement, are indispensable. Markets without such institutions for solving collective-action and coordination problems function poorly and are characterized by a low growth-high inequality economic equilibrium, where economic exchange does not develop beyond relatively simple economic exchange and is associated with high transaction costs.[5]

These are the basic elements of what I will call an institutional political economy approach for understanding the nexus between market economy and the state. The state might provide the right institutions for a thriving market economy or the state may not provide such institutions (Przeworski, 2003). This understanding of state and market is clearly at odds with neoliberal economic theory that explains dismal economic development by failures in state mechanisms and consequently advocates less state intervention for the promotion of growth. Institutional political economy is, however, also at odds with leftist[6] development theories, which see the basic problem in the failure of the market and the solution to this failure in state intervention. In contrast to these approaches an institutional political economy approach understands the market as embedded in institutions and therefore neither discards state-failures nor the short-comings of un-institutionalized markets. Or as formulated by the "father" of institutional economics, Douglass North:

> There is no great secret to the specification of property rights that broadly provide incentives for productive economic activity. As Professor Stiglitz pointed out, there is broad agreement as to their significance. The dilemma concerns their creation and enforcement. Take the characteristic of adaptive efficiency outlined above. Such a set of rules makes currently profitable and efficient enterprise less secure (thus the conflict between allocative and adaptive efficiency) by encouraging the creative destruction envisioned by Schumpeter. Not only do such rules encourage innovation and displacement, but they also wipe out losers. Now in that marvelous never-never land conjured up by welfare economists the gainers compensate the losers and all is well. But in our world they (for the most part) don't. And accordingly it is in the interests of existing firms, trade unions, farm groups, etc., to try to devise rules that protect their own (usually short-term) interest. Mancur Olson (1982) provides a portrait of the sclerotic consequences for economies that result from the long-run accumulation of such interest group pressures. But, unfortunately, he fails to provide any model of the polity that would give us insight into the political process that produces such adverse economic consequences. (North 1989:112)

The question is then: why do some states provide the right institutions and why do other states not?

The first relevant factor is their ability to provide third-party capabilities for solving collective action problems. A condition for the state to develop beyond the patrimonial form in which the state basically serves the personal interest of rulers, and provides third party action, is the establishment of some degree of rule of law which binds ruler as well as the ruled. In order to execute the law, formal judiciary and executive capabilities must be in place and undergirded by informal norms, such as a political and bureaucratic elite devoted to a minimum of public service. Internal and external accountability is likewise important, including civil control of the military.[7]

Second, the ability of the state to provide solutions to market-economy development will depend on the political inclination and outlook of rulers, or more specifically, how these rulers are embedded with private sector entrepreneurs and in particular with its industrialists. An intimate understanding of the problems and challenges of the private sector is crucial for the state to provide transformative and purposeful collective action to promote market-based economic development.[8]

I understand state-building structures as "big bang" historical events influencing subsequent path-dependent development which becomes locked into a mutually reinforcing political economy of endogenously induced interests (Kohli, 2004). But such political structures lose their legitimacy if they do not provide a minimum of socioeconomic welfare for the broader population and if they cannot sufficiently finance the spoils-system on which political patron-client relationships are based, and finance in particular as important a political gatekeeper as the military. In short, the fiscal basis of the state is crucial for the workings and inclination of the state. If the fiscal basis of state power is based on rent revenues, rulers will be less inclined to develop the economic foundations of society, and civil society's structural power vis-à-vis the state will be low (Chaudhry, 1997; Karl, 1997; Vandewalle, 1998). The third factor in explaining the developmental qualities of the state is therefore the fiscal foundations of the state.[9]

Capability of the Syrian State to Act as a Third Party

In an attempt to assess the Syrian state's ability to act as a third party, I will give a brief account of the country's modern state-building process. It was during the French Mandate period (1920–46) that the modern Syrian state was crafted. The French followed the Ottoman example in many ways. Neither invested either effort or capital in the country, and both were without ambitions to create a dynamic economy and polity in Syria.[10] Syria was granted *A* status as a mandate of the League of Nations. This meant that the objective of the mandate was to treat Syria as a protected state which was to be made independent as soon as possible. Although France clearly had its own thoughts on this, it ruled out the option of turning Syria into a full colony later to be incorporated into the French Commonwealth, as had happened with Algeria and other French colonies.[11] At the same time, the French had their hands full in North Africa and in Indochina clinging to colonies with large French settler populations and of greater economic interest than Syria. Finally, French politics during the 1930s were quite unstable, where governments from the left and the right respectively succeeded each other at short intervals. At the same time, the slump of the early 1930s discredited plans to expand commodity production in the colonies for an already overstocked international market, which is why the economic rationale of the Syrian mandate and by implication the argument for effective occupation and administration remained weak (Fieldhouse, 1981: 21 and 28).

The French Mandate was based on indirect rule. Syria was partitioned into four statelets according to sectarian identities.[12] The fiscal principle of the mandate was self-sufficiency. This last principle had the implication that only limited efforts were made to invest in physical infrastructure, administration or education. French colonialists did not settle in Syria, and it is fair to say that the French objective for their mandate was more strategic and prestige-related than economic, lacking direction and purpose (Yapp, 1996: 86).

During French rule mock democratic institutions were established in an attempt to link Syria to France in the same way as both Iraq and Jordan were linked to Great Britain. As a result, there neither developed a robust Syrian polity nor did the political institutions gain much legitimacy, and they were quickly discarded in the subsequent postcolonial period. Administratively, there was no serious attempt to build up an indigenous civil administration, and the mandate was basically run by a limited number of French military and administrative officials. Also in this regard, Syria was ill-prepared for the postcolonial period. This applies in particular to three aspects relating to the military, the administration, and political development.

First, the army was run by French officers making use of lower-rank military personnel from the indigenous "Troupes Spéciales," who were mainly recruited from the minorities: Christians, Alawites, Druzes, and Ismaili'is. When Syria obtained independence in 1946, it was in fact institutionally and politically ill-prepared for the tasks of modern statehood. The military was neither solidly anchored in either national institutions or identity due to its preponderance of the minorities nor organizationally or normatively under firm civilian rule. As a result, it did not take many years before the military dominated the fragmented Syrian polity and began to influence the choice of rulers and regime. Thereby, primordial bonds of loyalty and patronage played an increasing role, further exacerbating the fragmentation of the polity.

Second, the public administration did not have any tradition for acting as a neutral "third-party" tool of the state under political control. On the contrary, public bureaucrats were not chosen on basis of merits, but on the basis of the private influence of the economic elites and the military.

Third Syria was fragmented in political terms, producing a politically weak state that was unable to focus on economic development. Elites were split along sectarian, social and regional lines, and political energy was largely wasted in these distributional conflicts.[13] As an authoritarian state, Syria did not posses democratic political institutions which could facilitate conflict resolution, enable distributional losers to be compensated by winners, or strengthen cooperation by enabling positive-sum games on behalf of zero-sum games (Rodrik, 2001).

In conclusion, the Syrian postcolonial state was fragmented, weak, and had not developed effective means of projecting societal power. The Syrian state at the time of independence may indeed be characterized as a state with low developmental and transformative capability.

The Social Basis of the Baath Regime

To gauge the developmental capacity of the state, we not only have to asses the structural features of state and polity, but also the inclinations and outlook of rulers with regard to economic development. When the Baath came to power on a nationalist and populist (land redistribution and nationalization) program, it alienated at the same time the small group of entrepreneurs who had managed to develop industries and other private-sector operations between the two world wars. When the external politics in the Middle East during the Cold War drew Syria into the arms of the Soviet Union and its satellite states, the result was a deepening of the cleavage between the regime and the private sector. This cleavage has indeed persisted until today.

The late President Hafiz al-Asad was known to be a military man mainly interested in national security issues. In the highly authoritarian and hierarchical system which developed in particular during his rule, economic and development issues were given a clear secondary political role. Economic development was not an end in itself. Rather it was a means of both achieving the nationalist objectives of his regime and serving as a side-payment to the popular segments of the regime coalition (Waldner, 1999).

When the Baath state was established, the rapidly expanding bureaucracy was used politically in order to consolidate the rule of the Baath. This time recruitment was not based on the influence of the previous ruling land oligarchs, but rather on a combination of political loyalty and sectarian identity. Management of the bureaucracy on the basis of the principle of rational-legality was therefore ruled out, and the bureaucracy became further penetrated by patrimonial and particularistic private interests and developed into the unmanageable, corrupt, and penetrated public administration that we experience today in Syria. The use of the bureaucracy as yet another side-payment to coalition partners and a means of consolidating the political rule of the Baath of course further diminished the already low capability of the Syrian state to operate as a provider of collective goods and a third party in economic development.

Politically, the core constituency of the new regime was the military in alliance with a popular coalition with a distributive rather than transformational or developmental agenda. The rule of the Baath was the historical opportunity for the downtrodden peasants to be compensated for the long historical exploitation by the Syrian absentee landlords. But worker unions and public employees were important allies of this coalition, and on top of land distribution, an inflated public sector—based on nationalized industries and banks—and a protected industrial workforce soon put a burden on public expenses.[14] As a result many players in the industrial and financial private sector were deeply alienated from the new regime and fled the country in large numbers.

The class and sectarian character, as well as the narrow military outlook of the regime, alienated it from the private sector and in particular from the production-oriented private sector, which was dominated by business families who were well established, "honest," and had ties to the Islamic Ulema. Instead, a relationship that is based on a sort of "calculated trust" (Haddad, 2004: 49), characterized by mutually corrupt and exploitative relations has emerged between the new and speculation-oriented commercial bourgeoisie and the regime.

Finally, the mechanics of regional power, where the enemy of Syria, Israel, was supported by the United States, resulted in Syria establishing close ties with the Union of Soviet Socialist Republics (USSR), which ideologically consolidated the inclinations and outlook of the regime vis-à-vis the private sector.

As a result, we may conclude that the present Syrian state has low developmental capacities, a penetrated civil bureaucracy, a neopatrimonial ruling elite, and poorly institutionalized markets. The regime consists of self-serving politicians in coalition with a rent-seeking[15] private sector and without any economic transformational or ideological project able to mobilize a population which is subjected to economic and social hardship. This said, I will move on to look at the fiscal basis of the Baath state and the role of economic rent in maintaining its political economy.

The Fiscal Basis of the State

During the 1960s, when Syria still lacked a financier for its socialist-inspired development strategy of Import-Substitution-Industrialization, the economic results were relatively meager, with growth rates of four to five percent per year (Owen and Pamuk, 1998: 155). However, after the 1973 war with Israel, which Syria came out of with some honor and with oil prices rising spectacularly, Syria was awash in state-to-state development aid from the Gulf states. Military aid was at the same time handsomely provided by the USSR. and its satellite states.

State-directed and public sector–based development took off, and during the 1970s Syria experienced economic growth of an average of nine percent yearly. However, as figures from the IMF (2002) show (see table 7.1), Syria also experienced during the same period a steady decline in worker as well as capital productivity, and growth was increasingly based on capital input.

When oil prices went bust in 1983, Syria was hit hard by the resulting decline in aid from the Gulf countries, which coincided with its increasing macroeconomic imbalances, both in the state budget and in Syria's external exchange. Syria hit rock bottom in 1986, when it only possessed foreign exchange for a few months' expenditure of imports and could envisage a major economic meltdown if things were not radically altered. This was the time when the slow process of reengaging the private sector as an economic growth engine started.

Table 7.1 Determinants of growth (annual growth rates in percent)

Determinants of growth	1970–2000	1970s	1980s	1990s
GDP	5.7	9.9	1.9	5.3
TFP	−0.1	1.5	−1.5	−0.5
LP[a]	1.5	5.5	−1.5	0.9
CP[b]	−3.7	−7.5	−3.1	−0.4

Source: IMF, 2002: 12.
TFP (Total Factor Productivity).
LP[a] (Labor Productivity, defined as output per employee).
CP[b] (Capital Productivity, defined as output per unit of utilized capital).

Against the background of a penetrated public administration, a suspicious private sector, a regime with a narrow economic outlook,[16] a precarious social and sectarian legitimacy basis, and regime stability ultimately resting on the military, the private sector did not see the *infiraj* (relaxation) as anything but a short-term policy to retrieve the regime from a temporary economic bind.[17] The credibility of the Syrian government's economic liberalization measures were by implication low and institutionalized negotiation avenues between the private sector (in contrast to the influence of individual influential businessmen) were more or less absent. The result was that the openings quickly were exploited by rent-seeking businessmen, who, based on partnership between members of the regime and public officials, quickly turned the economic openings into rent havens. However, this time rent havens were based on the private sector instead of on the public sector. Economic liberalization resulted in new rent havens and not into a liberal economy that is based on formal rules and equal competition and on secure and enforceable property rights.

The result was a short-term surge in manufacturing exports based on barter-deals with the Soviet Union and its satellite states, which ended when the regimes of these states were overturned in 1991 and the Syrian private sector was left to supply the limited consumption needs of a protected Syrian market. Private sector exports dropped from 1.3 billion USD in 1990 to 700 million USD in 1992 and stayed at this level throughout the 1990s. However, at the same time the imports of the private sector increased steadily and reached a level of 2.5 billion USD in 2001, that is, causing a foreign exchange deficit of 1.8 billion USD. This deficit was made up by the corresponding foreign exchange earnings of the oil industry (Aita, 2002: Plate 27).

None of the basic elements of the socialist Import-Substitution-Industrialization system were changed: high external protection, a license system restricting business entry, credit and foreign exchange rationing, and intrusive and arbitrary state regulation. In combination with the lack of accountability and transparency of the public sector, this economic system gave politicians and officials plenty of opportunity to prey on the public sector or to collude with it in order to create private rent havens. The resulting relationship between the state and the private sector may be described as a mutually corrupt relationship and did not add to the development of a productive developmental Syrian capitalism.

In fact, the economic liberalization measures of the 1990s did not solve Syria's macroeconomic balance problems. Fortuitously, when the short-lived bonanza of the barter-based exports to the East Bloc ended, Syria discovered new significant oil fields, which quickly solved a number of its balance problems by providing 25 percent of GNP (Gross National

Product), 50 percent of state revenue and 85 percent of net foreign exchange earnings from the early 1990s until today (IMF, 2003: tables 25 and 26).

In this way, the regime was able to avoid the hard political-economy choices of state-building: making changes in relative prices, reducing and shifting public expenditure, balancing collective interests with particular-istic interests, and negotiating the social contract between state and society in order to allow this to happen. With oil revenues, the regime was able to circumvent this painful process.[18]

I will now provide six contemporary case studies in order to illustrate the interaction of state and market economy under state structures charac-terized by low capabilities regarding the provision of collective goods. At the end of the section, I will summarize the specific lessons of the case studies.

Case Studies of State-Economy Relations

The Mobile Phone Company

Syria was one of the last countries to introduce mobile phone services. In the year 2000, the Government licensed two private companies to supply the services: Syriatel and "94."[19] Syriatel was owned by the Egyptian com-pany Orascom (25 percent) and Rami Makhlouf (75 percent), who hap-pened to be a cousin of the Syrian President. Orascom provided the management. The license with the government was a build-own-transfer (BOT) contract for fifteen years.[20] The other mobile phone company, "94," was owned by the then Lebanese minister of communication Mekati, and by Rami Makhlouf. There is no competition on prices, as these are set by the state agency, the Syrian Telecommunication Establishment. Competition between the two companies is restricted to marketing, customer service, and signal coverage. The operation is hugely profitable.

In January 2002, Rami Makhlouf contended that he did not receive his proper share of profits made by Syriatel. Rami Makhlouf's representatives controlled the cashier department and stopped paying suppliers to the company. The court in Damascus decided in March 2002 to impose a legal guardian (*haaris al qidaai*) and appointed Naader Kalai (board member of Syriatel and representative of Makhlouf) as legal caretaker of the company until the dispute between the two owners was solved. The Syrian authorities started now to harass the Egyptian management: The Egyptian CEO (Chief Executive Officer) as well as the Egyptian marketing director received threats from the Syrian Mukhabaraat (Intelligence). The Lebanese lawyer of Orascom was not allowed to reenter Syria. Finally, in April 2002 the

CEO was given notice by the authorities to leave the country within three days. Orascom now filed a lawsuit in the United Kingdom against Rami Makhlouf since Orascom is registered in a UK dominion in the Bahamas. The case has recently been settled by agreement on reparation payments to Orascom.

This case shows that confiscatory activities are not confined to the public sector, but is also a widespread phenomenon in the private sector. The most important institutional remedy to confiscation is effective and enforceable property rights. In this case the economic actor (Rami Makhlouf) was able to mobilize the public authorities for private ends and make a mockery of the property rights of Orascom and expropriate its property.

The social costs of such insecure property rights (or more correctly: selective property rights) is considerable, as it scares potential investors (foreign and Syrian) away to the detriment of both other Syrian private companies and by implication to private sector–based economic development. As Volker Perthes has remarked:

> If an Egyptian company with good knowledge of the intricacies of doing business in the Middle East was not able to prevail in the Syrian market, international investors are unlikely to be optimistic about their prospects. (Perthes, 2004: 38)

In addition to the convenience of Rami Makhlouf's father being the brother of the President's mother, he is also the head of the state-run Real Estate Bank. Also, Makhlouf's uncle used to be the head of the Presidential Guards, whose sole objective is to protect the regime and, therefore, offers its leader considerable political leverage. Rami Makhlouf is in the process of expanding his business empire dramatically. The most spectacular of his activities is a chain of so-called duty-free shops at the borders, which in reality are shops that are not liable to customs and taxes like other shops selling imported goods. Rami Makhlouf's operations are all based on political 'arrangements' and indicate the degree to which predatory private interests have appropriated state institutions. The collapse of private and public interests indicate the development of the Syrian state into a neopatrimonial state type and imply the incapacity of the state to produce institutional collective goods.

Exporters vs. Domestic Market Producers: The Case of Thread

Walid Suuf is one of a number of small textile and garment producers.[21] Suuf exports knitted fabric made of mixes of synthetic fibers and cotton to

Jordan and Lebanon. Thread is used as an input in the production process. As a measure to promote exports, tariff rates on input commodities for export production were, in May 2001, reduced from 70 percent to 1 percent. Thread was classified as such as a production input and consequently only the 1 percent customs rate was charged. The lower customs rate enabled Suuf and other exporters to buy better and cheaper thread, which in turn strengthened their competitiveness in export markets, both price- and quality-wise. Textile and garment producers are small companies and not organized within a branch of industrial organization. The companies are numerous and many of them are engaged in exports. The two Syrian producers of thread and suppliers to the protected Syrian market are large companies and supply only the domestic market.

These two companies, whose owners had good relations with Government circles, felt the cold winds of increased competition. They petitioned the Government to move thread back into the high-custom category, which the Government did immediately and without consulting the exporting textile and garment producers. The effect was that the small advantage that the industry had gained in export markets disappeared.

Exports of textiles and garments are facing increased competition every year from Far Eastern producers. The international multifiber agreement expired in 2005, which is why Far Eastern producers no longer are under quota restrictions to the European market. As a result, Far Eastern producers' share of the European market will grow relative to other manufacturers who benefit from the previous quotas, which protect high-cost producers like Middle East producers.

First of all, the study illustrates Mancur Olson's point that "unless the number of individuals is quite small, or unless there is coercion or some other special device to make individuals act in their common interest, rational, self-interested individuals will not act to achieve their common or group interest" (Olson, 1965: 2). It seems safe to add that in polities where self-organization is repressed, this problems of large groups is exacerbated.

Second, the study illustrates the persistent strength of short-sighted rent-seeking coalitions between actors within the private sector and the Government (Krueger, 1993) and the ability of these coalitions to thwart Government intentions to solve medium-range macroeconomic balance problems by promoting exports. In this case, it did not take long for the vested, entrenched interests of the two protected home-market producers of thread to use their influence and move thread back into the high customs category.

The case study shows that, although the Syrian Government at the start had good intentions of helping exporters, it quickly acquiesced to the demands of politically well-connected business operators. Due to a combination of the political elite being captive of particularistic rent-seeking interests and the penetrated public administration, long-term collective interests lost out to the short-term particularistic interests of individual businessmen, who might very well not be able to hold their market share anyway during the next five to ten years, resulting in further economic decline.

The case may be described as an illustration of Government failure. Although Suuf would have been better off if the Government had not imposed any custom duties at all on textile industry inputs (as he is an exporter), he will in fact need complementary action by the Government (preferential treatment, legal and economic incentives to link up with global producers facilitating technology transfer, facilitate access to marketing outlets, create economy of scale, and so on) in order to survive the increasing competition on the European market.[22] On this basis, the solution to the case problem is to have a different state (an institutional problem) rather than doing away with the state (the neoliberal prescription).

Private Banks

A number of years ago, the Syrian Government announced its intention of allowing private banks to operate alongside the state-run Commercial Bank of Syria and three other smaller specialized state banks. In 2003, the Government finally permitted five private banks to start operating. At least 50 percent of the equity of these banks comes, as stipulated in the Syrian law on private banks, from Syrian nationals, while the remainder comes from Lebanese or Saudi private banks. The Government also enacted a new law on the role of the Central Bank to oversee these private banks and established a new board of Governors of the Central Bank with powers to fix interest rates and control exchange rates (Yazigi, 2003).

On paper, such a reform seems revolutionary compared to the previous banking system, which mainly bankrolled the state sector and where the banks operated more or less like general directorates under the ministries of Finance and Economy. Until June 2003, the state banks had applied the same interest rates for 22 years, whether this resulted in negative (which was the case for fifteen years) or very high positive (during the last 5 years when inflation has been negligible) real interest rates. Bank services[23] for private companies and individuals were in the past mainly provided by the private Lebanese banks located in the Lebanese border town, Shtura, only an hour's drive from Damascus. Financial intermediation took place via semi-legal private lenders who did not have access to official institutional adjudication and enforcement institutions. This resulted in short maturities and high interest rates because the high risks were discounted in the applied interest rate.

The lack of proper financial intermediation allowing longer-term and large private industrial investments seems to be an important element in explaining that the investment boom, triggered by Investment Law No. 10 of 1991, which gave tax and import incentives to private investments, predominantly resulted in investments in light industries with a short-term horizon, high-import content and low value-added transformation or commercial, tourism and speculative non-risk investments (Hopfinger and Boeckler, 1996).

However, the question is what these new banks will bring in addition to the convenience for Syrian businessmen of doing their banking in Damascus instead of in Lebanon?

First, these banks will not improve access to hard currency for investment purposes. In Syria, hard currency is basically earned by the state from its export of oil, and the revenue from this export will continue to flow through the Commercial Bank to cover the hard currency deficit of the state sector. In 1999 the private sector had, for example, a foreign exchange deficit in its external trade of two billion USD, while the public sector (oil) had a surplus of 1.5 billion USD (Aita, 2002: plate 27). Should public foreign exchange earnings be redirected to the private sector, this would without doubt cause a collapse of the state industrial sector and is indeed one of the hard political choices facing the regime.

Second, even if private domestic savings were provided for private investments, these would still be critically dependent on whether profitable investment opportunities indeed existed. All the existing protected, private semi-monopolists have majority shares in the new banks and it remains to be seen whether these banks would finance any new ventures that would increase domestic competition and ultimately threaten these same semi-monopolists.

Third, since the opening of private banks in 2002, only limited deposits have been received. This indicates a problem of confidence in these banks, which is critical for financial institutions. Will the Board of Governors (consisting of representatives of ministries and three "independent" experts nominated by the Government) call in the equity capital of a private bank should it default on its obligations toward its depositors? In answering this question, one should consider that these new private banks are owned by one or several of the hundred families which at the same time constitute the military-commercial elite that run the Syrian economy.

Fourth, how does the Government intend to improve the very limited technical capability of the Central Bank to monitor monetary and banking matters? The danger is that banks do not only attract risk-willing private capital to the private sector. They can also be utilized as a conduit to siphon out foreign exchange from Syria to overseas safe havens through scams like those witnessed in Russia, Albania, and other economies in transition to market economy.

Finally, it remains to be seen whether bank secrecy, on which Lebanese banks thrive (whether in relation to legal or illegal transactions), will be respected by the Syrian authorities, regardless of political expediency. Such critical issues will clearly have to be solved before confidence in the new private bank system can be established.

The bank reform is an example of a "stroke-of-the-pen" reform (Page and Van Gelder, 2001), the impact of which depends entirely on future painful political decisions. At the same time, the reform indicates that some parts of the state elite are aware of the problems with and the importance of the financial sector and that it attempts to address them.

But the technical launching of such a reform does not exonerate the regime from dealing with the political and institutional issues of financial intermediation. The hard choices are still pending to realize the economic gains of privatizing and liberalizing the financial sector.

Free Trade Agreement with the EU

In 2004, Syria and the EU agreed to sign an Association Agreement within the EU-Mediterranean Partnership framework.[24] Besides clauses on political issues (convergence of positions, democracy, and human rights) and civil security (antiterrorism) the agreement stipulates the gradual implementation of a Free Trade Zone between Syria and the EU for industrial goods. Free access for Syrian agricultural goods to the EU will be governed by a complicated quota system designed to minimize the harm to European agricultural producers.[25] Agricultural exports exceeding these quotas will be subject to standard tariffs for Most Favored Nation partners, equalling 6.5 percent on average, which the EU levies on Most Favored Nation partners (European Commission, 2003).

Syria already enjoys preferential status with the EU through the General System of Preferences scheme (GSP) by which the EU unilaterally gives tariff reductions to developing countries. However, the actual rate of utilization of the EU's GSP preferences by Syrian exporters is on an average only 30 percent and varies from sector to sector. Even for types of manu-factured products for which Syria is most competitive, the utilization rate is negligible. The utilization rate for "clothing," for example, is only 3.4 percent, with 0.2 percent for "textiles" and 30 percent for "leather goods." For the category of "live plants, flowers, fruits and vegetables," it is 60 percent (European Commission, 2003).

The limited use of GSP preferential access to the EU market suggests that tariff reductions are not enough to ensure export competitiveness. EU industries, who have only limited access to the Syrian market under the present highly protective trade regime, are, on the contrary, ready for competition with Syrian industries. It is expected that, during the period of the implementation of the agreement, a substantial part of the Syrian industrial production will cease as a result of this competition.[26]

Trade liberalization is a hallmark of the orthodox "Washington Consensus" approach to development. However, a number of studies have recently questioned the claim that there necessarily is a positive correlation between liberal trade regimes and economic growth (Rodriguez and Rodrik, 1999). These authors argue that a liberal trade regime is beneficial only if companies which become subjected to liberal trade regimes are competitive and that the process of becoming competitive historically has always involved antecedent discretionary state intervention, whether in trade regimes, credit policy, subventions or other specific incentives for export- or import-competitive industries. For a number of the successful Far Eastern states, export incentives were for a number of years combined with protective import regimes.

Trade liberalization in a situation without adequate strengthening of competitiveness of indigenous industries may in fact be a recipe for dein-dustrialization and the "stroke-of-the-pen" Free Trade Agreement which Syria has signed with the EU cannot serve as a substitute for hard and painful reforms.

Delta Food's Export of Bio-Dynamic Tomato Paste

Delta Food is a major agro-business in Syria involved in exports.[27] In the past, tomato farmers hardly used pesticides in their cultivation of toma-toes, which allowed the company to export bio-dynamic tomato paste to a booming market in Europe. After some years of exporting this product, the company experienced problems in ensuring the bio-dynamic quality of the tomatoes used for its production, as Syrian farmers also started to use pesticides. Although the company was willing to pay farmers a handsome bonus for bio-dynamic tomatoes, it has so far failed to secure a continuous supply of these types of tomatoes for its production. In dealing with the farmers, three particular problems emerged. First, the company tried to provide farmers with plastic boxes (and seeds) but soon the farmers brought tomatoes in dirty old wooden boxes again. Second, the company tried to make contracts with farmers at a fixed price, but when they came to collect the tomatoes the farmers had often already sold them if the current market price was higher than the contract price. Finally, the fixed price contract was often a problem for the company, as it produced on demand, that is, they did not know beforehand how much they would be producing and therefore how many tomatoes they would need to buy.

The supply of bio-dynamic tomatoes requires that farmers are taught about the requirements of bio-dynamic cultivation and that the production is supervised. Also, a payment and contract system is needed which penalizes production of sub-standard tomatoes and rewards the supply of tomatoes that comply with the standards.

Delta Food is a small company and the only company in Syria which produces bio-dynamic tomato paste. As a result, the company does not have the resources to provide farmers with the required instruction and to supervise them. Although the export of bio-dynamic tomato paste is a promising business, Delta Food is not by itself able to secure that the costs involved in ensuring the bio-dynamic quality of tomatoes are commensurate with the gains that will accrue to the company.

This is a classical externality problem, where the market is not able to internalize social benefits. Externality problems must be solved by a third party delivering the required extension services and assisting in establishing a minimum size market, which will allow the costs of specialized extension services to be recuperated. The problem in Syria is that the Government Agricultural Extension services are of no use, that the Ministry of Agriculture is not receptive to the problems of emerging export-oriented agro-businesses, and that there is not an efficient legal system which would allow companies to operate with contracts involving penalties and rewards in order to ensure the proper supply of bio-dynamic tomatoes. As a result, the potential of a promising business avenue, where Syria in principle has an advantage compared to other countries, has not been developed because of the absence of an adequate institutional framework and the lack of proper interventions by the state.

Grabbing Rent Havens: The Case of the Daimler-Benz Dealership

The "Omar Sankar & Sons Company" is an old Damascene company which, since mid- 2003, has been in a downward debt spiral.[28] The Sankar family is a well-known Damascene family belonging to the Sunni bourgeoisie, and for decades the family company has had the exclusive dealership of Daimler-Benz cars in Syria, which always has been a very profitable business.

Based on some trumped-up case of the company being in contract violation in relation to delivery of fire-fighting equipment to SPC (Syrian Petroleum Company), a legal order was issued prohibiting the company from continuing the Daimler-Benz dealership. According to reliable sources, the person trying to take over the dealership is Rami Makhlouf, the well-known cousin of President Asad. This case is an illustration of how regime-connected individuals use state institutions to grab lucrative rent havens. Furthermore, it indicates in which way the sectarian cleavages between the old Sunni bourgeoisie and the Alawi regime-connected new bourgeoisie are maintained.

Conclusions on the Case Studies

The first case study on the mobile phone company shows the effects of lack of separation between the private and the public realm as evidenced by the capture of state power by private individuals making a mockery of property rights. This phenomenon may be characterized as neo-patrimonialism, where the ruler (and his family) prey on society and appropriate its resources, but do not try to increase these resources by promoting economic development.

The second case study on the customs duties of thread indicates the influence of rent-seeking groups blocking the state from pursuing developmental policies. The Syrian state may be "strong" and "autonomous" in relation to controlling the broader Syrian population, but in relation to specific elite groups, it seems to be the opposite. This specific nexus between state and society seriously limits the state's developmental capacity.

The third case study on private banks underlines that if private institutions of financial intermediation are to promote economic growth they must be under-girded by efficient public institutions which in turn are based on hard political choices. As long as private banks are considered mere technical devices, they will at best not contribute to breaking the short-term and rent-seeking behavior of economic actors and at worst facilitate financial fraud.

The case study on the EU-Syria Free Trade Agreement shows that macro-economic reforms like a liberal free-trade regime will forfeit their developmental objective if they are not underpinned by micro-economic institutions and policies which are able to raise the competitiveness of the private sector. Yet, such underpinning of the private sector depends in the end on the political will and capacity on the side of the state.

The case study on bio-dynamic tomato paste illustrates the necessity of the state to complement the market by supplying public goods. The capacity of the state to deliver these goods is crucial for the development of a productive market economy.

Finally, the case of the Daimler-Benz dealership confirms the impression of widespread attempts of regime-connected private sector actors to confiscate other private sector actors' rent havens. Property rights, whether for rent-seeking businessmen or other actors, are quite insecure in Syria.

Conclusions

Syria's economic and political development has clearly reached an impasse, which at first glance seems "irrational" and difficult to explain. However, when the present zero-sum relationship between state and society is taken into account, this lack of development is far more explicable. The state is controlled by a coalition of private rent-seekers and predatory rulers, whose short-sighted interests seem to rule out any progress in allowing the state to perform its complementary role in the market economy, that is, to serve as a provider of coordination, institutions, and public goods.

In contrast to a country like Turkey,[29] the prospects of economic association with Europe have not had the effect of breaking up this distributive coalition. In addition, since the mid-1980s, Syria has maintained reasonably sound macroeconomic balances and therefore (so far) avoided hyperinflation, unstable foreign exchange rates, or a fiscal crisis. As a result, the distributive coalition in Syria has not been delegitimized by dramatic economic perturbations, as has happened in Turkey.

In recent decades, the productive capacity of the Syrian economy has, however, been allowed to deteriorate steadily. Currently, Syria is basically living off "oil and rain." The attraction of joining the European market is therefore limited, if not outright negative in the light of the competitive effects on Syria's protected industries. As a result, the attraction of joining the European market is weak for businessmen and industrial workers benefiting from the protection which the existing trade regime offers. Hardly any of the existing Syrian companies may expect to survive in a free-trade area with the EU. While the present EU strategy of providing preferential trade agreements and other economic incentives to promote development in Morocco and Tunisia seems to work due to its attraction to important members of the political coalitions behind the regimes of these countries, it seems quite inadequate for a country like Syria.

When the incapacity of the present regime to build a broad and long-term reform constituency which includes major political forces such as social organizations based on Islamic identity and the liberal, Sunni, production-based bourgeoisie is taken into account, the political and economic impasse seems far more explicable. Only a solid reform constituency including these major political forces would be able to establish the necessary positive-sum type relationship between state and market economy.

At the beginning of this chapter, I characterized the creation of institutions as "big bang" events where existing political deadlocks are shaken up by either external forces or violent social upheavals. The French mandate and the Baath revolution were examples of such "big bang" events in Syrian political history. It seems likewise difficult to envisage how the present dead-lock in Syria may be changed without yet another "big bang" transformation of its political economy (hopefully from inside), and in order to trigger such a transformation, a much more activist political intervention compared to the present economic strategy from the EU will be needed.

Notes

1. While the private sector's share of industrial, non-oil GDP in 1990 was only 45 percent, it grew to 82 percent in 1999 (Aita, 2002: plate 19).
2. I am not trying to claim there is a contradiction between democracy and the properties of a developmental state. However, while democracy might be beneficial to the properties of a developmental state, democracy alone is not sufficient to bring development about (cf. Kohli, 2002: 117).
3. Distributive conflicts may be on economic issues, as well as on identities, symbols, values, norms and ideologies.
4. Agonistic relationships are understood as competitive relations within a mutually accepted framework, while antagonistic relationships imply confrontation.
5. The thrust of the argument is here on explaining growth and lack of growth, rather than distribution of growth.
6. Whether Marxist or from the so-called "dependency school."
7. *External accountability* may be defined as citizens holding public officials accountable through e.g. voting, while *internal accountability* may be defined as one public agency holding another accountable, as when courts rule on the constitutionality of laws, when parliament votes against the executive, or when the audit agency investigates procurement by a ministry (World Bank, 2003: xvii). For the year 2000, Syria scored a value of eighteen out of 100 (higher is better) on the World Bank's index of public accountability, which is considered by the World Bank as a proxy value for external accountability. The average for Middle Eastern and North Africa states was 32, while the average of Low and Middle Income countries was 54. On the index for quality of administration—a proxy value for internal accountability—Syria scored 28 out of 100, while the average for Middle Eastern and North Africa states was 47, and 41 for Low and Middle Income countries.

8. The first and second factor in explaining whether the state provides market-friendly and development-oriented institutions are what Peter Evans calls "autonomy" and "embeddedness" in his claim that successful economic development hinges on the existence of "embedded autonomy" (Evans, 1995).

9. The fiscal basis of the state served in early rentier-state literature (Luciani, 1990) as a sort of economistic independent variable in explaining the non-developmental state. However, as the case of oil-rich Norway indicates (Karl, 1997), it is the combination of rent and state structures which explains the nexus between economy and state.

10. This may be contrasted with the effort of the British in India or the Japanese in Korea (Kohli, 2004).

11. Like the Caribbean colonies, Reunion, and Tahiti.

12. A statelet in Latakia and the Nusayria Mountains based on the Alawite community, a statelet in the Jebel Druze area based on the Druze community and two states based on Sunni-Muslim communities in Aleppo and Damascus were established.

13. Aleppo versus Damascus.

14. This is based on industrial relations and minimum wage regulation.

15. Rent has most precisely been defined by Adam Smith as follows: "Rent, it is to be observed, enters into the composition of the price of commodities in a different way from wages and profit. High or low wages and profit are the causes of thigh or low price; high or low rent is the effect of it. It is because high or low wages and profit must be paid, in order to bring a particular commodity to market, that its price is high or low. But it is because its price is high or low; a great deal more, or very little more or no more, than what is sufficient to pay those wages and profit, that it affords a high rent, or a low rent, or not rent at all" (Smith 2002: bk one, chap. 11). Captive markets, restriction of market entry, participation in trade protocol regimes (like the Iraqi-Syrian trade agreement), etc. are all measures which allow market participants to charge a price over and above the price which would be sufficient to bring the commodity to the market under efficient competition.

16. The ideology of the regime had narrowed down to nationalism. Socialist or re-distributional ideologies had more or less dissipated and been replaced by the naked self-interest of regime members.

17. In order not to be seen as emulating Egypt, Syria did not choose the Egyptian term for economic liberalization: *infitah* (opening).

18. The abandonment of economic reforms after some superficial measures were taken immediately after the take-over of Bashar al-Asad from his father in June 2000 (reduction of custom duties for manufacturing industries, import restrictions and export taxes, easing of foreign exchange dealings and allowing private universities) may to a large degree also be explained by the renewed rent opportunities in Iraq from 2000 (Perthes, 2004: 39).

19. The following is based on personal and confidential interviews in Damascus, December 2003.

20. Mobile phone services are natural mono- or oligopolies, as they are associated with high fixed costs, which mean that services will not be offered if market

entry is unrestricted. The ability to restrict rent opportunities in such markets depends of course on the capacity of the Government to auction off, regulate and monitor such mono- or oligopolies. It does not require much imagination to understand that the restricted mobile phone market in Syria lends itself to huge rent-seeking opportunities, given non-transparent auction procedures and the degree to which the bureaucracy is penetrated by the private interests.

21. Based on interviews with representatives of the company in December 2003. Names have been changed.

22. The role of the state in ensuring that economic liberalization result in economic growth is succinctly formulated by Pereira, Maravall and Przeworski (1993: 215): The state "should pursue measures that increase the rate of return to private projects. This role includes a selective industrial policy that would comprise preferential credit rates for high-technology industries, in which the market rate of return is much lower than the social rate; for projects that suffer from high costs of entry, substantial economies of scale, or steep learning curves; and projects that have potential spillovers across firms due to externalities and asymmetries of information between suppliers and buyers."

23. Like letter-of-credit and foreign exchange transactions.

24. However, at the time of writing (May 2005) the agreement had still not been approved by the EU Council of Minister because of disagreement between the two partners on Syria's engagement in Lebanon.

25. The quotas are subject to variations during the year and may be changed or rescinded by the EU depending on the production situation of European producers. Such a quota system is hardly the best incentive for long-term investments in the private agricultural sector in Syria.

26. The Delegation of the European Commission has informed the author that two-thirds of small and medium industries in Portugal closed down as a result of accession to the EU. However, at the same time a number of new Portuguese industries owed their existence to the accession and in total Portugal gained greatly from its membership.

27. Based on interviews with representatives of the company in December 2003.

28. The information on this case study is based on interviews with diplomatic staff in Damascus in December 2003.

29. Cf. Ziya Önis' chapter in this book.

References

Aita, Samir (2002) *Euro vs. US$. Private Sector vs. Public Sector. The Syrian Experience*, Mediterranean Dialogue Program, Casablanca, July 12–13.

Chaudhry, Kiren Aziz (1997) *The Price of Wealth: Economies and Institutions in the Middle East*, Ithaca, NY: Cornell University Press.

—— (2003) *Potential impact of a EU-Syria Association Agreement*, www.delsyr.cec.eu.int

Evans, Peter B. (1995) *Embedded Autonomy: States and Industrial Transformation*, Princeton, NJ: Princeton University Press.

Fieldhouse, D.K. (1981) *Colonialism, 1870–1945*, London: Weidenfeld and Nicolson.

Haddad, Bassam (2004) "The Formation and Development of Economic Networks in Syria: Implications for Economic and Fiscal Reforms, 1986–2000," in Steven Heydemann (ed.): *Networks of Privilege in the Middle East: The Politics of Economic Reform Revisited*, London: Palgrave Macmillan.

Hopfinger, Hans and Marc Boeckler (1996) "Step by Step to and Open Economic System: Syria Sets Course for Liberalization," *British Journal of Middle Eastern Studies*, 23 (2): 183–202.

IMF (2002) *Syrian Arab Republic—Staff Report of the 2002 Article IV Consultation*, Washington: IMF.

—— (2003) *Syrian Arab Republic. Selected Issues and Statistical Appendix*, Washington: IMF.

Karl, Terry Lynn (1997) *The Paradox of Plenty: Oil Booms and Petro-States*, Berkeley: University of California Press.

Kohli, Atul (2002) "State, Society, and Development," in Ira Katznelson and Helen V. Milner (eds.): *Political Science: The State of the Discipline*. New York/London: W.W. Norton & Company.

—— (2004) *State-directed Industrialization*, Cambridge: Cambridge University Press.

Krueger, Anne O. (1993) Political Economy of Policy Reform in Developing Countries, Cambridge, MA: MIT Press.

Luciani, Giacomo (1990) "Allocative vs. Production States: A Theoretical Framework," in Giacomo Luciani (ed.): *The Arab State*, Berkeley: University of California Press.

Mouffe, Chantal (2004) "10×10," *Politik*, 4 (7): 22–36.

North, Douglass C. (1989) "Comments 2," in Joseph Stiglitz *et al.* (eds.): *The Economic Role of the State*, Cambridge, MA: Basil Blackwell.

Olson, Mancur (1965) *The Logic of Collective Action. Public Goods and the Theory of Groups*, Cambridge, MA: Harvard University Press.

—— (1982) The Rise and Decline of Nations: Economic Growth, Stagflation and Social Rigidities, London and New Heaven: Yale University Press.

Owen, Roger and Sevket Pamuk (1998) *A History of Middle East Economies in the Twentieth Century*, London: I.B.Tauris.

Page, John and Linda Van Gelder (2001) "Missing Links: Institutional Capability, Policy reform, and Growth in the Middle East and North Africa," in H. Hakimian and Z. Moshaver (eds.): *The State and Global Change*, Surrey: Curzon Press.

Pereira, L.C., J.M. Maravall and A. Przeworski (1993) *Economic Reforms in New Democracies. A Social-Democratic Approach*, Cambridge MA: Cambridge University Press.

Perthes, Volker (2004) *Syria under Bashar al-Asad: Modernisation and the Limits of Change*, Oxford: Oxford University Press.

Poulsen, Jørgen (2004) "Zoon Politikon—Om statskundskabens grundlag," *Politik*, 3 (7): 96–110.

Przeworski, Adam (2003) *States and Markets. A Primer in Political Economy*, Cambridge, MA: Cambridge University Press.

Rodriguez, Francisco and Dani Rodrik (1999) "Trade Policy and Economic Growth: A Skeptic's Guide to the Cross-National Evidence," *NBER Working Paper 7081*, April.

Rodrik, Dani (2001) "Development Strategies for the Next Century," Paper presented at the Institute of Developing Economies, Chiba, Japan, January 2000.

Smith, Adam (2002) [1776] *An Inquiry into the Nature and Causes of the Wealth of Nations*, London: Methuen and Co (internet version accessed: 2002).

Stiglitz, Joseph E. (1989) "The Economic Role of the State: Efficiency and Effectiveness," in A. Heertje (ed.): *The Economic Role of the State*, London: Basil Blackwell and Bank Insinger de Beaufort NV.

Vandewalle, Dirk (1998) *Libya Since Independence: Oil and State-Building*, Itacha NY: Cornell University Press.

Vivvegaro, Anne (1993) Political Economy of Policy Reform in Developing Countries/Mass.: MIT Press.

Waldner, David (1999) *State Building and Late Development*, Ithaca NY: Cornell University Press.

World Bank (2003) *Better Governance for Development in the Middle East and North Africa. Enhancing Inclusiveness and Accountability*, Washington: World Bank.

—— (2004) *Unlocking the Employment Potential in the Middle East and North Africa*, Washington: World Bank.

Yapp M.E. (1996) *The Near East Since The First World War*, England: Pearson Education Limited

Yazigi, Jihad (2003) *Banking in Syria*, Paris: MEICA.

Conclusions

8

Democratizing the Middle East: A Means of Ensuring International Security or an End in Itself?

Dietrich Jung

For 60 years, my country, the United States, pursued stability at the expense of democracy in this region here in the Middle East—and we achieved neither. Now, we are taking a different course. We are supporting the democratic aspirations of all people.

—*U.S. Secretary of State Condoleezza Rice*

Introduction

This statement made by the U.S. Secretary of State, Condoleezza Rice, represents the credo of the current public discourse on democracy promotion in the Middle East.[1] Yet, does it announce a clear shift in U.S. foreign policy? Has the Bush administration really acknowledged the previous U.S. policy of prioritizing short-term stability over good governance as being a historical failure, as Oliver Schlumberger puts it in his contribution to this volume? Or is this new stress on democracy just an *ex post* justification for the U.S. invasion of Iraq (Rougier, 2005: 79)? Given the flux of events, it seems premature to aim at finding conclusive answers to these questions. At least in rhetoric, Condoleezza Rice's statement expresses something like a new consensus among Western foreign policy makers in their attitude toward the Middle East. For the time being, we should give credit to this new attitude, which was also expressed in the declaration of the "Partnership for Progress and a Common Future." This declaration, the G8 leaders released at their summit on Sea Island on June 7, 2004, thereby partly healing the rift that the Middle Eastern policies of the Bush administration had created with some of the United States's European allies.

According to the declaration of Sea Island, the G8 governments will work for the strengthening of freedom, democracy, and prosperity in the "Broader Middle East and North Africa," and this in "genuine cooperation with the region's governments, as well as business and civil society representatives."[2] The Sea Island declaration exemplifies well the new discourse on democracy promotion that has captured the debates on Middle Eastern affairs in academia, politics, and the media alike. It is in the context of this discourse that the research for this book has been conducted and the following conclusions have been written.[3] Instead of engaging in speculations about the "real motives" behind this new attitude of Western foreign policy makers, this final chapter will raise some questions regarding the atmosphere in which the current debate on democracy promotion takes place, its feasibility as a means of shaping international security policies, and the choice of appropriate partners for Western initiatives to promote democracy and market economy in the social environment of the Middle East.

Democratization as a Discourse and a Means of Ensuring International Security

The current discourse on democracy promotion in the Middle East highlights what Charles Taylor named the "benchmarks of modern political legitimacy": the values of liberty, equality, human rights and democracy (Taylor, 2004: 185). It is the application of these benchmarks on a global scale, their rising relevance in shaping both Western security and development policies, that Roland Paris has labeled a new *mission civilisatrice*, as the transplantation of "the values and institutions of the liberal democratic core into the domestic affairs of peripheral host states" (Paris, 2002: 638). While these policies of democracy promotion resonate well in Western societies, they undoubtedly evoke reminiscences of colonial hegemony in the Middle East. Given the long struggle between the "indirect powers" of colonialism and Arab and Islamic transnationalism, as Thomas Scheffler phrased it, regional actors listen to this Western rhetoric of democratic reform with marked apprehension. In contrast to Roland Paris, the majority of Arabs do not view the current Western policies of peacemaking and state-building as less mercenary than European colonialism was. Rather, Middle Eastern audiences interpret them as an historical extension of the colonial encounter. In a recent public opinion poll in six

Arab states, for instance, the overwhelming majority of the interviewees rejected outright the idea of present U.S. foreign policies as being driven by democratic values and principles. Instead, they perceived them as totally in line with the economic and strategic self-interest of the United States.[4]

In a similar way, the UNDP's Arab Human Development Report (AHDR), the third issue of which was published in spring 2005, indicates that Western foreign policy makers are engaged in an uphill struggle to prove the sincerity of their motives in promoting democracy and market economy in the Middle East.[5] While the Arab authors of the report join the general calls for democratic reform, they are very critical vis-à-vis the role that Western governments have been and ought to be playing in Middle Eastern politics. They blame both the incumbent Arab regimes and Western powers for the political failings in the Arab world. In particular the continuation of Israeli occupation and the invasion of Iraq finds their staunch criticism, and as an ideal scenario their report propagates indigenous reforms with as limited external intervention as possible.

From a scholarly perspective, however, this scenario of democratization by internal reform alone is wishful thinking, reminding us more of the out-dated ideals of Arab nationalism rather than proposing practicable avenues for reform in the future. In the brief theoretical discussion of the introductory chapter, I have stressed that also in Europe the distinction between external and internal processes in the formation of states and the democratization of their institutions only makes sense in retrospect. Only then can the observer apply the formal norms of a developed society of states to the historical process of this society's very evolution. Using concepts such as sovereignty and self-determination we should be conscious of the fact that these norms of international society have been under permanent negotiation and that individual processes of state- and nation-building have written the history of their frequent violation (cf. Krasner, 1999).

The case studies of this book emphasize the increasing scholarly irrelevance of this state-centered dichotomy between external and internal perspectives. In his analysis of the Turkish experience, Ziya Öniş meticulously shows the complex interplay of foreign and domestic forces in shaping the way of Turkey's religious political wing from the Islamist Refah Party to the so-called Muslim-conservative AKP. For the reform of Turkey's political and legal institutions, as well as for the democratization of its religious political movements, the EU anchor and contingent continuous foreign intervention have been indispensable. In investigating the economic scene in Syria, Søren Schmidt even comes to the conclusion that overcoming the current dead-lock in Syrian political economy demands more rather than less intervention from the European side. In a similar vain, Maye Kassem presents us an Egyptian regime maneuvering carefully in a political environment in which the division lines between outer and inner constraints increasingly have become blurred. The global discourse on democracy and human rights heavily impacts on all Middle Eastern regimes, and ideas of reform have been advocated by external and domestic actors. Prime amongst them, as Jakob Skovgaard-Petersen's chapter describes, are the new Arab media. They have been creating a new public space across state-borders and have become a part of domestic politics from outside. Against this background, the rhetoric of self-determination, sovereignty, local ownership, and equal partnership appears to be the application of—possibly necessary—semantic cosmetics in a political atmosphere poisoned by historically grounded suspicions on all sides.

In this atmosphere, not so much the alleged motivations as the results of Western foreign policy initiatives will count. On closer analysis, it is with regard to their outcomes and not their potential as role-models for concrete processes of reform that the essentially different cases of Japan, Germany, or Eastern Europe can teach us a certain lesson. In Germany and Japan the imposition of democratic political institutions from the outside was accepted because these foreign interventions were able to serve the key interests of these nations (Bellin, 2004–05: 606). With a similar attitude, eastern European states accepted conducting political and economic reforms according to the EU's demands. In principle, there is no given linkage between the imposition of democratic reforms and their subsequent success or failure. The crucial question is, therefore, in which way the current policies of democracy promotion will contribute to stability and prosperity in the Middle East and thereby strengthen international security. Looked at from a scholarly perspective, some qualification seems to be appropriate here.

First of all, there is no mutually accepted proof of the intrinsic relationship between the democratic structure of states and their peaceful interactions with each other. The current idea of democracy promotion as a means of achieving international security relies on some popularized assumptions of the theoretical school of "democratic" or "liberal peace." To a large extent this school in International Relations is based on the rather debatable statistical evidence that democratic states do not fight each other. Its basic assumption is that political institutions such as democratic liberties, the rule of law, electoral processes, and representative governments dramatically reduce the legitimacy of militaristic foreign policies, in particular among democracies based on market economies that recognize each other as being akin (cf. Brown et al., 1996; Kim and Rousseau, 2005; Maoz, 1997; Oneal and Russet, 1999, 2001; Russet 1993; Williams, 2001). Although it would be wrong to completely disregard the findings of this school, which can also claim roots in liberal political philosophy, it is equally flawed to take its assumptions for granted. Severe methodological problems concerning the applied definitions of democracies and the statistical viability of their samples have not yet been sorted out. So far, no academic consensus about the relationship between the democratic nature of and the peaceful interaction between states in the international system exists.

Second, and even more important, there is no evidence that policies of democratization will foster peace and stability. On the contrary, most scholars agree on the conflict-prone nature of democratization processes. Taking the case of post-revolutionary violence in France, Charles Taylor, for example, discerned in the link between democratic revolutions and the occurrence of scapegoating violence one of the "most disquieting features of modernity" (Taylor, 2004: 138). From a theoretical perspective, the formation and nationalization of state monopolies, as chapter 1 has shown is still an ongoing process in Middle Eastern state formation, has a high propensity to engender instability and political violence. With regard to the more narrow aim of short-term stability in the Middle East, Oliver Schlumberger even pessimistically suggests it might be wiser to disengage from the idea of democracy promotion at all. Moreover, his contribution reminds us of the failure of previous liberalization policies. They have neither enhanced personal liberties nor have they led to more democracy on the macrolevel. According to Schlumberger's analysis, the Western proponents of democracy promotion lack coherent political strategies that would allow donors to follow a clear path of engagement under the conditions of resilient authoritarianism that have characterized Middle Eastern politics so far.

Finally, it is flawed, if not even dangerous, to perceive policies of democracy promotion as the right means of fighting terrorism. On the one hand, we should recall that liberal democracies have not been free of terrorism themselves. In the 1970s and 1980s a number of European states were confronted with terrorist organizations whose members had been recruited from the post–Second World War generations. These political extremists did not suffer under authoritarian regimes and social depravation but in fact enjoyed the liberal rights and the social security of the democratic welfare state. On the other hand, in the aforementioned poisoned political atmosphere between the West and the Muslim world, the combination of coercive policies with an inflated discourse on democracy and human rights might even enhance the propensity among younger generations in the Middle East to pursue their political goals by violent means. The ongoing military struggles in Afghanistan and Iraq, as well as human rights violations in Abu Ghraib and Guantánamo, have clearly shown the discrepancies which can occur between the political rhetoric of democratization and the realities of military and other coercive actions. Aired and amplified by the new Arab satellite channels (cf. Jakob Skovgaard's chapter in this volume), these discrepancies have further strengthened the already existing deep sense of mistrust and hypocrisy with which the Arab world looks at Western foreign policies. Therefore, it is more than advisable not to justify applying coercive means in the fight against "rogue states" and terrorist groups with the argument of promoting democracy in the region.

From an analytical point of view, the relationship between international security, regional stability, and democracy promotion seems to be highly ambivalent to say the least. While established democracies might be more peaceful in their interactions with each other, the very process of democratization is prone to engender phases of instability and outbursts of collective violence. In this sense, democracy promotion seems indeed a questionable tool for enhancing security and stability in the short-term. In the long run, however, a politically and economically reformed Middle East might be an asset for international security. In addition, Western foreign policy initiatives in the Middle East have to overcome the deep mistrust on the side of the region's political opposition. Whether Islamists, nationalists, or liberals, political movements in the region share the suspicion that the Western discourse on democracy is only a means of achieving rather different hegemonic political ends (Rougier, 2005: 89). Against this background, the support for "the democratic aspirations of all people" in the region has to be a genuine goal of Western foreign policy. Therefore, democracy promotion should not be presented as a means of ensuring international security, but as an end in itself.

Rulers, Jurists, and the Civil Society

In a paradigmatic way, Maye Kassem's chapter on Egypt shows the adaptability of authoritarian regimes to changes in both the international and domestic contexts. The reforms of the legislative elections, the restructuring of President Mubarak's National Democratic Party (NDP), the establishment of a National Council for Human Rights, and the Amendment of Article 76 of the Egyptian Constitution in order to allow direct multicandidate presidential elections are analyzed as a series of liberal democratic reforms, the only serious purpose of which is to reinforce and stabilize authoritarian rule. In this way, the regime superficially joins in the global discourse on democracy and human rights in order to maintain international support and to dilute and/or coopt internal opposition. Policies of liberalization may thus be initiated as part of the survival strategies of incumbent regimes.

Ironically, after more than a decade of democracy promotion by international donors, the comparative level of illiberalism in the Arab world has increased (see Schlumberger's contribution). Yet it would be wrong to equate this resilience of authoritarian rule with a "lack of modernization." Modernity and democracy are by no means synonyms, as is also proved by European totalitarianism. Applying the concept of "multiple modernities" (Eisenstadt, 2000), Middle Eastern authoritarianism should, rather, be interpreted as the specific form in which political modernization in the region has evolved. Moreover, it is flawed to present the recent history of the Middle East as a mere period of political and social stagnation. Despite the continuation of authoritarian political structures, Middle Eastern societies have undergone dramatic changes. In order to promote democracy in the region, it is necessary to understand this interplay between continuity and change.

The liberalization policies of the Mubarak regime, for example, camouflage a very different daily practice that is based on extended networks of patronage. These networks, however, are carefully designed adaptations to modern social contexts rather than persisting forms of tradition. They are knitted into modern politics and the particular survival strategies of the respective regimes and the distributive coalitions (cf. Søren Schmidt's chapter) that have emerged around them. In principle, the current initiatives to promote liberal democracy and market economy in the region contradict these established social practices. Moreover, for decades the state-centered policies of Western governments have contributed to stabilizing and fueling the modern patronage machines of Middle Eastern states. Nevertheless, in the context of the global discourses on democracy and human rights, both the incumbent regimes and Western governments seemingly share a feeling for the need for reform and the necessity to avoid violent ruptures (cf. Schlumberger's chapter). In this setting, it is necessary to disentangle existing structures of patronage without destroying functioning state institutions. The situation in Iraq exemplifies that it takes years with high material and human costs to rebuild dissolved state structures. Therefore, Western policy makers have to find common ground with the incumbent regimes and include them in carefully designed and credible strategies for change. It is in this sense that democracy promotion in the Middle East necessarily implies "dancing with wolves."

International strategies to promote democracy in the Middle East entail engaging in multilateral negotiation processes that should aim at balancing the different and often contradictory interests of states, societies, and individuals. The reform process in Turkey is therefore an interesting and, so far, a comparatively successful example. Ziya Öniş's chapter gives us an understanding of the complex interplay of internal state repression, geostrategic changes, economic and political pluralization in Turkish society, and EU-imposed reforms that has transformed the authoritarian structures of the Turkish state as well as the undemocratic leanings of both Turkey's Kemalist establishment and its Islamist opponents. To be sure, Turkey's candidacy for EU full-membership makes it a special case. Nevertheless, this case tells us some lessons about the successful implementation of democratic reform in authoritarian contexts and the way in which the enormous gap between state and society might be bridged.

With regard to state-society relations, the judiciary plays a central role. In the emergence of democratic states, the growing independence of the juridical realm guaranteed the legally defined "private" space, that is, freedom from state intervention, in which civil society organizations could grow. In contrast to the present prioritization of electoral mechanisms in democracy promotion, Western initiatives might consider shifting their focus to the implementation of legally grounded forms of public spaces and mutually accepted mechanisms of political accountability. The mere introduction of electoral procedures often reproduces the established clientelist power relations in a new disguise. Egypt's multiparty system is an instructive example, and the introduction of elements of electoral democracy has not really changed state-society relations. The gradual establishment of legal arrangements, binding both state and society, by contrast, might open an avenue for reform that does not directly challenge the claim to power of incumbent regimes. While in some countries, for example in Turkey and Iran, the judiciary has been a core institution of the regime, strongly defending the existing authoritarian state structures and their respective Kemalist and Islamist ideologies against democratic reforms, in other cases the jurists play a much more contributive role. Maye Kassem's analysis points out this different attitude of the judiciary in Egypt, the only public institution that has been able to openly criticize President Mubarak and his ruling elite (Kienle, 2001: 10).

Taking legal aspects of globalization seriously, there is indeed a tendency to establish "rights across borders" (Jacobsen, 1996). Transnational law tribunals, for instance, remove the ability of states to perform gate-keeping functions in controlling the access to and the implementation of dispute resolution, making them "a protector of individual rights and benefits against the state" (Keohane et al., 2000: 482). Consequently, there are growing options of addressing the violation of individual rights by appealing to transnational legal bodies. This form of transnational litigation is just one example of the growing international discourse on law that could be much better utilized in strategies to promote patterns of legal accountability in authoritarian contexts. The gradual building-up of independent judiciaries whose legal standards are based on international conventions could serve as a normative standard for both societal interaction and the professional ethics of judges and lawyers. In this way, juridical reform would not only help to mitigate the distance between state and society but also contribute to the development of a political culture that leaves behind the regional legacy of patrimonial domination.

In this juridical manner of democracy promotion, the integration of religious jurisprudents should be an option. They play an important role not only in the legal systems of the region, whose personal status law has up to now remained under religious jurisdiction,[6] but also in the moral critique of the abuses of ruling power. In the context of Middle Eastern authoritarianism, we can observe an ambivalent function of Islamic law. On the one hand, authoritarian regimes and/or militant Islamists have largely been able to take over the right to interpret religious sources from the traditional institutions of Islamic knowledge. This weakening of traditional institutions has strengthened coercive authoritarianism in the Muslim world, as demonstrated by previous examples associated with the implementation of Koranic criminal punishments by Iran, Pakistan, or Sudan. In these cases sacred law degenerated into a mere instrument of power in the name of Machiavellian politics (Peters, 1994). On the other hand, the debate about the public function of Islamic law could also open a window of opportunity for reform. It might signal a step toward a reinterpretation of the canonic knowledge of classical Islamic jurisprudence that could serve as a moral basis for a break with the authoritarian heritage of Muslim states (cf. Arabi, 2001). In morally binding both rulers and ruled, Islamic law and religious jurists could contribute to facilitating the move toward more political accountability.

Turning to the civil society sector, the proponents of the G8 Partnership for Progress and a Common Future must acknowledge the social realities of the region. The overwhelming majority of grass-roots organizations and nonstate actors in the region have a religious background. To a large extent, the civil society of the region consists of Islamic organizations and it is counterproductive to address Middle Eastern civil societies from the vantage point of a wrongly understood concept of Western secularism. In his analysis of transnationalism in the region, Thomas Scheffler criticizes the growing disenchantment of Western foreign policy makers with becoming engaged with a civil society whose organizations predominately appear in religious attire. Yet any form of democracy promotion in the region has to take its Islamic culture seriously without turning religion into the sole explicative variable for the social and political developments in the Muslim world—a theoretical position which Maxime Rodinson once labeled theologocentrism, that is, the attempt to explain all empirical phenomena in the Muslim world by references to Islam (Rodinson,

1988: 104). In most Middle Eastern states, Islamic organizations supply public services that at least in Europe have been understood as tasks of the welfare state. In doing so, they often transcend ethnic, social, and tribal boundaries and provide social networks on which large parts of the population rely in organizing their everyday lives. Consequently, the indigenous political discourse is currently deeply molded by Islamic symbolism. In order to promote democracy in the region, understanding this is necessary to obtain a hearing within the framework of this indigenous discourse. The modern Middle East is also a religious Middle East.

Another crucial point concerns the economic side of civil society. Schlumberger's study indicates that previous structural adjustment policies have not unleashed politically bounded market forces, but rather tied the commercial interests of the regional bourgeoisie more closely to the self-interest of the regimes. In this way, the economic top segment of regional civil societies is also benefiting from the authoritarian status quo. With a series of short case studies, Søren Schmidt's chapter demonstrates the way in which under the conditions of authoritarian rule parts of Syrian civil society have been engaged in distributive coalitions with the state elite. It is this particular coalition that hampers democratic reform and suffocates economic development. In macro terms, the political economy of Middle Eastern states is indeed characterized by the huge gap between state and society, yet this does not exclude the coincidence of interests between some political and civil society actors on the microlevel. While the macrostructures provide the framework in which political and economic reforms take place, it is the particular microstructure of each country that, in the end, will decide about the success of these reforms.

Therefore, one-size-fits-all solutions such as the recurrent propagation of regional free-trade schemes and the integration of Middle Eastern economies into the European market are highly questionable. Schmidt's study, for instance, comes to the conclusion that current EU policies might fit the distributional coalitions in Morocco and Tunisia, but are detrimental for businesses in Syria. In this way, Western foreign policy initiatives often disregard the specific microstructures of the political economy of individual states.

Promoting democracy in the Middle East is not a simple task. Breaking up the entrenched structures of authoritarianism entails high political risks and needs meticulously calibrated strategies which address various regional and local actors. There is no blueprint for reform and no guarantee that democratization will automatically come along with security and stability. However, the negative balance of decades of state-centered security policies in the region, as Secretary of State Rice indicated, suggests taking the risk. Yet this shift in foreign policy only makes sense if democracy promotion becomes an end in itself. In the light of the atmosphere of suspicion and mistrust that so far has characterized the political climate between Western countries and the Middle East, it would be disastrous to view democracy promotion as a mere means of expedience for Western security interests.

In this context, it is the task of academics to provide policy makers and the wider public with analytically informed insights in the complexities at work; and it is their privilege to give policy advice without having the burden of making decisions. From the point of view of decision-makers, this might sometimes look like an all-too-comfortable position. However, it makes no sense to confuse the very different logics of policy making and academic analysis. While policy makers reduce complexities through decisions, scholars analyze historical events in retrospect and therewith the unintended consequences of these decisions. Having the benefit of hindsight, scholars should therefore be careful in their judgments when later discovering the "wrong decisions" which undoubtedly are also occurring in current policies to promote democracy in the Middle East.

Notes

1. Quoted from the speech of US Secretary of State Condoleezza Rice at the American University in Cairo, Egypt, June 20, 2005 (available at: www.stategov/secretary/rm/).
2. Quoted from the press release of the US Secretary of State "Broader Middle East/N. Africa Partnership," June 9, 2004 (available at: www.whitehouse.gov/news/releases/). The area defined as the Broader Middle East comprises the following states: Morocco, Mauritania, Algeria, Tunisia, Libya, Egypt, Sudan, Jordan Syria, Saudi Arabia, Yemen, Oman, the Gulf States, Iraq, Iran and Afghanistan.
3. These conclusions have been written on the basis of the research that is presented in the different chapters of this book. However, they only express the opinion of the editor and do not have the status of a joint conclusion of the authors of this book.
4. In a public opinion poll conducted in May 2004 by Zogby International and the University of Maryland, democracy scored lowest as motivation for the US intervention in Iraq. Most respondents viewed the intervention as being motivated by the desire to control Iraqi oil and to protect Israel, as well as by the intention to dominate and weaken the Muslim world ("Arab Attitudes Towards Political and Social Issues, Foreign Policy and the Media", accessed on August 1, 2005, under: www.bsos.umd.edu/SADAT/pub/).
5. Arab Human Development Report 2004. Towards Freedom in the Arab World, New York: UNDP.
6. The only exception is the Republic of Turkey, where the Kemalist reforms introduced secular civil codes in the 1920s.

References

Arabi, Oussama (2001) "The Dawning of the Third Millennium on Shari'a: Egypt's Law No. 1 of 2000, or Women May divorce at Will," *Arab Law Quarterly* 16 (1): 2–21.

Bellin, Eva (2004–05) "The Iraqi Intervention and Democracy in Comparative Historical Perspective," *Political Science Quarterly* 119 (4): 595–608

Brown, M.E., Lynn-Jones, S.M., and Miller, S.E. (eds.) (1996) *Debating the Democratic Peace*, Cambridge, Mass: MIT Press.

Eisenstadt, S.N. (2000) "Multiple Modernities," *Daedalus*, 129 (1): 1–29.

Jacobson, David (1996) *Rights Across Borders. Immigration and the Decline of Citizenship*, Baltimore and London: Johns Hopkins University Press.

Keohane, Robert O., Andrew Moravcsik and Anne-Marie Slaughter (2000) "Legalized Dispute Resolution: Interstate and Transnational," *International Organization* 54 (3): 457–488.

Kienle, Eberhard (2001) *A Grand Delusion. Democracy and Economic Reform in Egypt*, London: I.B. Tauris.

Kim, Hyung Min and David L. Rousseau (2005) "The Classical Liberals Were Half Right (or Half Wrong): New Tests of the 'Liberal Peace,' 1960–88," *Journal of Peace Research*, 42 (5): 523–543.

Krasner, David (1999) *Sovereignty: Organized Hypocrisy*, Princeton: Princeton University Press.

Maoz, Zeev (1997) "The Controversy over the Democratic Peace: Rearguard Action or Cracks in the Wall?" *International Security* 22 (1): 162–198.

Oneal, John R. and Bruce Russet (1999) "Assessing the Liberal Peace with Alternative Specifications: Trade Still Reduces Conflict," *Journal of Peace Research* 36 (4): 423–42.

—— (2001) *Triangulating Peace. Democracy Interdependence and International Organizations*, New York: W. W. Norton & Company.

Paris, Roland (2002) "International Peacebuilding and the « Mission Civilisatrice »," *Review of International Studies*, 28 (2002): 637–56.

Peters, Rudolph (1994) "The Islamization of Criminal Law: A Comparative Analysis," *Die Welt des Islams*, 34: 246–73.

Rodinson, Maxime (1988) *Europe and the Mystique of Islam*, translated by Roger Veinus (French 1980), London: I.B. Tauris.

Rougier, Bernard (2005) "Le Grand Moyen-Orient: un moment d'utopie internationale?" *Critique Internationale* 26 (janvier): 79–94.

Russet, Bruce (1993) *Grasping the Democratic Peace: Principles for a Post-Cold-War World*, Princeton: Princeton University Press.

Taylor Charles (2004) *Modern Social Imaginaries*, Durham and London: Duke University Press.

Williams, Michael (2001) "The Discipline of the Democratic Peace: Kant, Liberalism and the Social Construction of Security Communities," *European Journal of International Relations* 7 (4): 525–553.

Index